RENIA'S
DIARY

RENIA'S DIARY

Renia Spiegel

Preface, Afterword, and Notes by
Elizabeth Bellak
with Sarah Durand

Foreword by Deborah E. Lipstadt

Diary translation by Anna Blasiak and Marta Dziurosz

ST. MARTIN'S PRESS
NEW YORK

www.stmartins.com

Design by Jonathan Bennett

Maps by Jeffrey L. Ward

The Library of Congress Cataloging-in-Publication Data is available upon request.

ISBN 978-1-250-24402-4 (hardcover)
ISBN 978-1-250-25812-0 (international, sold outside the U.S., subject to rights availability)
ISBN 978-1-250-25612-6 (ebook)

Our books may be purchased in bulk for promotional, educational, or business use. Please contact your local bookseller or the Macmillan Corporate and Premium Sales Department at 1-800-221-7945, extension 5442, or by email at MacmillanSpecialMarkets@macmillan.com.

First Edition: September 2019

10 9 8 7 6 5 4

MAP OF POLAND 1939

SWEDEN

LATVIA

Baltic Sea

LITHUANIA

Danzig
free city

• Königsberg

Kaunas ★

Wilno •

EAST
PRUSSIA

• Minsk

Vistula R.

• Berlin

• Poznań

★ Warszawa

SOVIET
UNION

Dnieper River

GERMANY

• Łódź

POLAND

Breslau •

Vistula R.

San R.

• Kiev

Prague ★

OCCUPIED
CZECHOSLOVAKIA

• Kraków

• Przemyśl

• Lwów

CZECHOSLOVAKIA

Carpathian Mountains

Stawki •

Dniester River

Danube R

• Bratislava

OCCUPIED
AUSTRIA

★ Budapest

ROMANIA

HUNGARY

0 Miles 100 200 300

0 Kilometers 300

© 2019 Jeffrey L. Ward

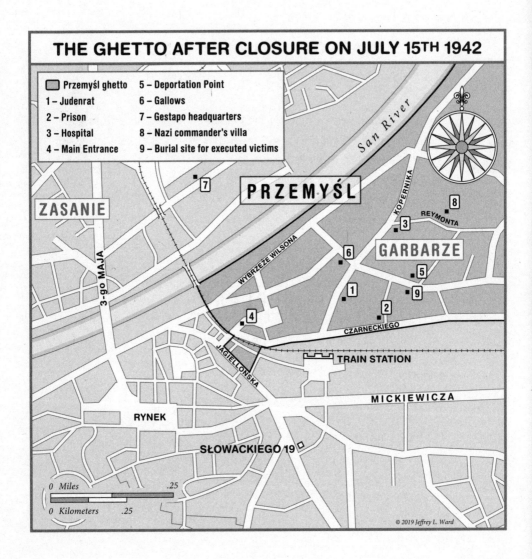

THE GHETTO AFTER CLOSURE ON JULY 15TH 1942

Przemyśl ghetto 5 – Deportation Point
1 – Judenrat 6 – Gallows
2 – Prison 7 – Gestapo headquarters
3 – Hospital 8 – Nazi commander's villa
4 – Main Entrance 9 – Burial site for executed victims

San River

ZASANIE

PRZEMYŚL

3-go MAJA

WYBRZEŻE WILSONA

KOPERNIKA

REYMONTA

GARBARZE

CZARNECKIEGO

JAGIELLOŃSKA

TRAIN STATION

MICKIEWICZA

RYNEK

SŁOWACKIEGO 19

0 Miles .25
0 Kilometers .25

© 2019 Jeffrey L. Ward

FOREWORD

In the past four decades, numerous Holocaust survivors have published their memoirs. Some waited to write until they reached an age at which people, in general, are more prone to reflect on the past. Some wrote because they felt the world was now more attuned to listening to what they had to say about this genocide. Others were urged to do so by their children, if not grandchildren. Since the 1980s so many memoirs have been published that it is easy to forget that this desire to "write and record" began far earlier.

In fact, Holocaust survivors have been writing their memoirs and giving their testimonies since the very end of the war. By the early 1960s, fifteen years after the end of the Holocaust, there were thousands of survivors' memoirs in print. In 1961, when Elie Wiesel sought an American publisher for *Night,* which had already been published in French, many rejected it because they believed there were too many memoirs in circulation. In his introduction to the French edition of *Night,* Nobel Prize winner François Mauriac acknowledged that Wiesel's was one among a myriad of Holocaust memoirs when he wrote, "this personal record *coming as it does after so many others*" (emphasis added).* Sadly, with the passing of the generation of survivors, that trend is nearing its end.

It is sometimes hard to imagine that these recollections, now much treasured and valued, were once eschewed by historians who preferred documents—despite the fact that most of these documents were products of the Third Reich—to personal accounts. These historians worried

---

* François Mauriac, "Introduction," *La Nuit,* by Elie Wiesel, as quoted in Ruth Franklin, *A Thousand Darknesses* (New York: Oxford University Press, 2011), p. 70.

that personal memories were not as "trustworthy" as documents. Today's historians recognize the value of these works, particularly when they are juxtaposed with the documentary and material evidence.

There are, of course, a number of methodological problems entailed in relying on these memoirs and testimonies. They are written ex post facto. Memory is elusive. It is impacted by more contemporary events. An individual's recollection of an event may be colored by how another person who was also present remembered it. A survivor may recount the details of an event in order to stress a particular point, a point whose importance only became evident to her well after the fact. This is true, of course, with any memoir or testimony. We write to make a point. It is particularly true when the memoir deals with a traumatic event. And what could have been more traumatic than the Holocaust?

Moreover, memoirs are the voices of those who survived, not those who did not. It was with good reason that David Boder, one of the first scholars to systematically record survivors' accounts of their experiences, entitled his work *I Did Not Interview the Dead*. He knew that the voices he recorded were of the ones who survived. The voices and recollections of those who were not lucky enough to endure were, in the main, lost to us forever.

I write "in the main" because we do have some of the voices of those who perished in the form of diaries such as Renia Spiegel's. Diaries are different, not only because they allow us to hear the voices of those who did not survive. They are different from memoirs because they do not pose these methodological challenges. Irrespective of whether they were written by someone who survived or someone who did not, they are fundamentally different from memoirs because they are contemporaneous accounts. Simply put, the author of the memoir knows the end of the story. The diarist does not. The diarist may well be unaware of the "bigger" picture of what she is experiencing. For example, is the creation of a ghetto in her town part of a broader policy of ghettoization or just something happening where she is? Whereas the person writing after an event may have a sense of how a particular German decree fit into overall Nazi policy, the diarist generally does not. What may seem to be of relatively little importance to the diarist may, in fact, turn out to be of great significance. And conversely, what may seem utterly traumatic to the diarist may pale in comparison to what will follow.

Most important, diaries offer us something that memoirs do not: an emotional immediacy. And it is this immediacy that is so very compelling. I am reminded of Hélène Berr, the Israeli young Parisian woman who kept a diary from 1942 through to the day she and her parents were rounded up in March 1944. Fortuitously, she begins to write but a short time before the decree that all Jews must wear a yellow star. She confides to the diary her struggle with whether to wear it or not. Was wearing it an act of compliance with a hateful regime or did it demonstrate a pride in one's Jewish identity? We read of her reactions to passersbys' comments. Some express solidarity and others pity. She reflects on them, not from a distance of many years, but on the day she encountered them. She does not—because she cannot—contextualize this act as the first step in an array of far worse persecution to come.

In reading Renia Spiegel's diary, I was also reminded, as will be many readers, of Anne Frank's iconic work. All three of these diaries— Spiegel's, Frank's, and Berr's—are filled with the seemingly mundane musings of young girls who are transfixed by first loves and filled with hopes for the future. Renia Spiegel's diary is replete with familiar expressions of teenage angst—first love, first kiss, and jealousies that, in retrospect, may seem meaningless but at the moment seem, at least to Renia, to be momentous. It is also filled with poetry that cannot help but touch the reader.

We who read her writings are possessed of something she did not have: knowledge of the outcome. At the outset of the diary she is distraught that she has been forced to go live with her grandparents and, therefore, has "no real home." It makes her "so sad that I have to cry." Not having a home will pale in comparison to what is to come. Had she written a memoir she would have known that fact and might have flattened this traumatic moment. She does not do so. In 1940, after the fall of Western Europe, she cries, "I'm here on my own, without Mama or Daddy, without a home, poked and laughed at. Oh, God, why did such a horrible birthday have to come? Wouldn't it be better to die? I look down from the height of my 16 years and I wonder whether I'll reach the end."

Were she writing a memoir, knowing what was in the offing, she might well have overlooked this moment of despondence. She might not have been so distraught when the luxury of fur clothing was taken from the Jews. "Yesterday coats, furs, collars, oversleeves, hats, boots were being taken away on the street. And now there's a new regulation that under pain of death it is forbidden to have even a scrap of fur at home."

Nor does she know that what may appear to be a terrible fate might, in fact, turn out to be a lifesaver for some victims. She describes the "fear, despair, abandon" experienced by those deported by the Soviets to Birobidzhan* and other parts of the Soviet interior. She is distraught that "they will travel in closed, dark carriages, 50 people in each. . . . in airless, dirty, infested conditions. They might even be hungry . . . with children among them dying out." Ironically, of course, these people had a far better chance of surviving than did those who would subsequently be forced by the Germans to travel in even worse conditions to an even direr fate.

Yet this young girl—for that is what she really is—with her dreams for her future, recognizes how the vise is closing in on her and her people. "Ghetto! That word is ringing in our ears, it terrifies, it torments. We don't know what will happen to us, where we'll go and what they'll let us take." Nonetheless, she continues to hope for the future. This tension between an increasingly bleak reality and optimism about what might still be possible cannot help but break the reader's heart.

But a few days before being caught and murdered by the Germans, she senses that the end might be coming. She writes with prescience, "My dear Diary, my good, beloved friend! We went through such terrible times together and now the worst moment is upon us. I could be afraid now. But the One who didn't leave us then will help us today too. He'll save us. Hear O, Israel,† save us, help us." Her prayer was for naught.

Renia Spiegel, a young girl so filled with a zest for life and possessed of an ability to describe in prose and in poetry the beauty of the world around

---

* A town in the USSR close to the border with China, administrative center of the Jewish Autonomous Oblast created in 1934.
† A reference to one of the most important prayers in Judaism, Shema Yisrael ("Hear, O, Israel: the Lord, our God, the Lord is one").

her, was denied with one bullet what she so wanted: a future. But for this diary she would have gone, together with millions of others, into the cruel oblivion that was the fate of most Holocaust victims. Those who saved the diary and those who worked to bring it to print have "rescued" her. They could not save her from a cruel fate, nor could they give her that future she so desired, but they have rescued her from the added pain of having been forgotten.

—Deborah E. Lipstadt,
Dorot Professor of Holocaust History at Emory University

PREFACE

My sister, Renia Spiegel, was born on June 18, 1924, in Uhryńkowce, in the Tarnopol province in southeastern Poland. This rural town is called *Uhrynkivtsi* in English, and it is now part of Ukraine. Before World War II ripped apart our family, our people, and our country, Uhryńkowce was in Poland.

I came along on November 18, 1930, six years after Renia. I was happily married to my Vienna, Austria–born husband, George Bellak, for fifty-three years, taught school in New York City for three decades, and am a happy mother of two and a grandmother to three wonderful boys. My sister only lived to be eighteen. She was murdered by the Nazis in 1942. Along with a few photos, some family heirlooms, and the memories I've turned over in my head for almost ninety years, the diary you're about to read is all I have left of her.

I couldn't always face this diary, though. I hid from it and from my past for many years until my daughter, Alexandra Renata, retrieved the diary from the safe-deposit box where it had lain, undisturbed, for over four decades. Realizing what an important work of history and literature it is, and how it could resonate with people around the world, she had it translated into English. She's still working tirelessly to have it published across the globe, helping to make it known why this story has value, even today. I thank her for bringing it—and my sister's memory—back to me.

When I was born, my parents made a stork out of paper, placed it in the window, and told my sister I was coming. By then, my family had moved to an estate in a town called Stawki (*Stavky* in English), which was near the Dniester River and close to the Romanian border, but Renia adored it just as much as her old home. She loved hearing the birds singing. She loved the wind. She loved the forest. I sometimes think the memories of those places—far away in the country, in another time—are what inspired the poetry she wrote in this diary. Her poems were quiet, peaceful thoughts taken down while she was surrounded by war.

War isn't what drove us away from our home in Stawki. I was a child actor, called "the Shirley Temple of Poland," and in 1938, my mom and I moved to Warsaw to promote me. She left Renia with her parents in her hometown of Przemyśl, a small city in southeastern Poland that is now on the border of Ukraine. In January 1939, Renia began her diary. That summer, I visited Renia and my grandparents for vacation, and my mom went back to Warsaw.

The German and Soviet armies invaded Poland in September 1939, and by the end of that month, Poland was divided into two zones of occupation: the German side to the west and the Soviet side to the east. Przemyśl spread across both banks of the river San, so it was split in two. My grandparents lived in the eastern, Soviet-occupied part. Our mother was in Warsaw, in the western, German-occupied part of Poland. We were not allowed to cross the San, so we were suddenly cut off from her. That's when Renia became a surrogate mother to me. We only saw our mom a few times in the next two years, and letters from her didn't arrive very often. Renia pined for her terribly. To this day, I wonder if this diary was a substitute for the mother she loved and missed so much.

Until my sister's boyfriend, Zygmunt, presented this diary to my mom in the early 1950s, I had no idea Renia had kept it. How she'd hidden seven hundred pages from me is a mystery, but it was her secret that she shared only with Zygmunt. Renia left her diary with Zygmunt just before she was killed, and he passed it to someone for safekeeping before he was sent away to the camps. The pages here survived just as he did, and a friend—we still don't know who—brought them to him in the United States. My mother died in 1969, and when I found the diary in her things, I locked it up in a safe-deposit box in a Chase Bank near my apartment. I couldn't bear to read it. It was just too emotional for me.

I've still only read a few parts, and they've made me sick or made me cry. But I know these pages are important, so I will share them with you. We live in a time when tolerance is sometimes hard to find, but it's so important. War is also difficult to figure out—especially if you're in the middle of it—but Renia was always so wise, and she did. I believe her thoughts, her struggles, and her death show us why the world needs peace and acceptance. So, I will let my sister's words and poems speak for themselves. At the end of the diary, I have written commentary that corresponds with particular entries and times of my life that I remember with my sister. I discuss history and what I recall about the last few years of Renia's life, and then I tell you how those of us who survived carried on after the war. My memories aren't as clear as they were eighty years ago, but I do my best. At some points, my thoughts and Renia's may feel scattered or not linear, but that's how a diary is. It's immediate and impulsive, and sometimes my memories are like that, too.

In the end, I know that my words are the legacy of the life my sister didn't get to have, while Renia's are the memories of a youth trapped forever in war.

—Elizabeth Leszczyńska Bellak, formerly Ariana Spiegel

JANUARY 31, 1939

Why did I decide to start my diary today? Did something important happen? Have I discovered that my friends are keeping diaries of their own? No! I just want a friend. I want somebody I can talk to about my everyday worries and joys. Somebody who will feel what I feel, believe what I say and never reveal my secrets. No human could ever be that kind of friend and that's why I have decided to look for a confidant in the form of a diary.

Today, my dear Diary, is the beginning of our deep friendship. Who knows how long it will last? It might even continue until the end of our lives. In any case I promise to always be honest with you, I'll be open and I'll tell you everything. In return you'll listen to my thoughts and my concerns, but never ever will you reveal them to anybody else, you'll remain silent like an enchanted book, locked up with an enchanted key and hidden in an enchanted castle. You won't betray me, if anything it'll be those small blue letters that people are able to recognize.

First of all, allow me to introduce myself. I'm in the third grade of the Maria Konopnicka Middle School for Girls.* My name is Renia, or at least that is what my friends call me. I have a little sister, Arianka,† who wants to be a movie star. (She's partially fulfilled this dream, as she's already been in some movies.)

Our mommy lives in Warsaw. I used to live in a beautiful manor house on the Dniester River. I loved it there. I think these were so far the happiest days of my life. There were storks on old linden trees, apples glistened in the orchard and I had a garden with neat, charming rows of flowers. But that's in the past now and those days will never return. There is no manor house anymore, no storks on old linden trees, no apples or flowers. All that remain are memories, sweet and lovely. And the Dniester River, which flows, distant, strange and cold—which hums, but not for me anymore.

---

* The Maria Konopnicka Girls' Middle School in Przemyśl at 4 Grodzka Street.
† Also *Ariana, Jarośka, Jarka, Jara, Jarusia, Jarosia, Jakusia.*

Now I live in Przemyśl, at my granny's house. But the truth is I have no real home. That's why sometimes I get so sad that I have to cry. I cry, though I don't miss anything, not the dresses, not sweets, not my strange and precious dreams. I only miss my Mama and her warm heart. I miss the house where we all lived together, like in the white manor house on the Dniester River.

> *Again the need to cry takes over me*
> *When I recall the days that used to be*
> *The linden trees, house, storks and butterflies*
> *Far . . . somewhere . . . too far for my eyes*
> *I see and hear what I miss*
> *The wind that used to lull old trees*
> *And nobody tells me anymore*
> *About the fog, about the silence*
> *The distance and darkness outside the door*
> *I'll always hear this lullaby*
> *See our house and pond laid by*
> *And linden trees against the sky . . .*

But I also have joyous moments, and there are so many of them . . . So many! I need to introduce my class to you, so that you can understand all our inside jokes.

My best friend, Norka,* sits next to me. Somebody might say that they don't like Nora, someone else might be delighted with her. I always like Norka, she's always the same sweet Norka to me. We share all the same thoughts, have the same views and opinions. At our school, the girls often get "crushes" on our teachers, so Norka and I have a crush, a real one (some girls do it just to butter the teachers up) on our Latin teacher, Mrs. Waleria Brzozowska née Brühl. We call her "Brühla." Brühla is the wife of a handsome officer who lives in Lwów. She goes to see him every other Sunday. We tried to get his address through the address bureau, but didn't succeed because we don't know his actual name. (We call him

---

* Also *Nora, Noruśka, Noreńka.*

"Zdzisław.") Brühla teaches Latin and we're good at this subject, which surely proves that we really love her.

The next girl in our row is Belka or "Belania"—fat and stocky like three hundred devils! She has an exceptional talent for academics and an even more exceptional talent for earning dislike. She has a terrible "crush" on Mrs. Skorska* and pulls stupid faces when looking at her.

Next comes Irka (ira-ae—anger). I don't like Irka and it's in my blood. I inherited this hatred: my mommy didn't like Irka's mother much when they were in middle school. I started disliking Irka even more when she began undermining me at school—all of this plus her unfair school report and disgusting sweet-talking, lying and insincerity made me genuinely hate her. What needs to be added to this mixture is also the fact that Brühla goes to visit Irka at home, which we investigated. And Irka's mother goes to visit Brühla at home, which we discovered peeking into the ground floor windows of Brühla's place, where I spent many an hour with Nora waiting for her. All of that means I can't stand the girl! But since we're in the same class, we have to get by. So Nora and I just clench our fists and wait for an opportunity.

When it comes to the girls sitting next to Irka, I either don't care about them at all or I like them a little bit. On the other hand I care a bit more about the girl sitting at the very back of the classroom, namely Luna, who sits behind me and constantly bombards my back. She thinks of herself as a very talented and unearthly creature. During parties and generally all the time she "pretends" to be this or that, tries to draw attention to her beauty (which she doesn't possess), her exceptional abilities (which are figments of her imagination) and her importance (which she's never had). Luna is always trying to get the attention from boys, so, being short, she wears high heels, pencils her eyebrows longer and powders her face. At first she "borrowed" Irka Łozińska's powder and did it supposedly "just for fun." And now she doesn't do it "for fun" at all, but entirely seriously.

Irka Łozińska must be the most beautiful girl in our class or perhaps even the whole school. You don't even mind her dark, almost orange skin tone (powder-related, of course) and her patronizing voice or harsh

---

* Olga Skorska.

words spoken by coral-red lips revealing beautiful, snow-white teeth. But Irka has the worst of all flaws; she has tuberculosis . . . Yes, sometimes she bleeds from the mouth and nose. I feel sorry for Irka. She has a boyfriend who loves her, but he doesn't know that his girlfriend's so seriously ill.

Irka sits at the very back of the classroom. Next to her there are two stony figures: Halina (very bad) with greatly coiffured hair and Sławka who always pulls surprised faces, never answers and hides Halina under her desk when she wants to avoid answering a teacher's question. Then there is the third Irka, thin as a rake and very ugly. Next to her sits Elza, my former neighbor. She plays all innocent but I know very well that it's just a game. She has decent grades, but her school report is always better than she deserves. Supposedly she always copies her Latin homework from the third Irka . . . but who cares.

Then there is the president of our class, Krzyśka. Krzyśka doesn't know anything and speaks as if she has dumplings filled with sand in her mouth, but she's pretty and always head-over-heels in love with all her Zbyszeks, Sławeks, Leszeks, Zdzisios, etc. She's friends with Luna.

In front of her the first Eda (there are three of them) bends and sways. Eda is a "lady with claws," she's engaged, has a great figure and all. The second Eda is Belka's former friend. She also has a crush on Mrs. Skorska, but she's not good at history, which makes me suspicious. The third Eda was our enemy as recently as several months ago. Just imagine, my dear Diary, some stranger, some "stray" from the sticks arrives and wants to be the boss, tries to show us we are slow and thinks of herself as an "all-around talent." Seriously?

Luśka and Dziunka sit in front of Eda. Dziunka makes "nervously tectonic" moves. I was on bad terms with her for over a year, but I got over it on Brühla's name day. Dziunka is considered the most boring person in the class and, indeed, she is one. Luśka is silly, stupid and backward. You can tell her whatever you want. But she's a fun one, she always dances the "Andrusovo" dance with me at parties. Once Luśka yelled during a math lesson, "Miss, miss, I haven't been called up for such a long time and I like math so much!" Nora's response to that was, "Luśka, come on, don't be stupid." "Not at all," Luśka answered, but then, when she realized what she'd done, she started stammering and widened her shiny eyes.

In front of them, in front of the first Eda, Luśka and Dziunka, there is a strange desk reserved for "antiques." Which means Janka. Janka is the best in the class at "playing stupid" and she only survives thanks to other people's help. When she gets called up to the blackboard, she has all the answers written on her nails. If, by any chance, the teacher notices something suspicious, Janka quickly licks the ink off and plays the saint. Janka knows how to cry, wail and even faint on demand, quite like the first Eda, who suddenly feels woozy when Pacuła is about to ask her to recite a poem. Janka is generally very talented when it comes to making scenes. Next to her sits Wisia, a little creature who's not even three and a half foot tall despite her fifteen years of age. The third in the row is Frejka or Salka. She gets nervous attacks every now and then, sometimes can't say a word when too upset, walks in comical steps and skips, and often "can't stand" sitting by her desk.

I should also mention Ninka, this unusual girl who looks completely innocent but receives poste restante letters from various "peoples," arranges meetings in dark streets, visits lonely men and is proud of it. She's quite nice. There are more girls like her in our class, but, as I said before, I either don't care about them or don't want to hang around with them, because I am a good girl.

We've been planning a party for months now. We've fought and disagreed, but the party is on this coming Saturday.

FEBRUARY 2, 1939[1]

My dear Diary! I have always been just average in gymnastics, so I practice at home to get better. I have just managed to pull off my first somersault. None of my friends can do it. I'm triumphant, though I've grazed my knee.

FEBRUARY 5, 1939

My dear Diary, it's after the party, finally! I'm so happy. It was a great party and everyone, especially Brühla, had a wonderful time. But some sadness awaited me after the party. And again, for the umpteenth time, I thought, "I wish Mama were here." What happened was that Irka's mother, Mrs. Oberhard, was all over Brühla, sweet-talking her as much as she could, which, of course, would be sure to benefit Irka and her younger sister in the near future. Oh, dear Diary, if you could only know how hard it is to want something so badly, to work so hard for it and then be denied it at the finishing line! What was it actually that I wanted? I don't know. I was given the highest praise by Pacuła, which I don't care about (she talked to us, me and Norka). Brühla was quite nice. But I'm still not satisfied.

Luna performed twice and so did I. Today I saw Brühla with Mrs. Oberhard, most likely walking back from hers. I nodded politely, walked past and said to Nora, "What do you think? She was at hers again, wasn't she?" And then I suddenly see her pulling a stupid face. I look around and see that Brühla is walking right behind us. She looks horrible, I don't know what's wrong with her, I would like to be of use to her, to help, perhaps to advise, but the abyss between us is so huge, so very, very huge . . . Perhaps even larger than the one separating me from Mama. She could help me too, she could advise. But it's much harder, oh so much harder to bridge this gap.

FEBRUARY 8, 1939

Dear Diary! It's been several days since I told you about my life, but actually nothing special has happened. Life goes on as normal, with few small exceptions. Brühla attended a Latin teachers' conference, so Latin was taught by Mr. Skorski. Mr. Dziedzic praised Irka very much (undeservedly), Belka got a bad grade, I got away with it, but I'm worried about tomorrow, as it could be a really bad day. That's all I needed to tell you.

FEBRUARY 11, 1939

It's raining today . . . Such a sad, gray day. But I don't feel very sad, I don't know why. Perhaps it's the idea of leaving for Canada, though it might not be so good there after all. Or perhaps it's because I'm making a Greek vase. Anyway I'm not as sad as I usually am on rainy days when I just stand by the window and count the tears trickling down the windowpane. There are plenty of them. One small one runs, then another larger one follows it closely, then the fifth, sixth . . . as well as two on my cheeks. They all run down, as if they wanted to drop onto the wet, muddy street, as if they wanted to make it even dirtier, as if they wanted to make this day ugly, even uglier than it already is. But today is a mystery. Like . . . like a rubbish bin. Everybody thinks it's nothing much, it's simply nothing. But it's not the case. I don't know. People might laugh at me, but you'll surely understand, my dear friend. The thing is sometimes I think inanimate objects can talk. (Actually, they are not inanimate at all. They have souls, just like people.) Sometimes I think waterworks giggle. And it's not just me thinking this, so it must be true. Other people call this giggle different names, but it never even crosses their minds that it's just that: a giggle. Or a rubbish bin:

Oh, the night! Darkness came at last!
I don't like it here! I'm feeling harassed!
It was better in the city,
With its comfort, light and warmth. What a pity,
A page came clean
From a weekly film magazine.
They only bought me yesterday
and I'm already in the garbage today!
You, at least something you've seen.
At least in the world you have been.
Your life was peaceful when at a newsagent's bound
While I had to run around
In the streets, shouting all the time.
It's better to be a weekly
Than a daily that passes quickly.
I was prepared and I'm not bitter
About ending up in the litter,
Said wrapping paper without a jitter.
I was a children's magazine, alas,
Beautifully illustrated en masse,
Full of color and class,
The trash can outlast.

7

I'm of a different kind,
Than a daily, I find
Or a film weekly for that matter,
Or even this . . . this wrapping paper.
So let me tell you, I don't like it here.
Stay away from me or I'll disappear!
That causes a proper commotion in the bin.
What?! What cheek! Aha! There you go, you mean!
And all the papers together
Flew out of the trash can like feathers.
People were surprised in the morning,
They took it as a warning
That somebody threw papers to begin
With, on the ground instead of in the bin.

Renia. I send you kisses, but now I have to sit down and cram.

FEBRUARY 13, 1939

Can there be a worse day than Monday the 13th? Monday on its own is usually quite bad, and now we have the number 13 added to it. Bad luck! It was definitely not a good day for me. On top of all other little pieces of bad luck, I'm at school. It's Latin and Brühla enters, so I think she'll do a test. But no. OK, better still (I think), I'm safe. But she wants us to write essays on little pieces of paper torn out of our notebooks. Mine went as well as it could on Monday the 13th. On a bad day it went really badly. Why? Humph . . . Good question, why?

Only a person who's not superstitious could ask this. Exactly, so first of all: I missed school and as a result didn't have certain forms; secondly: I was laughing my head off all the time; and thirdly: the essay was written on torn out pieces of paper which I didn't respect much, so I made light of it, not even thinking that Brühla might collect those pages. At geography we had a sudden and turbulent fight over the chairs, which I didn't take part in, but was still considered one of the castaways. We were supposed to move about the classroom. I said many times before that I'm not some kind of a loser. So I quietly moved with Nora to the last desk.

Gruca looks for me and tells me to move. I don't want to, I say I'm good where I am. She goes on and I go on.

"Move!"

"But I haven't done anything."

And so on and on. Finally I realize that I won't be able to get away with it, so I look for somewhere else to sit.

"There is a place there, please move," Gruca says.

"Oh, anywhere but there. I'm so delicate, I get colds easily. I might get too hot by the stove and get pneumonia," I reply.

It's time to end this.

"Fine, here then," Gruca says again.

"Oh, not by the door! How can I sit by the door, being so delicate."

The whole class is of course in stitches, howling and roaring with laughter.

I realize that I have no choice and I finally move, but it's only on her fourth attempt. Nora sits under the desk all this time and I keep knocking. I then tell Gruca that I can't see the map. And I continue knocking, pretending that a school inspector is coming. There was probably a thousand more adventures, but I'm glad that this exceptionally bad day's over now.

FEBRUARY 14, 1939

Parent-teacher conference today. It didn't go well, thanks to the dregs of yesterday. Brühla said my essay was terrible, so now I have something to worry about.

FEBRUARY 15, 1939

Nothing special today. Przemyśl is getting ready for a gas attack and I'm getting ready for a nervous attack. All because of last Monday! I was called up to the board at chemistry. I was prepared! Damn it, Dziedzic was trying to trick me.

FEBRUARY 26, 1939[2]

I've been busy for the last few days. Arianka is here. We have a gathering tomorrow and I need to write my report.

MARCH 28, 1939[3]

God, I'm so sad, so very sad . . . I'd just like to cry, wail and sob. How can I express how terrible I'm feeling? No . . . That's not possible. Mama just left and who knows when I'll see her again. I fell out with Nora several days ago so I need to hang out with Irka, which is not helping.

And then there are memories . . . They're always there and even though they make me cry, even though they break my heart, they're the sweetest. They're memories of the best time in my life. It's springtime already! Spring used to be so good there. Birds were singing, flowers were in bloom; it was all sky, heart and happiness! People there would be thinking of the holidays now. It was so different to everything here. So tranquil, warm and friendly; I loved it so much.

On the evening of the Passover Seder, I waited for Elijah. Maybe there was a time when this holy old man came to see happy children. But if he only came to see poor people, if he never stood in our wide-open doors, if he never let me see him, then he has to come now, when I have nothing. Nothing apart from memories. Grandpa's unwell. Mama's very worried about me. Oh! I'm so unhappy! Sometimes I don't eat on purpose to avoid . . .

It waits for me everywhere
It lurks, as I'm aware
Its ghastly, bony hands
Want to get me in their commands
It whispers into my ear
In every mouthful, all I hear
It waits for me, it calls me loudly
It shakes its hands so proudly
It wags its finger
It watches and lingers . . .

APRIL 2, 1939[4]

The religious retreat's over. I didn't enjoy those days. I'm still angry with Nora. And Irka didn't want to leave me alone, so I hung out with her a bit. Toward the end I didn't even have a good book to read. The holidays are coming. I'm learning French now and if there's no war I might go to France. I was supposed to go before, but Hitler took over Austria, then Sudetenland, Czechoslovakia, Klaipeda,* and who knows what he'll do next. He's affecting my life, too. I want to write a poem for Arianka. I'll be very happy if it comes out well.

> *A little hen was feeling sickly.*
> *She went to see a doctor quickly.*
> *She told him in no uncertain terms:*
> *"Help me, doctor, I have concerns.*
> *When I'm angry, something's tingling,*
> *Something's jabbing, something's stinging*
> *(So badly do I suffer, it keeps me busy!)*
> *All the time I'm feeling dizzy,*
> *I'm not hungry, my stomach's churning,*
> *I can't sleep at all till the morning.*
> *Then I'm tired in the daytime.*
> *Migraines mean I'm not in my prime.*
> *My face is a shade of prawn.*
> *And when my husband crows at dawn*
> *I go purple and black,*
> *I have a nervous attack.*
> *And let me also add, doctor dear*
> *That I get very sweaty, I fear."*
> *So many serious ailments*
> *Make the doctor head for derailment.*

---

* These were the territories annexed by Nazi Germany in 1938 and 1939, before World War II broke out.

He thought and thought about it hard,
He pored over many a book's card,
And finally he said to the hen:
"Go back to your pen.
I can't help you, it's time to die."
"Die? What say you? You surely lie!
My dear doctor, don't be a beast,
I'm not ill, not in the least!"

APRIL 7, 1939

Yes . . . Oh yes . . . A bird's song
It's been oh so long
So many hours did go by
It's all the same as time does fly

It's equally sad . . . tearful . . . heavy-hearted. I don't have a new coat and this one's old and worn down. I don't have new shoes, like all my friends. And even though I console myself that I have sweet thoughts and good dreams for the future, I'm still sad. The whole of Przemyśl is spruced up, every person shimmers from afar with their new, special shoes (you can tell by looking at the underside of a shoe and by listening to voices saying here and there, "Ooh, blisters!"). And everybody has a solemn face, as you should on festive days. I just don't know why this festive mood reminds me of the time when the air-raid training was taking place.

"Mr. Sztajner, I tell you, what a farce!"

"Unbelievable! Right! They made me some kind of commandant, good sir. I keep running around like a headless chicken all day long, good sir. And I don't even know what's what!"

"Yeah, yeah. 'Comediant' in the old age. Whatever else?"

You hear conversations like this one all over the city.

"Dear friend, let me tell you, it slightly stinks of war."

"Yup. The end of the world's coming . . . Heard something about bombs coming down. But people say it won't be a war, my friend, just that they'll keep having a go at each other, the ones from the bottom and the ones from the top."

"No war, you say?! But I think there'll be war. You, my friend, you don't know it, but they always put posters out before the war. They come and go and then, suddenly, my friend, war breaks out."

C: "Sirens?! An alarm! Turn the lights off! Draw the curtains in the windows! Kazio, grab a pan and whack it, quick," the commandant yells.

N: "What are you talking about, my dear neighbor? It clearly says that in case of an alarm one needs to bang on a rail," the neighbor says.

Neighbor 2: "What the hell? Are you crazy? In case of an alarm, one needs to do nothing, just stand quietly in the gateway."

C: "I think I am the commandant here and I know what to do! Here you are, everywhere there are gongs going, Kazio! A pan and a rail, whack them both."

N: "Sir, and what about an armband?"

C: "Excuse me?! Don't tell me what to do. If you keep opposing me, I'll immediately hand my resignation to the building overman. And you'll of course need to pay a fine."

Female neighbor: "Will you be quiet? I've only just put children to bed and you're making so much noise. What's going on? We need order. Let decent people live their lives. You are the commandant and instead of ensuring there is peace and quiet, you make noise in the neighborhood, keep children awake, get decent people out of beds?"

C: "My dear lady, there was an alarm . . ."

Female neighbor 3: "What alarm, what alarm?! Mrs. Pietroszkowa, have you heard it? I've only just managed to put children to bed. Henio is ill, doctor said he needs rest. And now all this commotion in the building in the middle of the night. Unheard of! Have you ever heard of anything quite like this?"

Mrs. Pietroszkowa: "Yes, my dear, that's a real rumpus."

Neighbor 2: "Didn't I say that what we need is stand here quietly and wait until . . ."

Zosia: "My Mom has a migraine. She said to be quiet right away or she'll call the police."

C: "I'm the commandant here, the responsibility lies with me, so I do what I think is right and I don't care about any ailments. Kazio, another blow on the barrel!"

Constable: "What's going on here? Go back to your flats. The alarm's long over. All this shouting! The racket! I'll make a note. All residents of 13 Nieszczęśliwska Street will pay a fine for making noise."

P: "Some commandant!"

MAY 4, 1939

I haven't told you anything for a while. Why? Do I know why? I study French now and I go to Jerschina.* I've written a paper on Roman painting and now plan or rather I've already started writing a German text. Yesterday, on May 3rd, I took part in a march, which is why I'm unwell today. I got soaked in the rain. Much has changed since my last conversation with you. Mama and Arianka went to Łódź. I'm on bad terms with Brühla. She didn't examine me at Greek and she told the Head that I just wander around with Nora all the time. That's what Irka told me, but Irka likes to spread gossip. There was a school dance, but I didn't take part. By contrast Luna was showing off as hard as she could. For some reason this idiot has imagined she's my rival! My rival! I couldn't care less about her recitation. No, I don't care at all, I just happen to know a little bit about it. I can't say I bragged about myself either. But my feeling is she'll one day become a cabaret artiste (you can tell by looking at her hair and movements), while I have different plans (I think), so our paths won't cross, so it's stupid to say that Luna could be my rival. Today I declare war—an internal war. I told her about it yesterday and I'll stick to it. What happened was she didn't want to let me into the row, where my place is. Finally the commandant arrived and told me to switch places with her, i.e., with Luna. So she says to me, "I knew you were right, but I wanted to spite you!" She wanted to spite me! Ha ha ha, that is simply funny. She, who fully depends on me at Latin and in general. So I told her, "You wanted to spite me, so now remember that I'll try to spite you too." I'll do just that, until the end, because that's what I want.

---

* Stanisław Jerschina—specialist in Polish studies, teacher, founder and director of the Teaching College in Kielce.

MAY 7, 1939

May. A very strange May it is. So sad . . . Brrr . . . It's raining. And to think it's May already, May, and I still haven't seen a tree in bloom, haven't smelled fields waking up, my fields . . . It rains. It's good that it's raining. Recently I like rain, because at least I know that it was like that there too, when it rained. Yesterday I went to a party and then talked to Nora about this and that, about different goals that people have in life, about the benefits of studying. I like talking so much when I know that somebody understands me . . .

> *The moon swims out in silence*
> *To shine in the sky, to shimmer for dreamers*
> *While below a street rumbles shrilly*
> *Crunching with labor, hot and weary*
> *Loud rat-tat-tat-tat of human steps*
> *Echoes from cobbled streets*
> *Gray carts and their wheels*
> *Groan and never miss a beat*
> *Taxis whoosh ahead*
> *And red tramways smoothly slide*
> *On their tracks of steel*
> *Stopping only sometimes*
> *To take in yet again*
> *Another mass of people*
> *Then leave without complaint*
> *Propelled by fiery heat*
> *Above in the azure sky*
> *The moon's silver disc moves too*
> *But nobody sees its flight*
> *Below a street hums, "Whoo"*
> *Chains of bright lights*
> *Illuminate the night*
> *So strangely draped*
> *In shop windows and posters staked*

Huge electric streetlights
Stand below the silver
Of the trembling moon
No one looks up with delight
The street below is way too bright

Renia

When I look behind my small window box
I see the same rooftops, same stationer's shops
I see the same gutters, nestled snugly into walls
And only people in the street change at all
Even the road, shimmering and slippery after rain
Even the people, neighbors from across are all the same
The spectacled lawyer and his daughter
The pharmacist above, the janitor in his quarters
Two servants and the gray-haired lady on the third floor
And here a girl, a doll, a clown, a monkey, toys galore
They always open their shutters the same way
And look down at the street, every day
The houses look out too, as do windowpanes, dozing cozily
And only the people in the street change, supposedly

JUNE 18, 1939[5]

It's my birthday today. I don't want to think about anything sad, about the fact that I'm not there . . . Hush! So instead I'm thinking about all the useful things I've done so far in my life.

A voice, "None."
Me, "I get good grades at school."
Voice, "You haven't earned it. What else?"
Me, "Nothing. I really want to go to France."
Voice, "You want to be famous?"
Me, "I'd like to be famous, but I won't be. So I want to be happy, very happy."

Tomorrow's the end of the school year, but I don't care. About anything... Anything... Anything.

I like Jerschina very much again, but Brühla less so. I didn't tell Nora about it, don't want to worry her. Tomorrow I'll tell you about our trip.

If a man had wings
If souls could be in all things
The world would lose its temper
The sun would shower us with embers
The people would dance beyond the beyond
Shouting, more! We want to abscond!
What we need is wind and speed
The world is dark, stifling, squeezed
Let it go to sweeping heights
Let it become great and bright
Let it cross into a boundless domain
Let it lose itself in its own vast reign
Supported by hundreds of limbs
Millions of hands, mighty wings
Let the time string go flash through
Until the darkness of the night descends anew
This powerful realm of the underworld
Until its flight slowing down occurred
Until, tired, exhausted and all
It will have to fall

AUGUST 15, 1939[5]

I haven't spoken to you for a while. The end of the school year is long gone, my summer vacation is almost over, and I haven't spoken to you. I went to see my aunt in the countryside, I went to Warsaw, saw Mama and now I'm back. But you don't know about any of that. You were lying here, left on your own with my thoughts and you don't even know that we have a secret mobilization, you don't know that the Russians have signed a treaty with the Germans. You don't know that people are stockpiling food, that everybody's on the alert, waiting for . . . war. When I was saying goodbye to Mama, I hugged her hard. I wanted to tell her everything with this silent hug. I wanted to take her soul and leave her my own, because—when?

> *Mother's embrace*
> *One and only, the last*
> *Will stay with me through all the days*
> *Through all tears, all ill fortunes*
> *Through all tough moments*
> *We will both get through, you and I*
> *And then a ray will glimmer*

I can't think logically today. Supposedly they call it "spleen." Something flies at a rapid pace and disappears into the mist. Zigzags, circles, stripes, fog . . . pink fog, greenish. No. I'm not curious of anything. One thought spins around my head, only one, the same one all the time. Mom . . . war . . . brown shoes . . . war . . . Mom.

SEPTEMBER 6, 1939

War broke out on Thursday! First on 30th or 31st of August Poland went to war with Germany. Then England and France also declared war on Hitler and surrounded him on three sides. But he isn't sitting idly. Enemy planes keep flying over Przemyśl, and every now and then there's an air raid siren. But, thank God, no bombs have fallen on our city so far. Other cities like Kraków, Lwów, Częstochowa and Warsaw have been partially destroyed.

But we are all fighting, we are all fighting, from young girls to soldiers. I've been taking part in female military training—digging air raid trenches, sewing gas masks. I've been serving as a runner. I have shifts serving tea to the soldiers. I walk around and collect food for the soldiers. In a word, I'm fighting alongside the rest of the Polish nation. I'm fighting and I'll win!

SEPTEMBER 10, 1939

Oh, God! My God! We've been on the road for three days now. Przemyśl was attacked. We had to flee. The three of us escaped: me, Arianka and Grandpa. We have left the burning, partially destroyed city in the middle of the night on foot, carrying our bags. Granny stayed behind. Lord, please protect her. We heard on the road that Przemyśl was being destroyed.

> *We left the city*
> *Like fugitives*
> *On our own, in the dark, dull night*
> *The city bade us farewell*
> *With the sound of buildings crashing down*
> *Darkness was above my head*
> *Mercy of good people*
> *Mother's embrace in the far distance*
> *Let them be our guidance*
> *Let them give us comfort and assistance*
> *We will walk through*
> *All our trials*
> *Until the day breaks, until it glints*
> *We are lonely fugitives*
> *Fugitives deserted by all since*

SEPTEMBER 18, 1939

We've been in Lwów for almost a week and we can't get through to Zaleszczyki. The city is surrounded. Food is in short supply. Sometimes I get up at dawn and stand in a long line to get bread. Apart from that, we've been spending all day in a bunker, a cellar, listening to the terrible whistling of bullets and explosions of bombs. God, please save us. Some bombs have destroyed several tenement houses, and three days later they dug people out from the rubble, alive. Some people are sleeping in the bunkers; those brave enough to sleep at home have to wake up several times each night and run downstairs to their cellars. This life is terrible. We're yellow, pale, from this cellar life—from the lack of water, comfortable beds and sleep.

But horrible thoughts are much worse, black as night, vulture-like. Granny stayed in Przemyśl, Daddy's in Zaleszczyki and Mom, my Mama, is in Warsaw. Warsaw is surrounded, defending itself bravely, resisting attack again and again. We Poles are fighting like knights in an open field where the enemy and God can see us. Not like the Germans, who bombard civilians' homes, who turn churches to ashes, who poison little children with toxic candy (contaminated with cholera and typhus) and balloons filled with mustard gas. We defend ourselves and we're winning, just like Warsaw, like the cities of Lwów and Przemyśl.

My Mama's in Warsaw. I love her the most in the world, my dearest soul, my most precious. I know if she sees children clinging to their mothers in bunkers, she must be feeling the same way we feel when we see it. Oh my God! The greatest, the one and only. God, please save my Mama, give her faith that we are alive. Merciful God, please make the war stop, make all people good and happy. Amen.

SEPTEMBER 22, 1939

My dear Diary! I had a strange day today. Lwów surrendered. Not to Germany, but to Russia. Polish soldiers were disarmed in the streets. Some, with tears in their eyes, just dropped their bayonets to the ground and watched the Russians break their rifles. Civilians took horses, saddles, blankets. I feel such grief, such great grief . . . Only a small handful are still fighting. Despite the order, defenders of Lwów are still continuing their heroic fight to die for their homeland.

> *The city's surrendered*
> *On its borders*
> *A handful continue the fight*
> *Without a command*
> *A handful continue the fight*
> *They won't surrender*
> *They are Lwów defenders*

SEPTEMBER 28, 1939

Russians have entered the city.* There are still shortages of food, clothing, shoes, everything. Long lines are forming in front of every shop. The Russians are especially eager to buy things. They've been organizing raids to get watches, textiles, shoes, etc.

This Red Army is strange. You can't tell a private from an officer. They all wear the same grayish-brown uniforms. They all speak the language I can't understand. They call each other *Tovarishch*.† Sometimes the officers' faces are more intelligent though. Poland has been totally flooded by the German and Russian armies. The only island still fighting is Warsaw. Our government has fled the country. And I had so much faith.

Where is Mama? What's happened to her? God! You listened to my prayer and there is no war anymore (or at least I can't see it). Please listen to the first part of my prayer, too, and protect my Mama from evil. Wherever she is, whatever is happening to her, please keep an eye on her and on us and help us in all our needs! Amen.

OCTOBER 27, 1939

I've been back in Przemyśl for a while now. I go to school. Life has gone back to its everyday routine, but at the same time it's different, so sad. There is no Mama. We haven't heard from her. I had a terrible dream that she's dead. I know it's not possible. I cry all the time, tormented by bad feelings. If only I knew that I would see her in two months' time, even a year, as long as I knew I would see her for sure. That's impossible. No, let me die. Holy God, please give me an easy death.

OCTOBER 28, 1939

School life is so strange. Yesterday we had a meeting, the day before—a march. Polish women riot when they hear people saluting Stalin. They

---

* The occupation of Lwów began the afternoon of September 22, 1939.
† Comrade (Russian).

refuse to join in. They write secret messages saying "Poland has not yet perished,"* even though, to be honest, it perished a long time ago. And now there is Western Ukraine here, there is "coomunism," everybody is equal and that's what hurts them. It hurts them that they can't say, "You lousy Yid." They still say it, but in secret.

Those Russians are such handsome boys (though not all of them). One of them was determined to marry me. "*Pajdyom baryshnya na moyu kvateru budem zhyly,*" etc. etc. France and England are fighting with the Germans and something's brewing here, but what do I care? I just want Mama to come, to be with us. Then I can face all my trials and tribulations.

One "auntie" died here, this silver-haired, thin, wrinkly old lady:

> *She lived so quietly . . .*
> *She was like a shadow*
> *One gloomy autumn, she just let go*
> *This gray-haired old lady, all wrinkles and wobbles*
> *Hunched, shriveled, coughing, always needing goggles*
> *She died . . . (as people do)*
> *And away from a calendar a card flew*
> *A new day arrived*
> *Nothing changed in life*
> *This life, that she held so dear*
> *The silver-haired lady, shed a tear*
> *For her, she was like a shadow*
> *And one gloomy autumn, she just let go*

NOVEMBER 1, 1939

I'm so angry today. Angry, as they say. But, truth be told, I'm sad, very, very sad.

There's a new youth club here now. Lots of boys and girls have been going there, and there's fun to be had (for some). I don't have a crush on Brühla anymore. I finally told Nora about it, and she told me she feels the

---

*"Jeszcze Polska nie zginęła" (Poland has not yet perished)—Polish national anthem.

same way. Now, according to the stages of a girl's development I should "fall in love" with a boy. I like Jurek. But Jurek doesn't know about it and won't ever figure it out. You know it, you and I, and . . .

The first day at the club was fun (I mean I had fun), but today I felt like a fish out of water. People played this flirting game (some game it is) and I didn't get even one card. I'm embarrassed to admit it even to you. Some boy named Julek (not Jurek) supposedly likes me, but why? Maybe because I'm so different from my friends. I'm not saying that's a good thing—it could even be a bad thing—but I'm very different from them. I don't even know how to laugh in a flirtatious way. When I laugh, it's for real, openly. I don't know how to "behave" around boys. That's why I miss the old days, the age of pink . . . blue . . . being carefree . . . When Mama was still with me, when I had my own home, when there was peace in the world, when everything was blue, bright, serene; when such weather prevailed in my heart.

> *I lived among some cheerful meadows*
> *Among fields painted with sunlight*
> *I smiled at the golden stars*
> *To pink emergence of daylight*
> *My life was also all in pink*
> *As bright as days filled with sun*
> *I didn't want it to end in a blink*
> *Being a happy echo was fun*
> *Sounding with silver glee*
> *Reflecting merrily off the sky*
> *In love with all, happy as can be*
> *I didn't know how much a heart could cry*
> *I didn't know the weeping of a soul*
> *I didn't know it could be different.*
> *Today I'm filled with regret*
> *And though I am still so young and whole*
> *I look back into recent past*
> *And cry. It's gone . . . Shame, I'm aghast . . .*

NOVEMBER 6, 1939[6]

I'm ill. I have a sore throat. But I am breathing more easily now. I know that Mama's alive, that she's in Warsaw. She'll come see me any day now. And I can't wait, can't wait . . . Ticio* sent a postcard; they have everything in abundance in Horodenka.† Daddy'll get a job as a farmer. He might bring us some provisions.

We have three days off. Anniversary of the revolution. There'll be morning assemblies at schools, young people's marches. Such a shame I can't be part of it. I'm ill . . .

DECEMBER 9, 1939

Holidays are coming. Daddy got a job in a sugar refinery. I might go there. Mama's in Warsaw, not planning to come here.

I might get a scholarship . . . Let's hope . . .

I love him, he's wonderful, just like I dream about, I love him—but I don't know if that's in fact love. He doesn't know of me and I only know that he's in Border Patrol. And one more thing, something terribly "teenagerish"—I'd love to kiss his lips, eyes, temples, just like you read in romance books.

Irka is passionate. She goes to Marysia's; there are plenty of beds there, with bed linen, and each couple goes to a separate room and . . . well, that makes you think. Belka said one mysterious sentence while we were working (Belka knows a lot), "Anyway look at Irka, at her broad walk . . ." Ugh . . . It's so disgusting. Truth be told, I'm not passionate. I'd like to have a pretty husband, like him . . . I'd like to live in Crimea in a pretty villa-house, have a golden-haired little boy, a son, be happy and love everything . . .

I have to write down a translation of a German poem. Oh, I've grown sick of school!

---

* *Ticio, Ticiu, Tusio*—Renia's father.
† A town in Stanisławów Voivodeship, an administrative center of the Horodenka district, at the time under Soviet occupation, later under German occupation.

Always at work, millions of hands
For thousand centuries, many decades
And every hand, which for an ax bends
Is like an Atlas, each the sky aids

Rattling and whirring, roaring and banging
This is the sound of our land's iron call
Crunching and quaking, booming and clanging
Immortal singing of work befalls

Plenty of cylinders must go in and out
And plenty of screw bolts must stay about
Hammers must strike the anvil with might
To make the world simmer, be alight

Thousands of people must be on fire
Brains must ignite and never tire
To keep this flame always ablaze
Filling the world with warm light for years

DECEMBER 10, 1939

"We work!" This is the title of our newspaper. "Work is power!," "Forward with work" and many more similar slogans I've heard. And I spent some time thinking about what work is. Every time I thought about it, various images came to mind. Here is a gray working army, these are workmen, I can see students with their heads bowed, I can see pilots in roaring planes, seamen somewhere out at sea. They are all part of the powerful working army; work goes on out at sea, on land and in the air. Yes, but what in fact is work?

Everything hums and roars around
Work's going on, never breaks down
It blares, it rattles and flutters in spades
Asking for soldiers for its work brigades!

Calls everybody on land and at sea
Those in the mines and those who fly free
To grab their axes, their chisels, their trowels
To join the workforces and not throw in the towel
To conquer the world as it is wide
To build a new one with work and to do it with pride ·

DECEMBER 15, 1939

The radio didn't mention an explosion in a middle school in Przemyśl, the papers didn't write about it, paperboys out in the streets didn't shout, "The Konopnicka School has been blown up with steam!" Nobody knew about anything, but "something" did happen. This "something" took place at a chemistry or physics lesson. It was, of course, before the war. Here's what happened: we had a guest at physics; we all shook like jelly, practiced all possible emergency measures, like "a wireless telephone line," nudging, kicking, clearing one's throat and other such methods, known only to us. Finally the new lesson started. And it was going well! But something was ticking! On the table there were plenty of little bottles, flasks, bowls, test tubes, stands, burners and other devices. It all looked rather impressive, powerful and very "scientific." Even more so, when it was all lined, connected—it was pretty. I can still hear this voice saying clearly, "But please remember to leave an opening for steam, this is very important." Of course! Certainly! Absolutely! All was going well, exceptionally well, the reactions were just like in the textbook, until . . . oh, what horror! In comparison to what happened next, Zeus sending a thunderbolt down was a quiet whisper and the clash of swords at Troy was a delicate rustle. Bottles, flasks, bowls, test tubes—first they all jumped up into the air and then landed on our poor tables, books and notebooks. The esteemed guest was of course outraged, etc. etc. . . . But let me keep that a secret, since the papers and the radio didn't talk about it. And I've already spilled the beans, so now I ask for your discretion. Let's keep this between us.

DECEMBER 26, 1939

Half of the school year is gone already. The time has passed in a flash. First I was elected to the committee as the head of the drama club, then we were supposed to have a party with boys, there were many searches in the city, there were four sexual murders. And now, tomorrow night, I can go to see Daddy at Horodenka. But before I have a meeting tomorrow and I'll go for a rehearsal at Słowacy.* There might even be a party. Shame I won't be there, since recently I'm feeling kind of . . . I'm going through silly, salad days and thoughts, which are quite pleasant. Just silly thoughts: life, buying powder compacts, taking photos, everything, everything is silly.

The meeting's tomorrow. I need to prepare a cabaret song about our class 4A based on "Suffer, my soul."†

> I
> *Suffer, my soul and you will be redeemed*
> *Don't suffer enough and you'll be condemned*
> *In our fourth grade*
> *Young girls in droves*
> *Dreaming, the whole brigade*
> *Sitting by a cold stove*
> *Suffer, my soul . . .*

> II
> *As soon as by the stove*
> *Rogues gather and hove*
> *Immediately the voices boom*
> *"Please leave the classroom!"*
> *Suffer, my soul . . .*
> *Even though our breaks*
> *Loudly reverberate with sound*

---

* The Juliusz Słowacki High School in Przemyśl.
† Title and first line of a folk song.

But during the hour
Everybody quietly cowers
Suffer, my soul . . .

III
Our class will compete
With such other suite
That our behavior pales
By comparison, it fails
Suffer, my soul . . .

DECEMBER 27, 1939

I
Round the corner
At Dworski Street
Not far from the Słowacki seat
A guy and a girl walk free
Just by the Christmas tree

II
I tell you, Rena,* just listen to me
Don't be as soft with yourself as can be
Grab some cash and go to school
Don't miss a party, don't be a fool

III
Józek Ciuchraj, listen to me in advance
Grab your accordion, play some Styrian dance
One, two, three, four, not a beat he misses
What a great party this is

---

* *Rena, Renusia, Renuśka*—variations of the name Renia. Also: *Aurelia*.

IV
Stop sending us glances
Go find somebody to dance with
Then run quickly home
Go to sleep, don't roam

JANUARY 9, 1940

The party's over. At the Christmas party I got an award for the best student, a chess set. Then we were preparing for a contest, and this contest is as early as tomorrow. I'm to recite a poem called "The Locomotive."* Let's hope it goes well.

Apart from that we are moving out of our school. Now we're going to be at a school with boys. Today we took everything from our classroom, our decorations, our inkpots, everything. This is supposed to be a seven-year school. Ugh, horrible. I hate everything, at first it promised to be something completely different, but I changed my mind a long time ago. I still live in fear of searches, of violence. And this whole thing of going to school with boys! Well, let's wait and see how that works out. The torture starts on the 11th, I'll tell you how that goes. Bye-bye, my dear Diary. Keep your fingers crossed for me. Let's hope it goes well!!!

I'm so incredibly stupid, what has happened to me? I've never been like that, people used to think me quite smart. How idiotic is it to fall in love with a komandir, to want to kiss him? Am I crazy? How can you dream of love in the form of some komandir? I don't go out with boys; that's the fact. I've never been in love either, but there is still time for it, I think. Although when I was at the party, I felt sorry that I didn't know anybody and I left with Nora, while Belka and the other girls stayed behind. Belka, she stayed, I was furious. But then Belka was jealous of me, jealous that I left. And she didn't party at all, she was angry and sad, I barely managed to lift her spirits a bit. And then I was angry that one scaredy cat turned around, the same one that I had a little bit of interest in. It's all so disgusting and stupid . . . I thought I was smarter than that . . .

---

* Julian Tuwim's poem.

JANUARY 12, 1940

It's all passed now. I mean everything that I've been pondering over here. I did perform at the contest. "The Locomotive" went so-so, but the contest went very well. So well, in fact, that when I came to school, boys called me "Four steps at a time."

But I've completely forgotten to tell you about the boys. The devil isn't as black as he's painted. At least that's what I think, for now. We have new teachers, but all our girls are together (I'm in 8C).

The boys are such innocent young things; they don't know much and they're very polite, they are rather swell. Other girls, our former colleagues, are even jealous of our set. The 8C boys aren't particularly attractive, with the exception of one very cute Ludwik P. and sweet Majorko S. They want us to mix up how we sit, i.e., a boy, a girl, another boy, but for now it isn't so.

On the day of the contest I got a letter from some komandir (of the Krasnaya Armya), summoning me on a rendezvous. I've decided to hide this letter, play a prank and write a reply.

Dear Diary, I do understand how important you are. I like browsing through your pages more and more often, looking for this feeling I felt then.

You know, I go through these different phases where I choose different husbands from among the young boys around me. I must have had around 60 of those phases in my life already. Or maybe even 100. And of course I keep finding new husbands (I mark people). Bye, kisses, Renia

JANUARY 19, 1940

Ein Jüngling liebt ein Mädchen,
Die hat einen Andern erwählt;
Der Andre liebt eine Andre,
Und hat sich mit dieser vermählt.

Es ist eine alte Geschichte,
Doch bleibt sie immer neu;

Und wem sie just passieret,
Dem bricht das Herz entzwei.*

You might not understand it, so I'll try to translate it into Polish for you. (Oh, Granny's been pestering me since midday. What does she want from me? I'm going crazy!)

A boy chose a girl as his dove
But she took somebody else as her true love
She cherishes the other one like her pearl
But the other one looks at yet another girl
He gave her his heart
And married her for a start
A story as old as time
Always a new mountain to climb
Whoever loved like this
Knows what a broken heart is

So in my case it's like this:

Łaba fell in love with Renia
But Renia is fond of Ludwik
Renia thinks Ludwik is a prize
While Ludwik to Krzysia turns his gorgeous eyes
He follows her everywhere, for her he is spoken
While Renia is deeply heartbroken
While Renia is furiously angry
But soon she'll leave that behind
A new love will capture her mind

Yes, that's the truest truth. What do I care about this Łaba, sitting there and staring at me for five hours until it makes me sick? What do I care about this or someone else who gawps at me? I like Ludwik. I turn around and look probably a bit too often, when I meet his gaze and sometimes a

___
* Heinrich Heine's poem.

31

little smile on his face. Is it possibly a joke? Possible, likely. Why haven't I said a word to him yet? Why do I flee when he's near? Why am I glad when he fools around? He in turn never recommends me when it comes to anything, a trip to the movies, a committee; and generally he treats me kind of badly. So why, when I turn back and look at him, why does he stare at me? A mystery. And anyway nowadays I am somewhat flighty; I like a different person all the time, that's natural. I told Nora that I need excitement and that I need to check our biology textbook to read about the mental state of 16-year-old girls. And she says to that, "Oh, if you need excitement, stop staring at books and find yourself a boyfriend." She is crazy! She's been terrible recently! Admittedly I too have a "dirty imagination" now, according to Auntie Lusia.

Majorko is a nice, swell boy, a friend. I'm impressed with Władek; I like him too. How do I know what to do?

They say spring will be hot and then they say it won't. I'm bored with those "liberators." It's the time for titmice now. As Tońko and Szczepko* said from France, "Release sparrows, keep canary birds, spring will bring titmice!"

JANUARY 26, 1940

Brrr . . . Brrr . . . Brrr . . . I can't even try to explain how terrible I'm feeling. I have troubles, like every normal human being. What on earth?! I'm no princess to feel bored, but I'm clearly bored. I've been struggling with a cold for several days. I haven't left home, I've been reading a bit and nobody, literally nobody, visited me but Eda. Nora hasn't been for a long while since the bombardments (Granny told her off once). In fact everything with Nora seems to be done and dusted. A friendship like this is good if it doesn't last too long. After all I only hang out with her because I don't have any other company, but I'll try to see her as little as possible outside of school. We don't share thoughts anymore; we don't

---

* At this point, Szczepko (Kazimierz Wajda) and Tońko (Henryk Vogelfänger), actors in the popular prewar radio program *Wesoła Lwowska Fala,* were in fact in Bucharest and only crossed the French border on March 9, 1940.

share opinions. There is nothing that connects us. And our liking for each other, as I realized, seems to be fizzling out, on her side too.

Now people seem to be only interested in material things. Which is not surprising at all, since a goose costs 100 złoty, and used to cost 4 złoty; a liter of milk costs 3.50 złoty, and used to cost 15 groszy; a pair of shoes—300 złoty, and it used to be 12 złoty.* So it doesn't surprise me at all. People pay (whoever can) and wait for the spring to come. It will! It'll come, I promise you.

I have decided to have a photo taken, as there isn't much one can do with money anyway. You peep out into the street and all you see is lines, lines everywhere, people waiting in lines to buy bread, butter, sugar, eggs, thread, shoes—everything. And if you think that after five hours of waiting you might get anything else on top of bread, you are very, so very wrong. And if you, by any chance, would like to buy two loaves of bread, better be careful, you profiteer.

> So listen, workmen
> celebrate, do
> never betray your treasure
> let smiles brighten your faces
> the red banner safe in your embraces
> Celebrate, do!
> No masters in workplaces
> You can do whatever you wish
> all made equal by the word tovarishch
> the red banner safe in your embraces
> Those who used to reside in grand manors
> now live in poor plain huts
> resigned to life in rags
> and what do you have? You have your wish
> you have the word tovarishch
> and the red banner in your embraces

---

* 1 złoty equals 100 groszy.

FEBRUARY 4, 1940

I'm so very sad! I'm singing, but that means nothing, I'm laughing, but that means nothing either. If I only could, I'd cry my eyes out. Granny took all her anger out on me. I know that they like Arianka better, they prefer her to me. I'm just a doormat. Mama loved us equally, there are others who prefer me, but she knows how to get on in life, she's like those people who know how to steal the show. And I was so happy today, wanted to write a poem, wanted to tell you something. But don't worry, all will be well again.

FEBRUARY 17, 1940[7]

I haven't told you anything for a long while, for such a long while . . . But don't think I haven't been thinking about you. I wanted to speak to you at every hour, but it so happened that I couldn't. So I'll tell you briefly what happened during those few days.

Daddy came here (he brought us provisions) and now he's gone again. A letter from Mama arrived. She might be in France already. I've enrolled myself in piano classes and decided to play.

Meanwhile, I'm not in love with Ludwik anymore. Which doesn't mean I don't like him, but I also like Jurek Nowak. Our class is nice, we have a class hero, Pieczonka, who lives on the same street. He walks me home, fools around, pulls my hood off my head, etc. Irka has started going after Ludwik in an impossible way. Since I sit right near them, I can see and hear everything. For example, "Irka, stop pinching me or I'll pinch you back hard." They flirt with each other like crazy. Our class is the best in our school. Though our attendance today was terrible. Only seven of us. We've already skipped out on physics three times. Pieczonka plays tricks, which makes us laugh. Łaba's still in love with me.

Mama said in her letter that she's been thinking of us constantly on her birthday. She said she was sorry she hasn't been getting any of my poems. I haven't been writing any; I'm so awful, so very awful. Granny and Grandpa are good to me. But I'm all on my own now. It's so hard being left on my own with my thoughts. It's so, so hard.

I feel compelled to draw nowadays; I find it irresistible. I keep seeing images, for example, of an archer. Begone, apparition! Ah! Ah! Ah!

A minute ticks second by second
Yet another hour beckons
Nobody knows when the end'll come
Or where it all started from
I don't know and you don't know
The world's beginning a long time ago
No beginning means no end
Earth's always sent round the sun to ascend
Millions of thousands of planets go round
Who in the world could swear it's not bound

MARCH 1, 1940

I had so much to tell you. Wednesday was a beautiful day, so our class played truant at 11:00 a.m. and escaped to the Castle. We threw snowballs, sang songs and composed poetry. I wrote a poem that's already in the school paper. Our class is really nice and sweet. We've become really close and we are good together. But because Nora and I aren't part of any gang, we've decided that I'll write verse.

I sway as if soused
with an abundance of spring incense
I'm up to my knees in water
dripping down from roofs and gutter
onto the passersby's heads, giving them shivers
flowing out in wide, wide rivers
humming and whistling on the corners
This cloudy, cheerful flood knows no borders
Houses dance in the streets, ice breaks on the walkways
trees, cobblestones, wooden fences, alleyways
From everywhere loud shouting arrives
Everything is springlike, dancing, alive

But I'm not happy at all
I'm not laughing, I'm crestfallen
like somebody who's just left their bunk
after sickness—I am drunk . . .

MARCH 16, 1940

A message from uncle in France. Mama wrote too.

Nora and I don't have much company, so we've decided to see what happens a year from today and ten years from today. So, wherever we are, still friends or angry at each other, healthy or ill, we are to meet or to write to each other and compare what'll have changed from now. So remember, 16 March 1950. We'll also write a diary together, but it won't be a diary filled with so many private thoughts, like this one here. You are and will remain my only friend.

I've started liking a boy from X class. I know that his name is Holender and he's from Zakopane. I like him very much. We've even been introduced to each other, but he's already forgotten me. He's well-built and broad-shouldered. He has pretty black eyes and falcon-like eyebrows. He's beautiful. There is a tale about a ship *Holender der fliegende Holender.**

You cross the wide ocean's waves
You wander around with no home
Known to all people on Earth
But in fact known to no one

Day and night you dash on slippery foam
Propelled by storm, by rain, by wind that's rotten
People talk about you often
But in fact you are all forgotten

Deviate from your winding course, Holender
Drift into lakes, rivers, waterways
You are so close to me, Holender
You are so far away . . .

---

* *The Flying Dutchman.*

Finally call at some port
Tired with storm, rain and wind
You are so dear to me, Holender
I love you with all my mind

Why do you roam aimlessly at sea?
Why do you have no home?
Known to all people on Earth
But in fact known to no one . . .
In dark, underground dungeons
In damp holes, rotten and pungent
With eyes burning with fever and agony
They dreamed of a communist destiny.
They waited . . .
And waited still . . .
Sick, shivery, crushed, out of steam
In hospitals, prisons—all with a dream
Until their red star lit up bold
With a sickle and hammer made of gold.
Their chains were dropped down
The gates opened wide to town
They marched out, shouting loud!
And froze, the whole crowd
This star, gold-plated star
(which left their lives so scarred)
was not red by far . . .
They saw it and cried the most
Over the freedom they lost
Over their dreamy idea
And the gray real life.

MARCH 31, 1940

I didn't tell you anything before, even though I should have. Our form tutor was Trelka, very learned and intelligent, more, an angel of a human being. He always defended us; made sure the classroom was warm; let us go home on the quiet. We got him a cake and a bottle of wine for Christ-mas, sent him a card. He didn't receive it in his office, but in the hospital. He broke his leg and now . . . he died. Today is his funeral. We are buying a wreath; we put an obituary up. I'm so very sorry, we've lost not just a form tutor, but a father. And now this disgusting Józia is our new form tutor. I can't stand her.

Runaways from Jarosław* have been here with us for a while. I'll tell you about it one day.

APRIL 24, 1940

It's been so long since we've spoken! Don't know where to start now; I have so many jumbled thoughts in my head, so many. I should perhaps start with the fact that terrible things have been happening. There were unexpected nighttime raids that lasted three days. People were rounded up and sent somewhere deep inside Russia. So many acquaintances of ours were taken away. Everybody was messed up. There was terrible screaming at school. Girls were crying. They say 50 people were packed into one cargo train car. You could only stand or lie on bunks. Every-body was singing *Poland has not yet perished*.

Now people are getting registered to the other side of the river San. It's a German commission, so many people get through. And those from there come here. It's terrible. I've been thinking about everything, but not about that.

About this Holender boy I have mentioned: I fell in love, I chased him like a madwoman, but he was interested in some girl named Basia. Despite that, I still like him, probably more than any other boy I know.

Irka's very popular.

At this point I've decided that if I can, one day I'll write a drama about Trelka's death, about how he wasn't in the coffin, but was taken away and then he suddenly came back. "If I only wanted . . ."† After

---

* Jarosław (Jaroslau)—a town near Przemyśl, at the time located in the general government.
† Reference to a sentence from Henryk Sienkiewicz's *With Fire and Sword*.

all I could have had it, but I didn't like them. And anyway . . . I don't want to. Though sometimes I feel this powerful, overwhelming need . . . maybe it's just my temperament. I should get married early so I can withstand it.

I wonder if Mama'll come back here. Isn't it better for her there? I never thought it would turn out this way here. Hell, perhaps I'll put something together!

> A voice on the radio rambles on
> Loudly, flatly, no uproar
> About what goes on in the world
> About what goes on in the war
>
> The world is not that important
> Spring has only just exploded
> And somewhere in faraway countries
> Cheerful life has unfolded
>
> Not much has happened at the front either
> The voice on the radio says calmly
> There was one single fatality
> Is that such a terrible blow?
> In view of many at war
> In view of many thousands
> Somebody cries softly some more
> Somebody whimpers in pain
> Somebody looks out the window
> Waiting, then dying in vain
> Somebody despairs even more
> One victim, is it such a blow?

FOR JARKA
THE DOLL AND THE CLOWN

The Clown:
Hello, hello, pretty Doll!

I've waited for you since the balmy morn.
Are you happy to see me?
Pray, tell.

The Doll:
Daddy, Mommy.

The Clown:
You don't believe me? I liked you
as soon as I saw you that summer.
And me? Do you like me as well?
Pray, tell.

The Doll:
Daddy, Mama.

The Clown:
Come, let's have a little dance.
What shall we dance together?
A mazurka? An oberek? A waltz?
Pray, tell.

The Doll:
Father, Mother.

The Clown:
Not a word from you?
You remain so stiff, so quiet
I understand you turn me down,
You don't like the ridiculous clown . . .

The Doll:
Don't think so badly of me.
I do understand everything.

But I am so very sorry,
I don't know how to dance, I worry.
(she cries) Poor me, poor, poor Doll,
troubled and lonely.
How could I give you a call,
When I'm so shy and so lowly?

The Clown:
Oh, don't cry, my little Doll.
Dry your tears.
Look! One step first,
then three more, it appears
then make a turn, lean your head to the side,
then bow low and jump with pride.

The Doll:
I'll cry no more, I will dry my tears.
So one step first,
then three more, as it appears
then I'll make a turn and lean my head to the side,
then bow low and jump with pride.

The Doll and the Clown:
Let's dance together.
Let's dance around.
It'll be joyous, it will be fun.
Great will be the world to discover
Where everybody understands each other.
It'll be joyous, it will be fun!
Let's dance together, let's dance around.
(they dance)

MAY 1, 1940

I would never have thought a year ago that exactly one year later, a long
and a short year later, I would be marching not on May 3 but on May 1 instead.* Only two days apart, but those two days mean so much. It means
I'm not in Poland but in the USSR. It means life; it means everything is
so . . . I'm so crazy for Holender! He's divine, adorable; he's amazing! But
what does that matter, since I don't know him? Tell me, will I ever be
contented? Will I ever have happy news to report to you about some boy?
Oh, please God. I'm always so disgruntled!

Finally shimmer, the eyes
that are dark, deep, tormenting
the wonderful eyes of a boy
wonderful, loving, enchanting

Dark, hot diamonds
Fiery, excruciating
The wonderful eyes of a boy
Wonderful, loving, enchanting.

Let them even be strict
Let them be bossy, unbending
The wonderful eyes of a boy
Wonderful, loving, enchanting.

MAY 3, 1940

They came out of a side street
from some inn or some gate,
the one they carried on stretchers
might've been ill, wounded or drunk.

---

* May 3–Poland's Constitution Day. May 1–International Workers' Day.

Their clothes were gray, torn, worn out
Their faces dark, haggard, washed out.
And the one on the stretchers
was also dressed like that
either ill, wounded or perhaps drunk.

They moved down the pavement,
people turned their heads away
Didn't want to look. Why should they?
A healthy boy walked in the way
Healthy, lively and joyful,
with an accordion like a beast
his eyes almost saying loudly,
Look at me at least.

With his fiery music
he dazzled the passersby.
He walked down the street, all cheery
Laughing and playing aloud.

MAY 10, 1940

Today was a gathering of *vidminniks,* i.e., the best students. Yes, Irka was elected. Nora went, this duffer Major went and I didn't. What do I deserve it for? You should know, my dear Diary, life is hardest for children without their parents, especially for those whose mothers are far away. Yes, know it, my dear Diary, and feel my pain, because I'm in pain too! How bitterly I cry sometimes. Let the school get something from me! If they need an article, let the *vidminniks* write it. Let them perform at contests too. Let's see!

Why does a child cry?
Lonely, on its own?
Why does it always yearn and is hurt, why?
Why isn't it comforted by its mother?
Why doesn't she caress it and give it cuddles?

MAY 23, 1940

It's over . . . I mean the school year's over, as is my love for Wilk.* It is now busy exam time for me. It's already begun. I've already had my algebra, geometry and biology exams. I think it went well. Let's see what happens next. I'm petrified by physics. You should know that I won't speak with you until after the exams. You'll have to wait a bit. I'll sit with you on 13th of June and I'll either be happy or . . . you'll get wet with tears. It's been a good day today. I got new shoes, which is a luxury nowadays. And also two light dresses. There is this one boy in my class who used to flirt with me, or so I thought. He's terribly ugly, but so very talented that . . . I like him. Let people talk, but I do like him, despite the fact that, apart from being a genius, he has few virtues. Ah, I forgot! I was made a *vidminnik*. You see, silly, how life changes? I told you once that something'll happen in the spring. It did, but it's something completely different than what I thought. Belgium and Holland are occupied, the Germans have taken over France, Mum's in Warsaw. Great Lord God, please make it be all right. See you on the 13th!

JUNE 13, 1940

Done! Finally! It's passed like a dream. The exams are over. It went very well, better than I expected. Bravo, Renia! It's late now; the streets are dark. Some alarm, it seems . . . Soldiers on horseback stampeding, komandirs getting up—there is a lot of commotion. We're going to go to Daddy's soon! Oh, who knows, there might be a new war? God save us. I might tell you something soon, wait for it!

JUNE 17, 1940

It's my birthday tomorrow. I'm turning 16. This is supposed to be the best time in my life. People often say, "Oh, to be 16 again!" And I am, yes, that's how old I am, but I'm so unhappy!

---

* *Wolf* in Polish. Most likely a reference to Holender.

France has capitulated. Hitler's army is flooding Europe. America is refusing to help. Who knows, they might even start a war with Russia.

I'm here on my own, without Mama or Daddy, without a home, poked and laughed at. Oh, God, why did such a horrible birthday have to come? Wouldn't it be better to die? I look down from the height of my 16 years and I wonder whether I'll reach the end. "Quietly like a razor through butter"* . . . this is death. Wouldn't it be better, at once? Then I'd have a long, sad funeral. They might cry. They wouldn't treat me with disdain, like today (Dzidziu,† "Nobody wants to go out with this old cow"). I'd only feel sorry for my Mom, my Mommy, my Mama . . . Why are you so far from me, so far away? I'd feel better otherwise, I wouldn't ever think about it. But I cry and I cry that it'll not be any different.

> *I walk along some empty streets*
> *my footsteps echo from gray cobbles*
> *the city seems to be transfixed*
> *as if it's fallen into slumber.*
> *Even the wind doesn't stir the leaves*
> *nothing moves, nothing rustles or flutters*
> *the only sound on the muffled street*
> *is deep, sorrowful weeping that somebody utters.*
> *I take a look, I look around*
> *who sobs so badly in the night?*
> *perhaps they need their mother now*
> *perhaps they miss home, warmth, a bright light?*
> *Why do they shed so many tears*
> *on their own, in the midst of dead silence?*
> *Nobody listens to you now, I fear*
> *or perhaps I'm wrong . . . someone does hear?*
> *I roam round dark streets*

---

* Most likely a reference to Julian Tuwim's "Śmierć" (Death): "Quietly like a razor through butter / Like a stone thrown into water."
† *Dzidziu*, also *Dido*—Renia's grandfather.

searching for the person I'm spying
but who do I search for?
it's me who is crying!

JULY 1, 1940

Listen, my birthday was a pretty good day. I got two bottles of perfume, flowers and lipsticks from Nora and Irka. The three of us are now on good terms—that is my sweet, my one and only Norka, Irka and I. This idyll has lasted since the beginning of the exams. Will it last long still? I don't know. Any thought can divide us, any row or any political wind can disperse our three-way truce. And let me tell you that the political wind is getting stronger. America has joined the war.* England counts on us, we don't know what to do and so on. My Mama is in Warsaw. My poor, one and only Mama. You don't know it, but she's the sweetest, the prettiest, the smartest and all the other "-ests" that exist in the world of women. Yes, I can see some flaws too, two flaws in fact, which I've always forgiven her for, which never mattered much to me. Only today, only now they affect me so badly that I need to take them as flaws, not virtues. Because, my dear Diary, what is my life?! It's just a handful of ashes of the past and some shells of the present. I hold them in my hand and I say, "What is bad'll fly away, what is good'll stay." And I blow. And what? All the shells and specks of ash fly away and all that is left is a whitish dust of temporary contentment such as sitting in a theater, getting a good school report, a letter from Mom, Brühla's smile. And everything else flew away? Yes, everything. So my life was sad? Yes, it was. And now let's be frank, let's get rid of all temporary contentment or joys, and let's classify. I've lived in Stawki. Was I happy there? No, there were worries, Mama was seriously ill, there were money issues, family quarrels and rows, first Daddy, then Mama. My home's fallen apart. Worse still. Arianka went to Warsaw, she struggled there, lost her childhood, it vanished and that was wrong. I was at Granny's and Grandpa's, I could've done

---

* While the United States didn't enter World War II until December 1941, President Franklin Roosevelt had begun mobilizing the war effort by denouncing Mussolini, increasing the U.S. production of war goods, and appointing two pro-interventionist secretaries of war.

something, I cried for Mama, I wasn't happy and looked like "a mother-less child." And that was wrong too. Another mistake was the fact that Mama let us, she simply got us to get used to life here. What life is it? Yes, Granny loves us very much, she tries very hard. They pay the price and we do too. They don't live a life of normal grandparents and we don't live a life of normal grandchildren. It's been like that and it still is like that. Such is life. Mama thought of us, she tried hard, she cared, but then there was her and there was Daddy. And we were left hanging. Arianka, poor kitten, and me, even poorer (because I don't know how to make it in life). And now there's the war. Arianka and I are on our own. What does poor Mama eat? They say there is famine there, my poor Mama dear, my poor, poor sad life. My sweet Mommy, if you were here with me, there would be so much less crying, I would be so much calmer with you, why are you so far away . . . ? Mama!!! But you know, when I finally get the goblet of happiness in my hands (even if it's short and small), I'll drink from it as much as I can, for all the happiness hidden in this tiny goblet.

JULY 2, 1940, WAR

> *A drop slowly follows another*
> *They'll soon form a stream together*

JULY 6, 1940

What a terrible night! Horrible! Dreadful. I lay there with my eyes wide open, my heart pounding, shivering like I had a fever; I was all ears. I could hear the clanking of wheels again. Oh, Lord God, please help us! A truck rolled by. I could hear a car horn beeping. Was it coming here? For us? Or for someone else? I listened, straining so hard it felt like everything in me was about to burst. I heard a jangling of keys, a gate being opened opposite. They went in. I waited some more. This was terrible. Then they came out, taking loads of people with them, children, old people. One lady was shaking so much she couldn't stand, couldn't sit down. The arrests were led by some fat hag who kept yelling in Russian,

"*Sadis', seychas sadis.*"* She loaded children onto the wagon. This night roundup was horrible. I couldn't wait for the dawn to come. And finally! Now! But it wasn't the end yet. Only now, in the light of day, I could see the despair, the violence, the lawlessness. Some people were crying, most of the children were asking for bread. They were told the journey would take four weeks. Poor children, parents, old people. Their eyes were filled with insane fear, despair, resignation. They took whatever they were able to carry on their slender backs to the place they would not reach. Poor "refugees" from the other side of the San. They are being taken to Birobidzhan.† They will travel in closed, dark carriages, 50 people in each. They will travel in airless, dirty, infested conditions. They might even be hungry. They will travel for many long weeks, with children among them dying out, they will travel through this happy, free country, the only one resounding with the song:

> Wide is my Motherland,
> Of her many forests, fields, and rivers!
> I know of no other such country
> Where a man can breathe so freely.‡

And how many will reach their destination? How many will die on their way from illness, infestation, longing? When they finally reach the end of their deportees' route somewhere far into Asia, they will be stuck in rotting mud huts, hungry, exhausted (like those who have already left) and in this slow dying ironically called life they'll admire the happy workers' paradise, listening to the song:

> A man stands as the master
> Over his vast motherland.

---

* *Sadis', seychas sadis* (садись, сейчас садись)—Sit, sit down now.
† A town in the USSR close to the border with China, administrative center of the Jewish Autonomous Oblast created in 1934.
‡ First lines of the famous Soviet patriotic "Song of the Motherland," composed by Issac Dunaevsky and with lyrics written by Vasily Lebedev-Kumach, first featured in the 1936 film *Circus*.

AUGUST 8, 1940

Oh! How much water has passed in the San (I say that, even though I can't see the San) since our last conversation? I was down with a stomach bug, a headache and other horrors.

Our trip to Ticiu has been put off day after day. Now we don't have much summer vacation left, but we're still going. I'll see Lila. But! But! Do you know Lila? No? Pity! Shame! She is my wonderful, golden-haired cousin and friend. Supposedly my real friend is Nora, but it is completely different. I share everything with Lila, while with Nora . . . well . . . not so much. I'm not ashamed of anything in front of Lila, I don't feel embarrassed of anything. My wonderful little cousin, the companion of my childhood, the creator of the scar on my right cheek next to my nose (but only a small one). We always have something to talk about. We find out "nice things" together, we pull pranks. Lila, oh, Lila! Do you remember? And there, ha ha ha . . .

I get messages from Mama often. Things look good there now, much better. I'm glad. I might see Mama soon. Aha! But I'm the only one who can know this. If it comes true, I will tell you. Because in fact it's stupid: a border. What is it? People just said so, put stones along, rammed posts in and said, "It's mine up to here!" And what does it matter that they have torn lands apart, that they have divided brothers, sent children's hearts far away from their mothers? "This is mine" or "The border is here"—I don't care about it at all! The clouds, the birds and the sun laugh at all these borders, at human beings, at their guns. They go back and forth, smuggling rain, blades of grass, rays of sunshine. And no one even thinks of banning them. If they even tried, the sun would burst out with bright laughter and they'd have to close their eyes. It'd cock a snook with its rays and cross "the border." The clouds, birds, and wind would follow. So would (quietly) one small human soul, and plenty of my thoughts. So I might go, what do you think?

AUGUST 21, 1940

And? Of course I went, I visited my auntie at Horodenka and then traveled all the way here, to Zabłotów.* So, so much has happened, that I find it difficult to relay. So let me start from the beginning. Auntie Lusia was supposed to take me there and that was the plan until the most important evening. On that most important evening, she was supposed to take me there, she was supposed to, and then suddenly no! Granny decided to take us there. Granny, poor Granny, suffered so terribly on the way, burned her face and then went back. It's a pity she went back; at least we wouldn't be so alone. So alone at our own father's place.

But from the beginning! We spent three days in Horodenka. Lila was so happy to see us! Sweet kitten, she's so poor. Just think, she visits some strangers and sees her own furniture . . . The same she was used to touching for so many years, which became part of her and the house. She returns to her tiny room full of remnants, she sees . . . those warm, nice, cozy rooms, the mirror over the washbasin, the head of a girl deep in thought on the most important shelf of the old sideboard, a lump of salt (for rain and good weather) and shiny, decorative cushions (which today decorate some strangers' rooms). She sees it all and thinks, "Oh, God, never again." Yes, that's what Lila feels, but she won't talk about it with anybody but me.

Ticiu came to pick us up from Horodenka. We had to ride for four hours in a horse-drawn cart. I've missed him so much. You can't call it anything else but longing. I've been pining for somebody close, oh, yes! I'm engulfed by this strange tenderness upon seeing Ticiu, both now and all the time. Generally I'm torn between two feelings. I came here and straightaway another feeling took over—some weird attitude of mine and Ticiu's to the house, and housekeeper's toward Ticiu. And it so happened that in the evening Lila thought the same thing and we started talking about how something was wrong. Attention! If two people notice

---

* A town in Stanisławów Voivodeship on the Prut River; between 1939 and 1941 under the Soviet occupation, then under the German occupation until 1944, then again occupied by the Soviets and in USSR.

the same thing, then surely it's not just a delusion or a mishearing. Oh no! The housekeeper tries hard to be polite, but to no avail. She knows exactly how old Bulczyk* is, she treats Tusio as if she were some feudal queen talking to her poorest vassal.

Ticio bought some fabric, but can't find it now; on top of this there is this "intrament" plus our laughter and her folly—it all meant we decided to run away. Yes, that's the only way to describe it. We have money, we're buying tickets and going back to auntie's. But even so, I still feel sorry for Ticiu, my poor Ticiu, but also . . . what? To . . . But I'm 16 already, ha ha ha! No, it's funny! So in such circumstances this dreamed-of family home, this red velvet tablecloth and the dresser with little curtains with the pattern of dolls and all of this—God, never again. Yes, but I won't tell anybody about it. Only you . . . and Lila . . . and Mom. Oh, Mom! Mom! Mom! Come to the rescue!

AUGUST 22, 1940

I spent half the night crying. I've decided to go. I feel so sorry for Ticiu, even though he keeps whistling cheerfully, but . . . what? Children flee from him as if . . . I would feel terrible. I told him, almost crying, "I know, Ticiu, that you had the best dreams, but this is not your home." This came to me in the night:

> *Will you, fantasies, all fade*
> *Just like the very first dreams?*
> *Will you flow with such small tears*
> *Leaving behind just weepy streams?*
> *Will my sun, so bright in my dreams*
> *And my life so full of colors*
> *Plunge and drown in dark themes*
> *And if so? Stop crying, alas,*
> *Stem the tear-filled stream's flow*
> *Even if dreams disappear*
> *Death will always be your beau!*

---

* *Bulczyk, Buluś, Bunia—Renia's mother.*

Wind, stop crumpling my petals
I'm an orphan, can you see?
Don't jerk me, don't bend down
I've enough suffering, let me be
I'm not from these parts, you know
But my heart is oh so strong
Delicate, silver petals
Not a little flower, I'm made as if of metal
Not like the wildflowers that grow here
Happy and playful and full of cheer
Among the silver fields of many sisters
Fate hurls me strangely, gives me jitters
Standing on my own is no fun
An orphan and not an orphan.

SEPTEMBER 10, 1940

Oh! So much water has passed in the Prut River in Zabłotów. And I just sit here in peace and go to school. Beautiful Miruś Moch is our math teacher and I shiver in front of him as if I were some kind of a scarecrow. We have a whole new set of teachers. We also have a new schoolmate, Luśka Fischler. She joined our threesome, known in the class as "the aristocratic three." They call her the fourth one for the bridge. There is one boy I like and Nora likes one too. We want to go to a party, in part because we want to get closer to that world—and we already made a step in this direction—and in part because Irka doesn't want us to come. There is very little time. We shall see . . .

SEPTEMBER 21, 1940

We didn't go to the party because there was no party. But! But! We made a big, huge step forward. Our class is calm. But! What do I care about the class when we are about to create a real gang with the boys! Mine is so wonderful! Wonderful! Wonderful! Mine, the most mine is Zygo S. Together we are ZSR.* I've met him already today! Nora admitted she liked him a lot, but she knew he was my type, she let go. Nora has cute, sweet Natek and Irka has Maciek. And? And I don't know how it's going to go and I don't really have much confidence in myself.

SEPTEMBER 30, 1940

It seems that our gang will not come about after all. I was terribly apathetic, but now my energy's coming back somehow, though slowly. It's all very strange. I know him, but he doesn't even say hello. Irka doesn't want to either. Nora doesn't want anything to do with Irka. There is something wrong with Nora too . . .

On Monday he smiled at her, so now she doesn't want anybody else. Or something, I don't know. Sometimes I feel terrible. Neither of us have it, I had more, but now it seems it's Nora. She tells me to leave him, because he's a lout . . . A lout, ha ha ha. And Natek's a gambler. Eh, life's nasty! Can it get better? Mom is not here. If only she were here, I wouldn't have so many worries.

OCTOBER 6, 1940

And another step forward. Again nothing. Before the mountaintop the heart aches, it's a time for waiting.

OCTOBER 12, 1940[8]

Today is Yom Kippur, the Day of Atonement. Yesterday everybody left the house; I was on my own with burning candles on the table in a huge, brass candlestick. Ah, a single moment of solitude. All memories came back and then I was able to think about all the things that get forgotten in the daily whirlwind, in the rumble, grating, splashing of the passing life.

Once again, I asked myself the same question I asked last year: Mama,

---

* Most likely a reference to *ZSSR*, the Polish-language abbreviation for *USSR*, though Renia shortened it to refer to "Zygmunt Schwarzer Renia."

when will I see you again? When will I hug you and tell you about what happened and tell you, Buluś, how terrible I'm feeling?! And you will tell me, "Don't worry, Renuśka!" Only you can say my name in such a warm, tender way.

Mom, I'm losing hope. How long, how long? I stared into those burning candles—Mama, what are you doing there? Are you thinking about us, too, about our torn hearts?

> *Who is stifled, killed, destroyed by you*
> *forever remains free*
> *but why do you hurt the living ones*
> *you furious devil, you're so angry?*
> *You bathe in the ocean of red blood*
> *livid with vendetta, seething with flames*
> *you'll set the whole world on fire*
> *and in its glow list dead people's names*
> *On battlefields and graveyards*
> *your bloodthirsty eyes shimmer with greed*
> *you creak, "more," and a plague erupts*
> *famine, misfortune suddenly freed*
> *A new heap thrown at the feet*
> *all fall with the same lethal wound*
> *those who're alive have broken hearts*
> *and the heap grows, in the sky its crown*
> *Ah, you've had enough of revenge*
> *a mocking laughter sounds about*
> *you howl, you infuriated beast,*
> *"More, I want blood to fill my snout."*

We see the boys out in town, we're close, we see Maciek almost every day. Only Zygo* and Natek are so distant. Zygo walked back from school with us today. He looked right at me. He has very powerful eyes and I went red in the face and didn't say anything. Oh, to hell with such nature! He flirts with Iśka, or perhaps I'm just imagining

---

* *Zygu, Zygo, Zyguś, Zyguśka*—variations of the name Zygmunt.

it. Anyway, should he flirt with me? I don't say anything. We're planning to go to a party soon—will I have fun? Nora more likely than me, since someone is in love with her. I don't believe in anything. Unless Bulczyk comes?

OCTOBER 19, 1940

We sat opposite each other at the Russian club this week. He stared at me, I stared at him. As soon as I turned my eyes away from him, I could feel his eyes on me. Then, when he said two words to me, I felt crazy, filled with hope. I felt as if a dream was coming true, as if the goblet was right by my lips.

But the goblet's still far away. A lot can happen before lips touch lips. So many things can happen to stop them from touching. This is the closest I've ever experienced to real love, because my victim is actually looking at me and saying two words, but then he is embracing Iśka. (By the way, Holender's getting married!! Well! Well! I'm not interested in him anymore. I haven't been for a while.)

Today at the history club Nora's Natek was talking to her all the time, he was laughing and he was very polite. Oh! She's in a much better position! I envy Norka! I mean, I want Zygo to be like that too. God permitting! God permitting! Mama! I came up with such an algorithm:

> *Whether you love or you don't*
> *There'll always be much crying*
> *Your bitter tears won't be drying*
> *Whether you love or you don't*
> *You will send your gaze around*
> *At times filled with longing, at times dumbfound*
>
> *Whether you love or you don't*
> *There'll always be much crying.*

I've written various nice things in Norka's diary today. They announced a competition at school today, entitled "School-free day." My dear Diary, I want to win it so much. Please help me. I'll try different approaches.

APPEARS

Like so many before, an ordinary day
Starts a bit gloomy and a bit gray
Then morning dawn shimmers and winks
The day becomes blue and orange and pink
And follows a different direction from then on
Along rumbling pavements through various town's sections
Not rushing to school to be there on time
Not getting there just when the bell chimes
This is not an ordinary day that looms
Full of silly pranks in the classroom
One that threatens with bad grades
One that roars with alarm sirens
One that rumbles with nonstop work
Full of rushing, blurry bottom to top
Counting minutes and hours in all detail
In factories—speedy, in schools—slow like a snail
One that is cheerful and in its glad rags
On the sunny warm day outside itself it drags
One that laughs easily at ace film comedies
That brings books, stamp collections and other commodities
One that brightens up the lives of its fans
For whom pupils like to stop a clock's hands
One that passes so quickly and is still succeeded
By another one that rumbles to school up the hill
An ordinary day, a bit gray, run-of-the-mill . . .

I will also try something else. I might win.

SCHOOL-FREE DAY

It slid down the sky at twilight
Rumbled down to earth all right
Filled with song, filled with twitter
Out of breath with all the jitter

A day—like a bird . . .
Splashing windowpanes with gold
Splashing eyes with sun and laughter
And then quickly gone, uncontrolled
Leaving just a worry thereafter
Leaving a shadow and then away
A meditation or a school-free day?

OCTOBER 23, 1940

This is a competition week, so I'm thinking about that more than about Zygo. Natek's hitting on Nora. I haven't been very lucky with him, but if all else fails, I'll always have you!

A person stares at a looking glass
sighs and says loudly,
"Wouldn't it be better alas
to have smaller lips and different eyes.
The nose also could have a resize!"
Not true, you stupid girl
Even if your beauty could outshine
that of Greek goddesses' line
Your fate will remain the same
Your life will not be reframed
Life doesn't care about your eyes
Your ugly lips
Nose the wrong size!

Mirror, mirror on the wall,
Tell me the truth you reflect and all.

OCTOBER 24, 1940

Why do we rush so badly
Why do we count the days
Saturday to Saturday, madly

In rain, drought, frost and haze
Fast, fast and faster still
We want the stream of life to flow
Through happy days, through tears, when ill
Day after day does go
From Saturday to Saturday, sadly
Let days leave shadows behind
Why do we run so madly
What do we want to find
Blinded and staring wildly
Into what's unknown and clouded
A pipe dream, rather untimely
A dream of a 16-year-old head.
We constantly speed away
Feverish, like in a nightmare
We get through short weeks, short days
Knocking them into the abyss without care
We speed ahead like crazed hurricanes
Out of breath, short-winded we race
As ever counting the days
And when we stop halfway to wait
Completely unfazed by all warnings
Life's now stepped up like crazy
And runs and runs ablaze

NOVEMBER 6, 1940

What a day I had today—I don't know if I should laugh or cry or scream, I really don't know. Mostly I feel like crying . . . It wouldn't have happened if I saw you three hours ago and told you everything, like I had already decided. "I'm going to a party tonight (do or die) and I know I won't dance and I know I won't be popular and Nora might be, but I won't let it worry me one little bit." I was supposed to tell you this, but no, I haven't, so when I escaped this party, I was on the verge of tears.

But *da capo*,* attention! I went to the party and, surprise, surprise, right before it I found out that I won first place in the competition and am to be given Mickiewicz's[†] works! My wonderful dream! Dear Diary, you helped me. My one and only, always so devoted!

So I come to the party and Maciek tells me about it in secret. Zygu congratulated me and spoke with me and only with me. Then, out of the blue, I got the award for my grades, for publishing the newspaper and for my 100% attendance.

Zygu was simply beautiful. All my hopes reverberated in me. Then the Head, with special emphasis, announced the winner of the competition. People clapped and congratulated me. Krela'll send it to Kiev, to *Głos Radziecki*,[‡] she'll also write about it in the school newspaper. And she, Krela, who's never happy with anything, she even praised me. Oh, what a triumph.

Then I went to that wretched party. Cukierman asked me. I said I couldn't dance, so he excused himself. Then Major. I didn't want to go, so I stood there on my own while Norka was dancing. I left. I walked through the wet streets, trying not to cry loudly. I thought, "This evening I won on the spiritual level, but I lost in life." I vowed I would not go to a party again. But no, I will! Shy or not, I need to win in this other arena. Even if that means my soul will lose, let life win!!! Believe me, this is going to be hard and sad. And again, I think for a thousandth time, I think I need to hum this sad song of my poor, orphaned heart.

> *Mama, why are you not here*
> *Such a long distance between us*
> *Far, far away you disappeared*
> *We both cry our eyes out*
>
> *Why do you sob, why do I weep*
> *Why has my life taken such a leap*
> *My heart follows comfort's traces*
> *And I seek mother's embraces!*

---

* From the beginning (Italian).
† Adam Mickiewicz (1798–1855), Polish poet, dramatist, essayist, and activist.
‡ *Głos Radziecki* (Soviet voice)—Polish-language Soviet newspaper published in Kiev between 1939 and 1941.

Mom! Why couldn't you be here today, to see my joys and be happy for me (as I know you are)? Why couldn't I then cry my heart out in your embrace?

I wrote a poem for the class paper, why not?

Blood pulsates and so do cobbles
Marching to big celebrations
A huge, gray crowd hobbles
Red banners . . . For the nation
This mass pushes through the city
Flows from suburbs, backstreets, dwellings
With new people constantly swelling
Joining others in the nitty-gritty
Roads are almost overflown
Like with lava flowing down
Like with liquid iron alloy
That can set at any time
Crushing this world in deep sleep
Tearing the old world down
Those red banners . . . The red sweep . . .

NOVEMBER 7, 1940

Listen, do you perhaps know if it's nice to have a lover? What do you think? I had this thought today! You know, I hate it when somebody talks about their future.

I don't want the sick ones to look for solace in me
I don't want to see hurt ones, as I'm hurt as can be
I want to live like some scoundrel, like a soul with no worry
I want to see good women carrying
The jobs of ministers, sailors at sea
Of diplomats, of those holding legal offices' keys
I want to see them as pilots, in action
To hear them delivering speeches with passion

I want to live with no trouble
My life to be a happy bubble
I want to write poems forever
And I want to have a lover!

NOVEMBER 9, 1940

I went for a walk with Zygu. Of course not on my own; it was the whole group. I might go to Irka's dance party. Zygu'll be there. I won't dance, but I'll go.

NOVEMBER 12, 1940

Just a few words, as it's late. I got a prize, hooray! Hooray! *Children* by Jan Brzoza.* I felt so haughty; it was so nice. Pity Buluś couldn't see it. I have a paper to deliver on it on 24 December. The day of Mama's birthday . . . Will you be here with me, Mama? I was also selected to the Mickiewicz event committee. I'll tell you about it later. Zygu teases me sometimes, but today he was sweet. On Saturday I'm going to a dance party at Irka's. He'll be there! If I don't party, then I don't! He is what matters!!!

NOVEMBER 18, 1940

Today I am under the spell of a film. Perhaps because I haven't been to the movies for a while or perhaps because, for sure because somehow I was in those images, people, views, incidents. Yes, some of my dreams were in it and that's exactly why I liked *Young Pushkin*.† I like Pushkin a lot, he is my hero; I might get his photo from somewhere.‡ Because, you know, I'm changing my whole plan and am starting to wonder if maybe it's better to be famous than happy after all. To be a poet like (not Konopnicka), but . . . like . . . Pushkin!!! Now I can compare his youth to

---

* Jan Brzoza (1900–1971)—Polish writer, publicist, radio host, communist activist, one of the founders of the proletarian literature in Poland. *Children,* published in 1936, describes the life of a Lwów paperboy.
† *Young Pushkin* (*Junost' poeta*)—1936 Soviet film directed by Abram Naroditsky, with Valentin Litowsky as Pushkin.
‡ Photography was invented in 1839, two years after Pushkin's death. The author most likely means a photograph of his painted portrait.

mine. It's clear he wasn't successful with women. It's a pity he died—I would shake his hand.

When Pushkin was in high school, he didn't study at all. He went on rendezvous with the other kids, went on moonlight walks on fragrant (even in the film) nights, picked white water lilies for his lover. He pined, dreamed, loved . . . Wasn't the world in his favor and could he become non-romantic? Wonderful, wonderful—ugly ape *obez'yana!** Pushkin! And the name! One utters his name with reverence.

But I could never become famous like that. I've been like a street urchin for four years now. All I see is gray, cracked cobblestones and cracked, thirsty lips. I don't see the sky, because the sky is just a moldy, dusty scrap of clouds. All I can see are ashes and soot that choke, that corrode the eyes, that stifle breathing. I can see people in the streets as sharp as stones steadily crushed with pickaxes and ground into sharp, stinging dust in coarse, rough fingers. No revolution will ever be able to fix this. Nothing will . . . Because those who have velvety voices and pleasant touch, those who lead silky soft, comfortable lives, they'll always remain . . . But I don't care, I detest the revolution, I, an average person (a phlegmatic), can't stand the rabid mob, so let it rather be the way it is. But you, Pushkin, what did you want?

> Look, how everything is distorted
> how fake, how wretched, how down-market
> It's new, but completely rotten despite
> red, red and white . . .

NOVEMBER 18, 1940†

My romance seems to be over. What a stupid, crude, arrogant idiot. He likes playing with me. And for all of this I could thank my dear friend Tusiek. What a vermin, damn it! But you know what? He's not worth writing about. Naturally I'll have my revenge; I'll find a way. There'll be another reading evening, oh, I'd like that so much! Will you help me again?

---

* *Obez'yana*, обезьяна—a monkey (Russian).
† Renia wrote this date for two separate entries.

I am coming to you
I'm on my way!
A train rumbles on the tracks
across bridges, along archways
through fields and towns, it doesn't relax
It glides ahead, it hisses, it speeds
Along the slippery steel rails
At a high speed it proceeds!

Colors are red and yellow
with some black, green and blue
The evening lights are so mellow
Scattered around each day anew
I hear the long-drawn-out toot
The locomotive wheezes and puffs
I'm coming to you, I'm en route
Following the trail on the map . . .

NOVEMBER 20, 1940

I've had my revenge today. I wrote him an offensive poem. He got annoyed. Now he'll leave me alone. I can't stand him. "Rhymester" is what he called me today. It'll be even worse now, he'll . . . I wish I were dead! You know, sometimes all of it is so stupid, and so important. No, it doesn't matter. It'll always be "I'll never know what happiness looks like." Miraculous God, please, don't let it be a prophecy. I'm so low, so low . . . so very low.

NOVEMBER 24, 1940

I went to the theater today. Everybody said I looked very smart. But Zygu wasn't there. I act really indifferent now and he's surprised, angry, says this or that to me, and I still do nothing. (Nora says this is only a beginning.) All I say is, who knows!

Nora's Maciek lives on the fifth floor. She constantly stares at it.

Is it made golden with the light of dawn?
Is it surrounded by darkness?
Why are you so far withdrawn?
Why is the whole world between us?
Why does this terrible river
Divide us like a shiver?

NOVEMBER 28, 1940, THURSDAY

Tomorrow is a math demonstration lesson, I'm so terribly scared. I've had strange feelings toward Nora those last few days. I feel she's terribly fake. As soon as she notices that Z wants to say something to me, she purposefully interferes. Yes, it's all because of Waldek. And anyway she's temperamental and whimsical and I, thank God, seem to not meet her requirements anymore. She was so happy that people thought she liked Z. She liked it, even though she knew it was not true. Ha ha ha!

NOVEMBER 30, 1940

The lesson is over. It went pretty well, I was prepared. I'm in a paper. I'm falling out of love with Zygu, as I don't have any stimulation from him. Nora has sprained her ankle. I wrote an article about it and a poem too. I'll write it down for her. It's not so bad with Nora after all. I created it, so I'll write it down. I'd like it in *Piszemy sami.** Something must be wrong with me!

DECEMBER 8, 1940, WEDNESDAY†

Suddenly, I love him like crazy. Just think, everything was about to go dormant and today it sprang back to life. Nothing happened—but still so much! He played with my hood, stroked it, came closer! But I'm vain. I think of a thousand projects. Fralalalalala! Wonderful Zygu, wonderful, so wonderful!!! This is what I wrote once:

---

* *Piszemy sami* (We write)—most likely a newspaper
† The author made several mistakes with dates and days of the week. December 8, 1940, was a Sunday.

Hey, let's drink our wine
Let's drink from our lips
And when the cup runs dry
Let's switch to drinking blood
Wanting and yearning
Inspiration and love burning
Let them start a fire
Let rage burn like a pyre
But remember, girl, that flames
travel in your veins
that blood can burst you from inside
Wanting and yearning
Inspiration and love burning
Let them start a fire
Let rage burn like a pyre
Both wine and lips are red
One life before you are dead
Our hearts are hungry, young, on fire
Only for each other beating.
Remember, girl, that flames
travel in your veins

WHAT IS BEING ROMANTIC?

It's a horse that gallops through the steppes
It's a high cloud that swiftly follows
Moving smoothly, steeped in a deep red glow
Shrouding white swan's down in golden twilight
It's a Lover on the edge of a deep abyss
Sliding down the rope from the great height
A bunch of roses red in his embrace.

RIFFRAFF, OR CHILDREN OF MACHINES

Among the rattling and grating of iron
Among the racket of collapsing chunks
Among the whirring and birring of workshops
With sharp, piercing dust that in the air hangs

burning our hearts and our dreams
we grew up, we, working children
people machines

In the roaring fire of forges
Crucibles engorged with molten metal
In the swelter of slag slurry treacle
We got tempered, we, steel people

Our hands are rough and mighty
Our hands like iron springs
Our hearts like slag—hot, flighty . . .
Seething, boiling power of teens
Working people—children of machines

DECEMBER 9, 1940

I love, I desire, I'm crazy for Zygu!!!

DECEMBER 10, 1940

I went to the second floor today. Zygu said to me, "How are you, girl," or something along those lines, and he pulled my hair. You know, recently, when I see him, I have this blissful, pleasant feeling that's unpleasant at the same time. Something paralyzes me. Ah, that idiot, if he only knew how much I love him. There's an invisible thread connecting us. It could break, but no . . . If we could really be together, it would be wonderful and terrible at the same time! "The chocolate box may be empty, but there is lots of sweetness in your lips." I don't know. I have no idea what's happening to me.

Oh, age, you! When one loves like never before
The one who knows you, can't ever find peace
The one who knows you, is drunk with ardor
And life only starts when the other heart is seized.

The one in love can never wake up
Stuck in a tormenting dream, in a feverish shake
Only to fall asleep when the dawn erupts
And dream of loving and heartache.

DECEMBER 11, 1940

Today I stayed at home. I'm to write a paper. I'm to write for the competition. Because Krela told the Teich girl that she expects something great from me. What should I write?

FROST

The air is windy and foggy . . .
The sky Decemberish gray . . .
Feathery balls of sparrows, all groggy
Bounce off glassy roads all day . . .

It's somewhat sleepy outside.
Snow falls softly and slides
Along invisible lines
Grayish clouds blossom everywhere
As if cigarette smoke was in the air.

HEINE*

Leise zieht durch mein Gemüt
Liebliches Geläute,
Klinge, kleines Frühlingslied,
Kling hinaus ins Weite.
Kling hinaus bis an das Haus,
Wo die Blumen sprießen,
Wenn du eine Rose schaust,
Sag, ich laß sie grüßen.

Slowly cutting through my musings
This lovely, this tinkling sound

---

* From *Neue Gedichte* (1844), by Heinrich Heine (1797–1856).

Jingle, spring song, chime your music
And travel far off, be unbound.
Fly all the way to the house
Dozing among pretty flowers
And when you see a rose there
Give my greetings to her.

DECEMBER 20, 1940

So what, that I can write nice poems and I can say that I'm . . . well, you'll see for yourself (I'll paste a photo) and that my couplets are so cheerful that the whole school sings them, that girls and boys like me—I'm not happy with my school life. Jara—ah! I always want what's best for her. I once even decided to keep trying to convince her to practice (so that she can become a pianist). But sometimes, almost all the time, she embarrasses me. God! She flirts with my male friends. In fact she has this shrewdness, this ability to win people's liking. She has a very good heart, but not a crystal personality. She's very talented when it comes to music, also when it comes to acting, but she's not very clever, she doesn't have this thing, this innate thing, this something. And she's a woman, oh, a real, horrible woman, like Aunt Hela—just slightly . . . And you know what I'm like. Mama and you—you two know! I can't fight for them because I'm dispirited, both for fighting and for life. So far my skills have paved my path for me, but now there is this terrible possibility of the two of us, poor, lonely souls, getting separated! God! Jealousy—no, I don't want, do you hear me, I don't want it, I want to love her without a shadow of resentment, I want this, I love my only little sister!!! But she, she . . . No, I can't. She's aware of her successes and now she started talking to me with half smiles, ironic semi-words. She's happy she can go with Zygu, she wants to impress me this way and when I call her, she pretends not to hear me. Once she told me, "Rena, I'll get married before you anyway!" But it's not about that. Lord, You've separated me from my mother, don't separate me from my sister!!!

DECEMBER 25, 1940[9]

It was your birthday yesterday, Buluś. This was the second birthday of yours we didn't spend together. When will this torture finally end, when?! My longing gets stronger, I feel worse and worse. Sometimes it feels so terrible, I feel so empty that it's like my life is almost over— when, in fact, my life is just beginning. I can't see anything ahead of me. There's nothing, just suffering and fighting, and it's all going to end in defeat. I laugh during the daytime, but it's just a mask, it's like an oblivion (people don't like tears), but now I think that you, my Mama, are so far away, that you live in a ghetto, that you are unhappy and that I can't help you, because I'm not even ready for life myself. That's what Krela says.

Today there was a rehearsal for a variety show at Irka's. I've written couplets. I also take part in the show. Krela knows so much, she knows the whole of Europe, speaks so many languages. She's very clever, intelligent and swell. She told the boys that they're not ready for life and then she mentioned the girls too. Irka's mother said that Irka would manage all right in life. Irka is so smart! Krela said that Maryśka Filagrowicz is the sweetest girl in the school. I barely know her. And the smartest and most well-read boy is Zygu! Him again. It's always like that—I may think he doesn't matter to me, but he surreptitiously crosses my path again and I go crazy for him again. I suffer terribly. I keep crying all the time, because I'm in love.

Oh, Maciek keeps paying me compliments and saying lots of other things (which he says to everybody), but that's something completely different. And Waldek is yet another story altogether. When it comes to moments like this, no boys matter to me and I'm left with Zygu . . . Him again . . . "You need to wait patiently, God willing, you will meet." Yes, but when? God, why not now? If You want to bring us together, will it be a long time from now? Will our hearts, filled with bitterness, regret and longing, survive this? And what if one of them breaks? Then the other one'll die too. Lord God, please, help!!!

DECEMBER 28, 1940, SUNDAY*

Am I a sinner? Yes! Because even when I'm supposedly close to some-thing, my nature intervenes and stops me from going and ... that's it ... It just so happens—could it be any better? Zygu is going to be in the variety show! In fact, he and I are going to be in the same scene. It was so wonderful when Krela said, "Spiegel and Schwarzer would be best for that" and ... (what do I care about the rest). So we're reading from the same page. Irka says he listened admiringly when I sang couplets (I thought the opposite, but oh well!).

Then we went to school. It so happened that Luśka dragged him out, but Irka was cleverer and as a result I walked with him arm in arm. First he waited for me to grab him, but I was too embarrassed, so he took my hand, ah! It felt like my hand didn't quite belong to me. Or it did, but it felt completely different from my other hand. Some very nice shivers went up and down it, so nice that ah ... ! Earlier, when he was standing there reading his part, I couldn't tear my eyes away from his wonderful red lips, I'm embarrassed to admit.

At school he suggested I should sit next to him and it would be great! If only ... If only what happened today didn't happen. Because today, damn it, I blushed so badly. (Damn it! To hell with such nature!) Then he sat next to me, mumbled something and said to Luśka that he didn't know anything about her and that we were together onstage. And I, what an idiot, I messed it all up, because I removed myself. I made him angry at me, forced him to start talking to Luśka to spite me. What's more, he threatened that he wouldn't take part in it. "Do you hear, Rena?" And I told him that I didn't care! What can I do that I'm so stupid?!!!

DECEMBER 29, 1940

Today again! I've just been to a rehearsal. He was wonderful. He said that nobody sings cabaret songs like I do and that he didn't realize I was

---

* December 28, 1940, was a Saturday.

so talented. We talked and talked, he was so wonderful and lovely, my divine Zygu!

DECEMBER 31, 1940[10]

New Year's Eve! We put on the variety show. I was very popular. Backstage, Zygu took my cape off and untangled my hair. When the dancing started, I quickly left. They really wanted me to stay. Poldek, Rysiek, Julek and Tusiek. But I didn't want to stay and that was that. Zygo's so wonderful, divine, so charming. It was all so exciting; I told Norka everything. But she and Maciek aren't so close anymore, so she envies me. I feel sorry for her. Oh! I'm not surprised at all and I really understand her. Do you remember how terrible I felt for the same reason? Now she feels like that. She even cried, poor kitten. I would have perhaps stayed a bit longer to watch, but I left because of her.

When I was about to leave, Zygu ran up to me and asked if I would go to a party with him tomorrow. I told him that I don't dance, but he went on something about getting an invite and Jara said, "Yes, yes, she does dance." So I'm going. I am, why not, after all I told him that I might not dance. Aha! Wait, a day before yesterday at a rehearsal he invited me to go with him to drawing lessons with the XB class. So we went, but we had to leave quickly. Aha! I am a *vidminna*,* I was the only one who had everything, etc. Aha!

What else? Today is the last day of 1940. Tomorrow is the beginning of a new year, which will bring new regrets, new laughter (perhaps), new worries, new struggles. My dearest wish is to get my poor beloved Mama back. I also wish for good political relations and for "something" with Zygu. Let it be like I have described it in the final of our variety show:

> Be gone, worries, tears and upheaval
> Let all be carefree and good humored
> So, good night and let's hope winter isn't evil
> That's what we wish you, rest assured.

---

* *Vidminna* (відмінна)—feminine form for *excellent, superb* (Ukrainian).

Just remember, don't be chancing
Start the New Year in full joy
With singing, laughter and dancing
Take the first step, don't be coy.

I want this new year to be cheerful and happy. Nice to all in the world and to me as well.

Take all in kind embraces
Let it be friendly and warm all round
Paint happiness on people's faces
Call them into the future with a cheery sound
Let them walk briskly through life

With love for it and with real zest
And let my dreams come true, don't strive
That's more than gold, that's the best.

The last day of 1940. The last page in the diary. I'll greet the new year on a new page.

JANUARY 1, 1941, WEDNESDAY

I went to the party. It went wonderfully well, it couldn't have gone any better, I think. I danced with everybody. Mostly with Poldek and Zygu! Do you hear it? I hope the whole year goes as nicely as today's party! Zygu talked so much; he was so charming. We didn't dance too well, but it was so sweet. "It's my fault," "I knew you would come," "Pity the lights are so bright," etc. And when Irka said at the end that she was hoarse, he announced, "Rena's hoarse too." Hooray! "The first step always matters the most." I'll go to parties from now on.

JANUARY 3, 1941, FRIDAY

It was only the day before yesterday! And I am going crazy as if I haven't seen him for a year. The closer we get the more I feel I love him. For example today I've been trembling since the morning. Every time I think of that evening, I'm gripped by something I've never felt before.

So how was the party? Everything was sweet. What was the best moment? Was it when he spoke to me while we were dancing? Or when he draped his arm around me as I stumbled in a waltz? Or when he smiled wonderfully and asked, "Rena, why are you running away from me?" Or when he led me gently by the arm after each dance? He smelled so amazing! And when he touched me . . . brrr . . . ah . . . so great! So sweet, so good! We sat and talked together. What an evening.

And Poldek likes me too? But I didn't know he liked me so much. He was adamant about seeing me today; he keeps walking me home, annoying me. In fact I didn't say goodbye to anybody, but Zygu approached me and made a special effort to say goodbye. I can barely contain myself.

Today we've had a terrible blizzard; it's been snowing all day long. But I'd walk through any blizzard, snowstorm, hurricane, downpour with him—as long as we were together. My wonderful, my golden boy, my lover. I have to finish a paper to turn in tomorrow, but I just want to see Zygu. I'm going crazy. And at the same time I don't want to see him, because I'm so scared that something will go wrong, that this wonderful, sweet, fragrant memory will get spoiled.

JANUARY 5, 1941, SUNDAY

And? Didn't I say it was better not to see him? I was so regretful, but tough. It always so happens that when you love somebody, you tease them. The greetings were sweet, but then he didn't dance with me, he sat there fuming, in a bad mood, but tough, after all (oh, God) love can (i.e., must!!!) sulk too. Today I'm in bed; I'm unwell. Oh, I so hope that everything pans out well!! Please, Great One! I find evidence of his liking even in anger.

A 16-YEAR-OLD

When you're 16 years old
you dearly love the whole world
with all its parties, pranks and jokes
and especially with your favorite folks.

When you hide your crumpled diary
from your mother's strict inquiries.
When you sing love songs
Then you are 16 years old.

JANUARY 8, 1941, WEDNESDAY

All is well again, or even better than that. Irka insists that Zygu's in love with me. He said he would fight a duel with Poldek over me. That's because Poldek is head over heels in love with me. He came here once when I was ill.

Zygu didn't want to go to the movies when he found out I wasn't coming. And today he said he would go and I would go, so perhaps we might manage to go together? I was planning to go to a match (because Zygu plays and he invited me and asked through Irka to come). I made arrangements with Irka, but on my way back from the post office, I turned around and somebody said, "Rena, where have you been? Aren't you ashamed to be ill? You have really high welling-ton boots and you still caught a cold? Come with me to the match." Come and come. And I couldn't go, because, damn it, I made arrange-ments with Irka. He also said this and that; he was sweet, wonderful. For example he said he'd go on the pitch first, because he didn't want me to see it, etc. etc.

Zygu won the match and I congratulated him. I wasn't able to con-tain my worry that he might be joining the army. And Zygu? Zygu was very happy about it. Then we walked together, cracked jokes, teased each other like lovers do (or so I thought). And tomorrow? I'll see him at the match! I'll tell you more.

JANUARY 9, 1941, THURSDAY

Today . . . Oh, I'm even scared to say it—I went to the match. Nothing special happened. (Just once a ball hit my wonderful, dear Zygu on the jaw; it was so bad he crouched down in pain. My poor darling. I was very worried.) But after the match! Ooooh! We walked together and I told him that I was very upset during the match. He asked, "Why?" I said, "Just because." He persisted, "But why?" I said, "I was just upset. Let me be." "Spit it out." He simply wanted me to say, "Because you were playing."

Irka was walking in front of us with Genek, but Zygu arranged it so that we split. Finally alone! And what did fate have in store for us? Fate wanted us to see Arianka on the ice. We went down to the ice and the pipsqueak wouldn't give up and joined us. But Zygu didn't say anything. He was upbeat the whole time, mumbling something in Yiddish and asking why he hadn't seen me the other year. And he asked when we could go to the movies and this and that.

Naturally Giza saw me in town and she pulled the stupidest face. Then Poldek saw us too and naturally he wouldn't leave us alone.

Zygu is planning to study medicine and he said, "Rena, what are we going to do next year? You'll come to Lwów and we'll study together." Hooray! Hooray! Zygu is a wonderful boy and he says such sweet things! If only Mom were here—I could easily count these days as my happiest so far. (He's only just slightly naughty, not like other boys, who are vulgar.)

JANUARY 10, 1941, FRIDAY

I love him, I'm crazy for him! I haven't seen him all day long today. It drives me mad. If he goes to the party at the Socialist Club tomorrow, I'll go too.

Irka gave me an elephant. She blew on it for good luck for me and Zygu. Let it be so!

JANUARY 12, 1941, SUNDAY

What shall I tell you? I feel so strange; it's all so hard and so sickening . . . As if there were pawns moving around us, as if there was a pair of black eyes shining in the dark.

I saw him today, we even walked together in town, but it was because of Irka, it was her doing. Then he walked me home, admittedly on his own accord, but again, it was thanks to Irka that we were left alone. We both felt weary. He was quite polite, but it felt like he wanted to stay with Irka.

Yes, presently I am in such a state that I can barely hold a pen in my hand. I don't know what's being said to me, I forget everything, I don't write and at night I just lie in bed with my eyes wide open and think . . . think . . . Mama, I'd so like to cry my eyes out with you. Mama! Mama! Come!

> *A net of interlacing cords*
> *A brown ball bouncing up and down*
> *A whistle . . .*
> *And many arms stretched out*
> *A rumble as if walls were coming down*
> *One circle full of colors*
> *Fans are in uproar and they scream,*
> *"Not true," "Crazy referee," "Go"*
> *Out, service—and another whistle*
> *The ball bounces—that's a match, I know!!!*

I can't even mention Zygu. I feel faint, it's so terrible . . . Mama! Help me!

JANUARY 14, 1941, TUESDAY

I delivered a paper today. Finally. Everybody liked it, the room was very quiet, everybody was enthralled. Krela then said something, but in fact she didn't have anything to add.

It was quite sweet with Zygu today; he congratulated me afterward. But no matter, he said, "Rena, what do you think? I have my draft card." He read something out to me and, because I didn't understand what it meant, he said, "Am I married?" He laughed and then we walked arm in arm upstairs. A surprise awaited me there. They wanted me to become the president of the literary club. They started shouting, "Spiegel girl!" and one after another they nominated me. Zygu nominated me too. We voted and naturally I had the biggest amount of votes. And when Krela asked who they wanted to be the president, they all shouted that it was me. But that wasn't important. Zygu was nice, pulled faces at me and when Krela was speaking we were almost in stitches . . . And all would have been well, we would have been alone etc., but unfortunately one guy from IXA wouldn't leave me be. Zygu was furious and so was I. Zygu suddenly said goodbye, mumbled something and left . . . What a shame! Well, let's hope there'll be another chance . . . for us to be finally alone.

JANUARY 17, 1941, SATURDAY*

I've been ill for three days now. I'm struggling terribly with this poem. Oh, what a tough birth, as my sweet Mama says. I have a plan, oh! I have just got two letters from my dear Mama. I'm so happy, God! She wants to come, my wonderful, sweet, good Mama. She might come, I hope it will all pan out.

It's been a good day today. Today Arianka has started the fifth grade. A letter from Mama. Kasia might be back. What will Irka and Norka say about . . . (about whom?).

JANUARY 21, 1941, WEDNESDAY†

Ah, wonderful Wednesday! It was Wednesday then too. I seem to be lucky with Wednesdays.

> *Long live every Wednesday*
> *good humor and fair play*
> *Long live, in all the truth*
> *everything about youth*
> *about carefree laughter*
> *about hope with no restraint*
> *which always takes you after*
> *to parties, no complaint*
> *to dates and walks in town*
> *for cakes and to entertain*
> *and even home, when in your gown*
> *those words you make on the windowpane*

---

* January 17, 1941, was a Friday.
† January 21, 1941, was a Tuesday.

the arrows and those letters
the word that in your diary
blushes in red and is allowed
the one you always carry
the one that always rings aloud
So long live every Wednesday
good humor and fair play
Long live, above all
everything that's called love.

The party was on Wednesday and today... Make a guess, because I'm breathless. Words want to jump out of my throat. So today... Zygu came to visit me. He came, he was sweet, lovely. He looked at me, all the time hypnotizing me with his eyes. I didn't pretend to be unhappy. He spent so much time with me and said so much. The most important thing was that when Maciek asked, "Who has the most beautiful eyes?" Zygu went sheepish (and so did I), then he (my wonderful one) blushed and said, "Rena." Maciek winked at me, said loads of things in relation to love. And Zygu was sheepish.

My writing is bad today, because I have German measles. That's why Maciek, Poldek and Zygu came for a visit. Poldek, I know it, is very much in love with me. Maciek, as I know, likes me a lot too and Z is a mystery, a Sphinx.

He is an Apollo
with his stature, his skin
so brown and smooth
He is a Sphinx
with his impenetrable eyes
hiding an uncouth mystery, I think

All three of them told me that if I don't go to the party, they wouldn't go either, so I said that I would prefer to feel better and go, and that they should go too.

They've been gossiping terribly about Nora, those brats. I'm curious what they want from her (leg, stocking, nose). They've been at logger-heads with Maciek for a while. I was angry at him and today he paid me back for this wrongdoing out in town. Maciek is as good as an angel, he could be jealous, but no.

JANUARY 23, 1941, THURSDAY

Irka insists that I write something in her diary. In verse, of course. I'll try.

JANUARY 27, 1941

I didn't finish the entry last time, because Norka came over. Then there were visits from Poldek and Maciek, and Nora with Irka. It varied; some-times it was nice, sometimes boring (and once there was even an un-pleasant situation).

On Saturday Zygu was supposed to come, but he didn't, because his mother arrived.

And me? I live off memories; I'm astounded that I remember his every word, every smile, every face he pulled. When I remember something new, it feels like . . . I don't know myself. I can't talk or think of anything else. It's becoming a real mania.

Yesterday Uncle Maciek (whom I like very much) went for a visit to theirs. He loved Zygu—himself and his behavior. Zygu left two note-books in the room, so he knocked, apologized and went in to pick them up.

God! Why are they telling me all of this? As it is, I can barely control my heart, which wants to jump out of my breast. Irka already says quite directly that Zygu's in love with me, but I don't believe it, no! I don't believe just yet! That'd be a miracle! And I already . . . God, God, God, please! And you, Buluś . . .

JANUARY 30, 1941

Today . . . Today was a good day. First at school . . . well, nothing impor-tant. In the afternoon there was a LOPP exam (Airborne and Antigas

Defence League)* and naturally I, not even knowing what *Osoaviakhim*†
was, decided to try. Zygu trained me a bit. He came after his exam but
before mine. He was wonderfully sweet and there are no words in the
world to describe his eyes. He kept talking to me, laughing, paying me
compliments (he's so witty) and at some point he grabbed my chin (that's
his tender gesture) and he almost k . . . me, but I gently pushed him away
(perhaps next time. Lord God! Buluś!).

I said that eating hen meat spoiled my skin, to which Maciek replied
that a rooster would sort me out. Maciek is a pig. He even called Zygu
over and repeated the joke to him. And I? I pretended not to understand.

During my exam Cukierman was cracking up.

I have a new rival, Dziunka. Today she noticed that we like each other
(when we were cuddling on the bench). She was furious and eager to
mess things up. Poor me. Haven't I been in her shoes once? But now I can
tell you that I'm in a better position and, God willing, if fate allows, it'll
get even better? Well? Well? Well?

FEBRUARY 1, 1941

It was a so-so day. He was sweet, talked to me, we were even supposed to
go to Irka's together, but he was ready to go home and he was tired.

There is something very friendly, very intimate. But he is so proud
(why wouldn't he be if everybody keeps suggesting that I'm his?). Bloody
rascal, he didn't even want to invite me to sit down. He laughed, saying
that when I see him in his gray shirt, what then? Ah, Buluś, Buluś,
help me.

Irka has given me this to cheer me up and for good luck. It looks funny
phrased like that, but what do I know?

---

* Airborne and Antigas Defence League existed until 1939.
† OSOAVIAKhIM (Union of Societies of Assistance to Defence and Aviation-Chemical
Construction of the USSR)was a paramilitary Soviet organization established in 1927,
concerned mainly with weapons, automobiles, and aviation. In 1951, it was renamed as
DOSAAF (Volunteer Society for Cooperation with the Army, Aviation, and Navy).

FEBRUARY 4, 1941, TUESDAY

It was a strange day today. Nora had an argument with Maciek—she cried. Krela yelled at me. She really had a go at me. It's all her fault anyway. He was just staring and staring, which paralyzed me.

In the morning Zygo stroked my face in front of Irka, Tuśka and Ela, he took my face into his hands and called me Renusia. I just had a thought that he did it on purpose, to flummox me. Briefly everything seemed to be going well. He took me under my arm and said, "Why don't you want to be the president? I worked so hard to get you on the board!" Then he sat down with me, pulled my hood off my head and we talked all the time. Then Krela had a go at me for various reasons but mainly because I talked during the meeting. Zygu consoled me and said that Krela told him off too. And when Krela said, "Let's see who could be the husband killer in *Lilies?*"* he said, "Renusia" (damn this "Renusia"!), "You are not good for a husband killer." And "I want to be Rena's son" and this and that and I started thinking that he was mocking me, which really unnerved me.

He didn't wait for me, he didn't say goodbye—as if he wanted me to follow him. But, actually, what's my problem? He was sweet after all. And if he wanted to make fun of me? God, You know how much that would hurt! He just stared and stared, which paralyzed me.

FEBRUARY 5, 1941, WEDNESDAY

I'm so blue! I'm so low. I'm in love and mocked by the object of my love. I even cried. Such a blow. And so well aimed. I've taken offense. I've heard Zygu telling Maciek, "Rena is angry at me." He said that to me at school and I confirmed. Angry, is that what it is?! I'm not angry, I'm very, very sad and concerned. He told me this awful, "Look at how she holds her leg, just like Nora does." When he said "Renusia," I instinctively turned around, immediately. And then he said that I was angry. I heard him saying on purpose that Irka was pretty. I heard it all and I cried, not

---

* Adam Mickiewicz's ballad.

with tears, but I could feel those tears inside me, stifling me, flooding my heart. Mama! I felt so bad, so very bad! But love's stronger than anything and when I went sad, Zygu laughed and said, "Rena, what is it?" So, trying to pull an offended face, I laughed. If he really mocks me like that, if he really says it, then . . .

I will draw two tiny hearts
two hearts linked by love
and a wide black arrow or dart
that pierces the red buds from above
One heart will be true and full of life
honest and hot—that one is mine
the other one I'll make alive
I'll give it love to drink like wine
I'll feed it smiles and happy noise
I'll feed it words, gentle touches and looks
I'll give it silly things (the most precious joys)
my unsatisfied dreams flowing down brooks
It will be bright like radiant sunshine
It will be red like a pretty poppy
And then when the other's ready to decline
The red one will whisper, "Yes! Let's be happy."

Pavements move, glide ahead
as do stars, tarmac and streetlights
I sleepwalk around the city
embraced by silver moonlight
I wander around, looking, looking
into infinite depths I stare
Is a tiny love seedling
perhaps hiding somewhere in there?

Don't worry, no matter, there, there
Not everything will be surely lost
"Why do you cry, silly girl?
It's perfectly normal, don't be cross."

Oh, cry as much as you like
Perhaps sobbing'll make you weary
You might forget and sleep'll strike
I cling to hanging ropes, it's scary
to trees, wires, bells a-ringing
I cling to church bell towers
to thunder's and lightning's stinging
I go there, into the sky, into starry showers
fueled by unearthly force, kind of
I go, I fly, I soar
Oh, I am so much, so deeply in love!!!

Strange thoughts tremble inside
cloudy, half-sleeping, dreary
jumbled into a nightmarish ride
wobbly and clumsy and blurry
spring water comes as if from a gutter
there are red, juicy berries
and this misguided, drunken thought—water
The lips' effort is a futile flurry
The effort of brain throat cracked dry lips
Words don't want to sound out
Nobody hears the lamenting apocalypse
Just those entangled thoughts all out
Splashing of water, forest-grown berries
And this unspoken out loud
Word—water—that carries!!!
For once in my life I'm surely allowed
To ride the vehicles of airstreams
To crack, to whoosh, to shine through clouds
to fly straight to the stars that gleam
For once in my life I'm surely allowed
To speed merrily through celestial expanses
To climb rainbows, moons and clouds
To roll down with the morning dawn, to take chances
For once in my life I'm surely allowed

To enjoy this thrilling ride
To jump onto a star in style
to look at the stars from the other side
For once in my life I'm surely allowed
To get lost in this crazy love
To love with passion and with pride
Even if . . . this love is not returned . . .

FEBRUARY 7, 1941, FRIDAY

Oh! It's so much better! It's almost good. I've had a long conversation with him in the red corner. And somehow my heart tells me that he went to town because of me (though how he walked—God, have mercy on him). And I had to leave him in the midst of it and go study Polish. Such is life (ish). But I'm not complaining at all. I would just like it to open its wings and frrr . . .

Maciek tells me today, "Aurelia S., née Spiegel . . . I'd like the two of you to get married, because I like you and I like him." So I tell him, "What's that to you? You would be a friend of the house," to which Maciek says, "Yes, and perhaps you might get bored in time . . ." No, I couldn't get bored with Zygu! Everybody likes him so much that I think I might go crazy with jealousy! Lord . . . don't abandon me, and you, dear Mama!

FEBRUARY 8, 1941, SATURDAY

Today is Saturday, February 8, I had a sweet day. At school Zygu assured me that he would vote for me, as he's a member of the jury, and that he would give me all possible points. Later, after the match I waited for him and we walked together. Together, you hear? There was this other boy walking too, but he didn't count and left soon anyway.

When we got to the red corner, one of my numerous rivals soon left. I couldn't count all those looks he gave me. But he does it in a kind of conspiratorial way, as if not wanting me to notice. Eh! He's a wonderful boy, the prettiest in the school! Please, God and Buluś, let it continue in such manner, like this . . .

And now I need to get busy. I have a poem to write, praising Mickie-wicz. I should write it, but am I able to? Will my words be worthy of the man? I'm not sure if I can, I doubt . . . but still . . . perhaps . . .

Mankind erects a shrine to your memory
It is to be worthy of you, it is to thrive
It is to look at the world with reverie
to grow, make you famous—be alive!

It is to proudly soar into the sky
fueled by burning love and admiration
to become a symbol and a cry
of what you used to call liberation

To be a beacon for the world
To last for years, for centuries
An endless memorial is unfurled
Huge, powerful, in your memory

At its top there is a place of yours
To look down on earth below
To see what you suffered for
And what you loved even more.

FEBRUARY 10, 1941

Today is Sunday, February 10.* The Teich girl has found out about my love and told me, "I would prefer if you were to fall in love with Maciek. Because Zygu is handsome, wise, intelligent, but he's no good and he'll really wear you down. He's this and then that, and you'll never know why." Yes! God, the second part rings so true. No good, oh no! Zygu, you? You are the best, best, best, best.

---

* February 10, 1941, was a Monday.

FEBRUARY 11, 1941, MONDAY*

Lord God, my poor Mama is so far away! Poor her, it's bad there, she's all on her own. I would very much like her to come to us, as I have a big problem and I'm so sad, and that terrible person is wearing me down! The Teich girl was right. He tortures me morally, he simply exercises me: contracting and stretching. Today he took offense over what? Over nothing—he pulled a sweet face and I went into the classroom first and only then approached him. And not the other way round. Naturally he didn't come to the rehearsal in the afternoon and after the rehearsal he sent me such a look that blood curdled in my veins with fear. And then he yelled, "Leave it!" to Poldek, so that . . . well. God, what does he want? Zygu, have mercy, why do you tease me so much?! Stop it, I can't take it anymore! Holy God, help me!

FEBRUARY 12, 1941, WEDNESDAY

Mama can't come; it's so bad there, famine. Zygu's angry with me, doesn't come to the rehearsals. God! God! Help me!

FEBRUARY 13, 1941, THURSDAY

Hooray! I have to force myself to explain everything properly to you. There were apologies at school. But how? As if nothing had happened. He approached me, embraced me so sweetly and we had a good talk which lasted the entire break. The whole school could see us, damn it! People were pulling idiotic faces. The Teich girl was laughing under her breath. Zygo came to the rehearsal and then we went, I mean, I and him, to the red corner. Elu came too and we laughed our heads off; it was very nice. And then I talked to Zygu on my own (ah, those newspapers, what fuss), then Stela came, my number one rival. Of course I understood her mood. So then I say to Zygu to go and we went. Waldek, sweet, poor Waldek, he's a bit not right in the head, he wanted to leave us alone and go on his own, but I didn't let him. We said goodbye in town. And then I

---

* February 11, 1941, was a Tuesday.

was left with Zygu. I met our Norka, Belka, Helka and other people from town. We talked about most trivial things in the world (thank God for the existence of Kubrakiewicz). Then I met Maciek, Poldek and Julek. Maciek almost gave me a peck in the middle of the street, as a joke. Of course he was full of jibes about Zygu and me. Then we walked on our own again and again talked about nice things. In fact I don't know if that's how it's going to be till the end of the world? Do you have such ordinary conversations? I need to ask. At some point Zyguś thought I took offense. "Renusia, are you angry at me?"

Zyguś walked me home and we made plans to go to the movies on Saturday.

Oh, I lived today! Nothing . . . but still . . . Buluś, you helped me, I feel better now, even though tomorrow he might still be angry at me. And I'm so ugly—how can I be attractive? Wonderful Zyguś, don't be angry at me, be good, like today and . . . even better. Mama, if you could only see him! Keep helping me, Buluś, and You, God . . .

FEBRUARY 14, 1941, FRIDAY

I'm such a stupid idiot, a moron and the rest! I've arranged to go to the movies with Zygu. And I meant to go with him on Saturday, but I went today with Maciek and Poldek. Ah! I understand Zygu. I would take terrible offense too. God, what am I going to do? Will we go to the movies or perhaps to a concert or nothing at all? "I know I am worth the punishment," but . . . not quite—I wanted to know what the film was about to explain everything to him. And everything went topsy-turvy. I had good intentions, but it turned out so, so badly. Lord, I'm scared of tomorrow! Help me, God, and you, Buluś . . .

FEBRUARY 16, 1941, SATURDAY*

I'm trembling all over today. No, it wasn't a terrible Saturday, though it didn't promise to be too good. I went to a match. Zygu first pretended he

---

* February 16, 1941, was a Sunday, so it's not clear if Renia wrote this on Saturday, February 15, or on Sunday, February 16.

didn't see me and invited Irka to sit with him, inquiring (so that I could hear him), "Irka, are you going to the concert?" and when she asked him whether he wasn't going to the movies, he replied, "What good is a movie today?!" And I felt so bad, so terrible, so awful . . .

The first breaking of the ice took place when he pulled my hood off my head. He was still a bit angry. But later everything went well, wonderfully well! We walked together (he adjusted my hair in the street), then at Irka's and later at the concert—this was the culmination. No, not yet, no. But at the concert we sat together on one and a half chairs, ah! And we talked all the time and I realized how wonderful, how gentle, how decent he is! All the time together, a wonderful Saturday afternoon together. He walked me home, him and another one, and . . . when he was saying his goodbyes, he held my hand in such a way; he held it and said, "Bye, Renusia." And then I said suddenly, surprisingly, as if it wasn't me, "Bye, kitten." And still, it was me. God! I said this, this fire which has tormented me for so long suddenly leaped out and congealed together, forming this one word. And Zyguś . . . He laughed (perhaps even a bit glad?), he laughed so wonderfully . . .

We were supposed to go to the movies tomorrow, but he just said, "12 o'clock tomorrow, in town." Tomorrow, ah! Thank you, God and you, wonderful Buluś, and you, Zygu, for this Saturday.

For me now nothing matters
boredom, rumpus, scandal, chatters
physics and mathematics
little Purcel's mad dramatics
Auntie Józka with meniscus
Salcia and Breit and hibiscus
Krela with her big mouth
all other creatures about
they don't matter to me now
I'm also not bothered to even look
what grades I have in the mark book
I yawn terribly in the classroom
thoughts filled with doom and gloom

Good or bad ways are not a thing
one thing that matters—is loving

I wrote this today at physics, in secret—isn't it wise?

Today I had this flutter inside
I was taken over by this strange tide
Everything pulsated and twitched
Today my heart was bewitched.

FEBRUARY 16, 1941, SUNDAY*

I didn't want to tell you at all that Z was out in town with his buddies and I was with Julek K. and we pretended not to see each other and this idiot didn't even approach me. I didn't want to tell you that this other one, the one who walked me home with Z and already interfered once—remember? He is in love with me! What a fine kettle of fish! Wait a second, and Zygu? I can't say either way—it's a very strange story. I just wanted to tell you that something terrible is happening to me. Some dark, crude force is seizing me. I keep looking for ambiguity in everything, I can be easily persuaded when I can't see, can't I? I'm reading Tuwim's poems, also the indecent ones. I wrote in Irka's diary.

Blood pumps, spring is about
And spring makes hearts open
It makes them grow and swell and sprout
eyes shine, the world dissolves into laughter
lips, breasts, hips enlarge
Spring is lavish, spring gives freely
Doesn't spare anything, by and large
Lips and eyelids kisses silly
Refreshes with sweet caresses
Spring's coming, be ready for its excesses

---

* This entry is in fact from February 17.

I want this power to seize me, to lift me
I want to write lopsided verses
Clumsy and savage, raunchy as can be
It simply must be so
I feel my blood boiling
I feel my heart beat faster
Spring storms are broiling
I want wind and bluster
I want my face slapped
Hit me, beat me, poison, torture
Bite me, throttle, kiss me, strap
Hellish power inside me's surging
So tie me up, be like a tyrant
Curb this force that is in me
'Cause I toss and turn in crisis
my blood shouts like some banshee
You have to overpower me
Or I will overtake you

You see, just look, this is still nothing. I find some wild, sadistic plea-sure in people saying, "Rena is seeing Z." People talk about it at school, but I'd like to write something so indecent . . . and then find pleasure in it . . . I'm ashamed . . . God, help me again and you, Buluś, please, make those people be right in what they say. Give me courage.

FEBRUARY 18, 1941

Oh, what a wonderful, happy day! I don't think Z was ever as wonderful as today. I met him on the stairs. He said to me, "My poppet, my sweet-ness" etc. We spent the whole break standing on the stairs. So stupid. Ah, he really didn't see me in town, because he asked me where I was then. Girls from the 8th grade passing by said, "Aaah!" Zygu burst out laugh-ing and said we should go somewhere else.

It's really hard, you have to understand that I can't even describe it in words. It should be written on a blue sky with spring fantasies, sighs and whatever ticks, whatever vibrates inside . . .

He was supposed to get me *Kordian*.* And he tried. We sang something for fun at the club. He said I would be his mascot during matches. (Do I really have eyes like Valentino—big, blue, burning? What is he saying?) And even though he left early, I, for the first time, am feeling something. Touch wood, it's true. It's something and nothing, but still. I heard Jerzyk saying, "I have a feeling that a new couple is forming at school." Not sure if it was about us, but perhaps . . . Let's hope so. God, God and my wonderful Buluś, keep me in Your thoughts, now and forever.

FEBRUARY 19, 1941, WEDNESDAY

You know, I'm starting to believe. At school he behaves in such a way—I absolutely cannot describe to you how it is. We walked along the corridor together, he asked me to recite a poem, so sweet! Dziunka saw me. And when Kubrakiewicz approached us and started saying something about my eyes, something, something, Zygu added his bit too. Suddenly old Kubrakiewicz shouted, "See how he's looking at her? He's flirting with her! But no matter. Nice couple!" If Kubrakiewicz realized that, then something must be the matter, though he's quick with those things. But if this old, wizened Aunt Józka noticed something in the red corner, even though it was nothing special . . . Ah, after Kubrakiewicz's announcement Zyguś went terribly sheepish and said, "I'm embarrassed."

Aha, and then the poem, the poem, this and that . . . Today I wrote in Ewa's diary on the same page as Z, the same one. And I drew a heart. Tra la la! How he was excusing himself for his untidy writing in Ewa's diary!

In the evening we walked together and this Tadek constantly wanted to be next to me, but I and Nora outfoxed him. Z and I stayed behind, walking together, just the two of us and it was wonderful, simply wonderful!! "Sweetheart" and smiles and looks and "Renusia, study maths" etc.; can't even list it all. He was supposed to go home, but he walked me, and when I left for Irka's, he turned around and went straight home— he was gone a moment later. What matters is how he said goodbye— he shook my hand and held it awhile (as is typical for him), and then

---

* Juliusz Słowacki's drama.

he did this . . . strangely, intuitively I sensed it . . . I didn't know what it meant . . . I asked Ariana and she knew. It means, it is, eh!—it's a calling. I don't know if he did it by accident? Have I imagined it? Have I? Because I know that Z's not vulgar or anything. Or perhaps, perhaps this is just a mask, perhaps this liking is all pretend?

> *Perhaps, perhaps, perhaps*
> *Who can really tell*
> *Help me see through cracks*
> *Mama and You, God, as well!*

It's so sweet, so good, so light and strange.

FEBRUARY 20, 1941, THURSDAY

I've been dreaming about Mama all night long. Together with Zygu we were rescuing her, looking for her in Warsaw. And today I remembered all those painful, burning things, so . . . be quiet. When it comes to it, it's not quite working and it's partially his and partially my fault. Let's hope things get sorted by Saturday!! I'm worried about the weekend; things always go wrong then. Help me, God Almighty. Help me, my one and only true friend, my wonderful, distant and close Mama . . .

FEBRUARY 21, 1941, FRIDAY

So far today all is well (only everybody keeps calling me "Mrs. Schwarzer"). He was so cute, shaved, handsome. Today, but . . . what about tomorrow???

I have four rivals already. But please, God, and you, my wonderful Mama, you love me and understand me, please make tomorrow be . . . be . . . be . . . good. And let me tell you all about it. I have such terrible stage fright!!

FEBRUARY 22, 1941, SATURDAY

I had stage fright, but perhaps it wasn't worth it. But still. A bow in the cloakroom, a handshake in the classroom and *Balladina*,* then again, after the break and then in the corridor in the morning. Exactly. The two of us stood there and I can only imagine what we looked like—everybody was looking at us. Eda approached us (his former love) and I, stupidly, like some idiotic moron, went beetroot red! Zygu laughed his head off! Damn it! Stupid blushing . . .

I went to the match, I got in when he was changing, so I apologized, but he just grabbed me, like only he can, he grabbed my chin with both his hands and asked about my hairdo. Later I went to school on my own without saying goodbye. Strange enough! At school Zygu was reproach-ful because of my running away. During the rehearsal it got very nice, finally. It's not possible to describe it; you need to feel it in every single nerve in your body. And remember that we sat together all this time, and we walked and walked, just the two of us, and that he was hell-bent on going to the concert and this and that . . . at 9 p.m., and then he didn't want to and made plans to go to a party and when we were standing there, I lowered my head over my watch and our foreheads met. I think his hand trembled a bit when we were saying goodbye. He held my hand for a long time . . . for so long . . . and then he did it again (or so I think) . . . But it might all be just for show, oh! Perhaps it's nothing. After all he would sooner say something ambiguous in the presence of Irka and . . . No. Buluś, I'm going through a spiritual tragedy. Let's hope to God it ends well! Lord, please give me back my Mama. Mama, come and help me!!!

> It hurts like searing heat
> Wild jealousy is eating me
> It jerks me, it wrenches hard
> Like some sharp, rough shard
> Listen—spring is near
> And I'm more and more jealous here

---

* Juliusz Słowacki's drama.

I squirm and writhe, I'm hyper
Why did you give me this viper?
to grab my peace from me?
to torment me, eat me, see?
to make me swear like a sailor?
I can taste jealousy's flavor
Oh, all those sleepless nights
All those thoughts and dreams alight
Stifling words—unsaid
Burning tears—unshed
All the teasing, taunting torments
I'm so jealous right this moment
because I love to a crazy extent!!!
Perhaps when rivers flow wide
With a turbulent and raging tide
Perhaps when the orchard glistens in the distance
Morning dawn'll embrace me, give assistance
And when clouds in pink will fly
And roll down from the azure sky
Your eyes'll shine for me
My black-eyed prince!
Perhaps when sun glimmers
With hot, blinding shimmers
Or when night descends
Filled with spring's stifling scent
And when birds' joyous screaming
In the empty valley go a-ringing
Your lips will touch me
My red-lipped prince!
Perhaps like a flower that declined
leaving the memory of its smell behind
You will also soon be gone casually
I'll be left with longing and waiting and a fantasy . . .

No! No! No! Mama, no!

FEBRUARY 23, 1941

I'm so very tired. So just quickly. At night I get up, sure that Zygu is next to me. I start shaking him, calling, "Zygu! Zygu!" But it was Arianka, who was scared and came to me. War! Field games at war—together all the time—Zygu throws himself onto his back in the present and yells, "Rena, down!" and then we walk together. Rysiek screams, "Rena has a crush on you, Zygu!" Zygu mumbles something under his breath, "Stop it." We're having a party tomorrow! Ah, my second one. You know, I have terrible stage fright. I'm scared of everything. Will I have a good time? Will Zygu dance with me? Will "something" happen?

Damn it, this idiot Nacek has a thing for Lidka, that's all we need. Nora is down. Poor her, I was hoping things would work out in the end, but now . . . Nora bet it all on the party, but Lidka'll be there too.

Norka! I hope you don't get disappointed! Z and M and the rest tease her. But this Nacek, this stupid, presumptuous, horrible brat . . . If it were me, I would smack him on the face angrily. What a great, smug piece of S.

Irka's Feluś is sweet and Irka is great (my matchmaker). And Irka's Feluś, though far away, keeps kissing her on the pages of her diary.

I will write when . . . oh, it'll be so long (or perhaps never), when . . . I'm worried about tomorrow's party. Mama, help me, send me your blessings, bring your little daughter back to life. God, Buluś, please, help me! Help me!

FEBRUARY 24, 1941, MONDAY (SECOND PARTY!!!)

Oh! Ah! Eh! I'm so terribly tired. But I definitely have enough energy to tell you what I want to tell you. Mom! Mama dear, if only I could tell you everything, every single thing, and kiss you and get your advice and tell you everything. You'd surely understand me, you'd be happy for your daughter who is so . . . well . . . ("let sleeping dogs lie") . . . contented.

At school—nothing; then—yes; then the party. I danced with Zygu the whole time, my wonderful, one and only, sweet-smelling Zygu. Roma, my rival number four, was there as well and suddenly she said, "Look, he is dancing with her for the seventh time. If he takes it to 10, I'm leaving." Zygu laughed and told me that Roma was still there and added, "Now she can count to 20." And there were a lot of pleasantries apropos this. Then he bought me a bagel in the canteen and put it in my mouth in such a sweet gesture . . . Then, when Maciek said, "This is Zygu's love for one night," Zygu immediately consoled me, saying, "No, that's not true." And he pulled such a sweet face saying this. Everybody, even a blind person, could see that something was the matter when we danced together. One thing though—I was terribly jealous (even though he danced with the others only three, four times). But he called Irka "sweetheart" and she took him under the arm after their dance (I sometimes walk with him that way too). Zyguś called Elza "Elzuś" and asked her jokingly to sit in his lap. When our hands got sweaty in the dance, we held each other by our elbows. Wonderful, wonderful Zyguś. Of course I'm now called "Mrs. Schwarzer" all the time. Even in front of Zygu.

We walked arm in arm from the party, with Irka on the other side. It was sweet, but it could've been better . . . no! I'm sinning by saying this; it was great, thank You, God! I could see from the beginning that he wanted to ask me, but Poldek was faster and asked Nora. Oh, Nora, poor Norka, it was terrible! Nacek and Lidka flirted with each other. She was in a bad mood, didn't dance (Zygu, when he saw she was not having fun, even sent Julek—he's that nice).

Poor Nora, it was a tragic evening for her. She just told me, "You are so happy." (No, I shouldn't sin by being jealous or anything. Zygu walked me home on his own and even though he didn't . . . he was always sweet, polite and good.)

Norka, I'm so sorry for her, I'm so very sorry, she left without saying goodbye before the end of the party. I've heard Nacek saying that she was sitting there on her own, so he asked her out of pity! He's horrible! Maciek also said that Nora didn't have a good time. Even this W. didn't ask her, since she said no. It is better to stay on friendly terms with every-body after all.

Something's going on between Irka and Maciek again. But I don't want to be jealous of Irka, she wishes me well. Though not as much as you do, my Mama, not like You, good God! Thank You so much and please keep helping me . . .

Around! Around! Stars shine brightly
Take me strongly by the hand
Let them play wild music, lightly
Let dance pull us deep into its land
Until death in waltz embraces
Dancing, waltzing left and right
Like at a party, at other places
All of life is fun, a delight
Let's dance lightly, smoothly, swiftly
Let's dance fiercely with panache
All life, on floors silver, shiny, shifty
Let the house be a ballroom afresh
To forget about the world that's small
To flash into the realm of night, sun bright
Nothing matters, I'm dancing with you after all
this waltz with no end, no end in sight

FEBRUARY 25, 1941, TUESDAY

Zyguś! My wonderful! Wonderful! Wonderful! He came to the classroom looking for me, my dear "pet!" We stood in the corridor (while Roma was cussing me in her classroom), then I shared my wafers with him. He put a piece into my mouth. And he said to Irka, "Rena is in the foreground," so he lent me his copy of *Balladina*. And this and that. "Rena, you are under a bad influence." His, of course. Then, "Renusia" and he almost whacked Rysiek for flirting with me. Aha! But that's not all! I still have a hum in my ears after the party—play, fanfare!! Irka told me that Zygu stood with her in the corridor and said, "Rena is so pretty" and when she asked him if he had a good time, he said, "And what do you think?" and "Who did Rena come for?'" And when Irka told him, that I came to have a good time, he laughed with disbelief! I'll see him tonight at 6 p.m. Mama, dear, it's so good to be in love. Lord God, please, let things continue, please . . .

Let's spread our arms out wide
Let's walk through life with joy and pride

Let our song reverberate
Let our tears dry at a quick rate
Let's have a ring of cheer inside
With a scarlet banner of love let us stride
Arm in arm, together, two of us folks
(the world will vibrate with our jokes)
Let the world become a garden
Let spring last and never darken
Such joy in our souls, in us, ever after!
Let's walk through life with lots of laughter
Two of us, we will always cheer
We will throw the word high in the air
We will spark hot bronze and steel
Listen to love, feel what we feel

He stood in the corridor, reading the poem, and he said, "This is Rena's poem." Maciek told me this.

Nora's really low right now.

FEBRUARY 26, 1941, WEDNESDAY

I shouldn't doubt him anymore. Didn't he ask me today, so sweetly, if I was going to the club? Didn't he come only because I was going, too? Didn't he carry my schoolbag and help me down the stairs? Didn't he wait outside the school? When I shared my halva with him, he said that he couldn't have it, but then took a piece without asking—it was so intimate, so nice. He took the page with the homework. But do you know what I like thinking of most? I don't know why, but I like recalling this sweet moment when my Zygu bought me a bagel and put a piece of it into my mouth. Because, you know, you understand, that apart from sweetness, there was something so . . . masculine about it . . . so husband-like. Oh, this scene, I remember it.

You know why I never draw him? Because I can't make him beautiful enough; because I'm scared, not able to. Perhaps I'll get a photo? Maybe, Zyguś mentioned it once.

For now they tease us, they make fun. I'm sorry, but ... let's hope they'll have a basis for it soon ...

God, Mama, thank you! Help! So, so much ...

I'm so happy he isn't like Nacek! No! I can't stand it anymore. Even though I have homework to do, I need to tell you. I thought that was all for today, but ... Irka came with Zygu! With Zygu, do you hear me? We sat together for three hours or so, then out to town. Zygu wanted to go for a walk and Irka wanted to go home. To which my wonderful Zyguś said, "Up to Rena." Then we were on our own. A ha ha ha!

I have a photo, two photos—stolen, but still. When they asked him who he was in love with, Zygu said with me (he was standing behind me). Ah! Oh! Ah! I'm so happy ... I'm feeling silly, affectionate and strange. When we were finally going back, I told him I took the photo and Zygu said, "But I wanted to give you a different one, larger, prettier. In my opinion it's disrespectful to give you a photo like this one!" Isn't he wonderful? You don't know, you can't know it, but I'm ready to burst, I'm exploding, yeah! Look! Look! Look! He's so wonderful! Admire him all day long and all night long, just like I do. Mama and You, wonderful God, lead me ...

P.S. When I told him that I'm scared of my rival number four, Roma, he said not to be scared and that he would defend me and that we should do something about her, perhaps send her to Kulparków.*

> *Flowers nearby*
> *Stars high in the sky*
> *It's all for you*
> *All for you*
> *Sleepless nights*
> *Poems fiery and bright*
> *Tears, bitterness anew*
> *It's all for you!*

---

* Kulparków is a district of Lwów, famous for a psychiatric facility.

FEBRUARY 27, 1941, THURSDAY

School was good. And later it was so nice too! We met in the afternoon, I mean I met him in the red corner. Roma and Ewa were there too, we couldn't get rid of them. They followed us all the time, went to Irka's, where a farce took place—I ran away upstairs, Maciek to Zygo K's; Zygu was looking for me etc. He then joined Maciek at K's and they were supposed to do homework. Then they whistled at me and we went for a walk. Zyguś took me sweetly by my arm and then dropped hints of this and that. But he was terribly lovely. We met Nacek who said something about the Spiegel girl and the Schwarzer boy, don't know what he meant. On our way back they began an academic discussion on sexual matters. I felt a bit embarrassed. But they started explaining that if I am to study medicine then this and that. They think I'm still such a child and Zygu doesn't let them tell any vulgar jokes (I mean, to me).

We were making plans for our time at university—they'll be downstairs and Irka and I upstairs. Zygu wanted to lend me one book, "Which you can learn a bit from."

He generally has become very forceful recently (which I like terribly). He tells me, for example, "Rena! Learn that German poem! Now!" or "Rena is to go to a drama school" and he gave Rysiek a beating for teasing me. He was furious at W for his "Can I come with you?" "Rena, about turn, fetch the coat!" And when I took offense, he said, "Well then, will you do an about turn and I will give you your coat?" When they were in the red corner Zygu said that as soon as he mentions me, I appear in the window. He keeps staring at me, so sweetly. When Maciek said that one needed a friend, he replied that one needed to find one then.

I could fill whole notebooks with just one conversation. That's why I'm not writing everything, just thinking . . . thinking . . . that God is good and my Mama loves me very much and they'll both help me with everything . . .

FEBRUARY 28, 1941, FRIDAY

God! Saturday tomorrow already? How quickly this week has passed! It's Saturday tomorrow. What'll happen at this time of the day?! I'm so scared. Lord God, help me, and you, my one and only Mama!!

MARCH 1, 1941, SATURDAY

School was sweet! Zygu asked if Prochaska calls me Mrs. Schwarzer (so using his surname). He even says it himself. I'm not sad. It's not a sin. I turn myself over to Your care, Buluś and God.

MARCH 2, 1941, SUNDAY

It was such a pretty day today! Springlike! Sunny! I saw Zygu in town, walking with some ramblers, he bowed, sent me a burning look. What an idiot! Couldn't he approach me? He laughed, silly billy! But it doesn't matter; we're both in love (only me) and young. Irka wrote this and if it rubs off then . . . well. And it's starting to wear off already, but we don't. Oh, you know, I recall thousands of things, thousands of nice, intimate things. Otherwise I'll go crazy—and cold—and everything will go to nothing.

Irka loves Feluś. I wrote a poem for her yesterday.

Is it really nothing? This week it's Irka's birthday. There might be a dance party. Will it be sweet? Will I dance with Zygu? It's so good now, I have his photo and can stare at it for hours, stare and stare. I won't see him again today.

Good night, dear Diary. I'm jealous of you, because you can spend a whole day with my thoughts about him and his image . . . Well, let's see what happens next, Buluś. Bye . . .

SMALL, STIFLING FLATS

The day is autumnal, gray and dripping
I stand by the window tightly wrapped
Listening to the old clock's loud ticking
Watching the street in the rain trapped

It's cold and it's so deserted
My nose runs, I have shivers
I feel like many people, I'm certain
When autumn rains deliver
Everything's the same, but then not quite
Dusk sneaks in, I hear crickets chirping
I'm reading my diary in the dim light
A spring page. I'm returning

"Happy days are near
filled with sun, light, bliss
I'm so joyous, full of cheer
glad for early spring like this!
Let's open windows wide
Let's unlock doors and gates
Let's stand with spring side by side
Let's assist it, link our fates
Come! Why don't you? On our way!"
We run armed with songs and play

With flowers in many bouquets
Wait, I'm coming, with you I belong!
I'm so happy, I'm so merry
So bright, warm and so amorous
I want to open my heart, to unbury
And walk toward the glamorous spring!
I read those impassioned lines
Words filled with sun and fragrance
Sounding of carefree delight

Dirty windows cry with tears
The autumnal sky is weeping
I read and I think to myself
That something else might've happened
Sun, happiness, smiles, I bet
Now—it's so dreadful, so inapt

This autumnal day, gray and wet
I stand by the window tightly wrapped

Perhaps at some point in my life
On some sad autumnal day
When the moment is quite right
I'll read my spring, sun-filled diary!

What spell do you cast on me?
Because of you I do nothing
Like thunder you rule my eyes, me
I can't live because of you

What is it, God! Mama!

MARCH 3, 1941, MONDAY

Irka's birthday. Actually Zygu's a swine, but he's so sweet and lovely that I forgive him everything. He approached me and greeted me sweetly at school, he told me he was "dragged to a party," but that he was terribly bored. Aha! When Tusiek was trying to convince him to come along to the party, he said, "I would rather go to town to see somebody." See whom? Rena. They teased him terribly about me, he didn't dance and today at school he said, poor him, "Not only do they call me Rena's husband, but also Arianka's brother-in-law." Oh, his words were so wonderful. "Rena, you look like you just got out of bed." And then, "What about the newspaper?" and "You must have written something about me" and then this look and this and that and the other.

I arranged with him to come to Irka's, but he didn't come, this wonderful boor.

Nora avoids people, even us. She holds a grudge against us, especially against me. I understand that, I'm not angry. She seems to think people laugh at her and in fact she's right. But she doesn't even realize how bad it is. This Nacek . . . And today to Irka—anyway he also told her something at the party. I'd like to know what it was. What could he have told her, this vulgar lout? She might feel relieved if she were to tell me, but as it is . . . poor, poor Norka . . . God, Buluś, please take care of me. There is something about us like a solid relationship, like a marriage. Mama, why aren't you here with me now?

FEBRUARY 5, 1941, WEDNESDAY*

Ah, Wednesday again! Mama, if you were here, I wouldn't be lacking for anything, I don't think! It would be so good, but . . . There is always some kind of a "but" . . . When will you come?

Now there are long walks, goodbyes and meetings—I can't even describe it all. Anyway, in the morning he bought some gingerbread from the canteen and let me have a bite, in fact pushed it almost whole into my mouth. He told me about Roma, how she came to see him at 7 a.m. when he was still in bed. And Irka told me that he must have asked a hundred times about me during the match etc. etc. He keeps going on about how beautiful my eyes are, these eyes, eyes, eyes (he likes my personality as well—Maciek has told me and he was right). Zygu says, "Rena, nothing can help you, it's all in your eyes" or "I'm under the spell of somebody's eyes." He said something about my skin too, so I asked if he was being ironic, to which Z took offense and said . . . Ah, he's so wonderful . . . He stroked my hair. He said, "Why does Irka's hair stay up so easily?" and that he won't jump higher than 1.48 m, and that I should switch to sport. And that we'll go to a party together on Saturday. "Rena, you better learn how to swing dance." "You are to start reading papers as of today." It was so sweet, so wonderful when they teased us in town and he said, "Rena, what an alliance!" and "Roma doesn't compete with you directly because she senses your superiority."

I really can't write it all down. He said we need to find somebody for Nora, but I told him to leave it, because she's so low. Zyguś, wonderful Zyguś . . . And still so very shy . . . Mama, if only you could come. God, please keep helping me. I give myself into Your care . . . Ah, one part of my wish is beginning to come true, let's just hope for the other . . . Oh, Lord!

---

* This is in fact the March 5 entry.

FEBRUARY 6, 1941, THURSDAY*

He came to the classroom after his classes today. But at the break he was plotting something with Irka. They laughed a lot, I was very curious. And Irka told me what it was about. Zygu told her in secret that he was in love with me, that I have wonderful eyes (I'm fed up with the eyes thing) and teeth like pearls, eyelashes like curtains and nose and everything else and doesn't Irka by chance know if I love him too? Of course he asked her to be discreet, because he wants to tell me himself or something along those lines. He said he would be happy with me.

I'm torn, not sure if I should believe Irka, but she swears it's true . . . Ah!!! If that's the case, then Zygu is a total fool! He's an oaf! He's a boor! Who deals with such a delicate issue through a third person?! Can't he just tell me? What a baby! And he still knows how to ask about my time of the month. Sweet, sweet, wonderful Zyguś! Mama, come! God, Buluś, under Your protective wings I look for shelter . . .

> *I'm waiting and waiting, I worry*
> *Time goes on. It's not filled with bliss*
> *The inscription is getting blurry*
> *And Zygu's still in no hurry to give me a . . .*

FEBRUARY 7, 1941, FRIDAY†

We almost . . . Today after class, he pushed me (gently) against a wall and brought his lips close to mine . . . He said, he said, "My sweet poppet" and also, "What shall I do with those eyes?" I told him to get me sunglasses. He asked why I was so evil? That was too much, I was outraged. "What, Zygu? Am I evil?" He took my hands and repeated sweetly, no, no, no! And asked about the plans for tomorrow.

Tomorrow can be whatever he wants. We're going to Irka's, but will

---

* This is in fact the March 6 entry.
† This is in fact the March 7 entry.

everything be the way I want it? I'm not so very scared anymore . . . But will I get disappointed???

I feel strange. I might go to his place. Will it all work out, at least a little bit? I pray to God and Buluś. I ask You earnestly to take care of me . . .

MARCH 9, 1941[11]

He was sweet at school on Saturday, he called me "my sweetness" and said that he must look like a "sweetness." I wonder if he really likes me? But he wasn't at Irka's, he didn't come . . . and I waited . . . Perhaps it wasn't his fault, as he wasn't properly invited, but still. He was himself looking forward to Saturday and . . .

> *Each moment gave me hope*
> *Each strike and chime of the clock*
> *A doorbell, steps, knocking—a shiver*
> *Raised the scope of my anticipation*
> *You didn't come. Why didn't you knock?*
>
> *Today I don't miss the hum and laughter*
> *A shame you weren't there*
> *I'm glad it is the day after*
> *It's all gone and I don't care*
> *Gone are the dancing couples, quiet all the voices*
> *And I can think sweetly*
> *Of kissing you, brushing your hair, rejoicing*
> *It feels so good, completely!*

Something strange happened today. I kind of knew something was the matter, but I still didn't think it was so bad! Maciek is in love with me! So now I understand what it all means, that he walks me home, that he constantly has something to whisper in my ear, or a speck to brush off me, that he raves about my lips, eyes, that he embraces me and yesterday he even kissed me. I didn't want to tell you, because I didn't think it was anything special. All his meaningful hints I took as "Well, he says that, but it's just gossip." But now I don't know myself, or rather I know that Zygu didn't come to the dance party because he was jealous, very jealous in fact—and I so understand him. Wonderful poor stupid Zygu! Don't you see you are the only one I love? I tell you this with my every move, every look I send you! You! You! You! It's true, I like Maciek, I like him very much, but how can you compare those two feelings, liking and loving?!!! He is jealous. Really!

I went to Irka's today and we had a vigorous discussion about it, while Zygu and Maciek were at my place. Zygu wrote in Arianka's diary "For my girlfriend's sister," so he now officially calls me his girlfriend, oh merciful heavens! They left me a note, which I paste below. They came to my place, what a shame I wasn't home! Zyguś was here, my wonderful Zyguś, Mama! Ah, Buluś, if only you were here . . . You will help me, Buluś, and You, God . . .

MARCH 11, 1941, TUESDAY

Wonderful! Divine! Good! First at school with chocolate. Then in the afternoon he came to the Shevchenko club.* It was so good to sit together and talk a lot. Everybody was pulling knowing faces. Then we left. At first Maciek and Poldek hung around, annoyingly, but soon they were gone and we were on our own. We spent maybe two, three hours walking. It was so nice. Zygu is very tactful and delicate—like nobody else! He sang, "*Du hast die schönste Augen. Mein Liebchen (Mädchen) was wils du noch mehr.*"†

I don't remember it all exactly. I only know I was happy. It feels so good to be with him. He was really sorry for not coming on Saturday. He apologized and promised that this Saturday we will party together for sure. Aha! And we made arrangements to go to the movies on Thursday! Zyguś, you are so wonderful! Wonderful! Mama, I wish you could meet him soon . . . You will help me, Buluś and God . . .

---

* Taras Shevchenko (1814–1862), Ukrainian national poet.
† Should be: "*Du hast [Diamanten und Perlen] [. . .] die schönsten Augen— / Mein Liebchen, was willst du mehr?*" From *Die Heimkehr,* LXII by Heinrich Heine (1827).

MARCH 12, 1941, WEDNESDAY

I heard people teasing him after school. Irka met him after he said goodbye to me. She said he was very irritated and when she asked him what he was doing for so long with me, he replied, "What's the problem? I can't? With my Renuśka?" And he told Irka she would make a caring wife, but then he added that I would not make such a caring wife, because I like daydreaming.

> *I'll be such a daydreamer*
> *A fantastic, poetic wife*
> *I'll watch the sky a-shimmer*
> *And count stars all my life*
> *I'll invite butterfly swarms*
> *I will practice playing clarinet*
> *I will gather flowers in my arms*
> *And make sure you never fret*
> *Fragrant ambrosia I will stew*
> *I'll dust with clouds, mend clothes with sunrays*
> *I will be loving and pining and true*
> *A fantastic, poetic wife, always*
> *Somebody might tell you—half-witted*
> *That it is really not permitted*
> *To have some crazy, insane wife*
> *Don't let them talk, don't waste your life*
> *I will fill both of my hands*
> *With blossom of lilies, apples, cherry*
> *I will drape them, make garlands*
> *I'll make each moment merry*
> *complete with a poem's amazing flow.*
> *I'll grab the wide, seven-color rainbow*
> *I'll write directly on the sky's blue*
> *That, Zyguś, that I . . . I love you*
> *So hush, you magpies so outraged*
> *With such a crazy wife*

Burn piles of meat on the stage
What matters is your eyes, your life
And your brow, unclouded, under your hat
So, tell me, Zygu . . . Do you want a wife like that?

MARCH 13, 1941, THURSDAY

I'm breathless, you know?! If I only could, I'd scream with all my might, brightly, springlike!!! Just think, a whole afternoon with him! First at the movies he paid for my ticket and he also bought a ticket for some poor child. He is so good, my Zygu! You know, I'm saying it, or rather writing, rather dryly, but you should have seen it, this gesture and his sweet, wonderful face. Zygu! He's such a good person; he doesn't say anything bad about anybody, even his enemies, even his rivals.

Then we spent two hours at my place (I think he stole my photo), then at Irka's. We were, you know, like a real couple. It's better than I dared to dream! Ah, my wonderful Mama, if only you were here with me now!

Then, on our way back home, Zygu wanted to find out something about Maciek. He knows a bit, he figured out a bit more . . . But, you know, he's in . . . I know what he wanted, here, at Rejtan Street, and then, when we were saying goodbye . . . ahhh (thiiis again). I knew he was irritated. At the end he said, *"mein Liebchen."* I won't even tell you that we walk arm in arm all the time and we are officially an item.

> Ich bin din
> Du bist min*
> *I wanted to punish you hard*
> *To imprison you in my heart*
> *You will stay forever there*
> *'Cause I lost the key somewhere . . .*

I can't even tell you what it's like . . . Mama and Great Lord God, I'm so very grateful to You and I love You. And I'm submitting myself to Your care.

---

* I am yours / You are mine (German).

MARCH 14, 1941

It's Saturday tomorrow . . . As usual I await it and I'm scared . . . I love, love more and more . . . Buluś, God, You will help me!

MARCH 15, 1941, SATURDAY

He was wonderful today at school! And he said he would give me all of today's afternoon. And he crossed his fingers for my schoolwork. He was wonderful, wonderful, wonderful. As a result we forgot to make plans and I only saw him in the evening in town. He was with friends—he excused himself and approached me. "You know, Irka's right when she says that we're like a 'pretend' married couple." Zygu tells me that if I don't do my hair, he'll not shave, so because I'm going to the hairdresser's, Z'll shave.

There is a dance party tomorrow. Z asked if I'm going to have a good time. Oh! How could I know that? By the gate he told me, "Rena, the gate's locked, os stel og yats ni a letoh."*

He makes me so happy . . . Aha! We are to meet at midday, I suggested it, but he said he needed to see my hair. A "What else do you want?" kind of provocation. Mama, please be with me tomorrow and always. I'll be happy or sad . . . Good night, till tomorrow . . .

MARCH 16, 1941, SUNDAY

It's today already. Or rather it is gone, like another stage of this beautiful, spring dream. We met in the morning like a regular couple does, i.e., he waited, I arrived and we walked until 2 p.m. in town. And today at Olga's picnic it was also wonderful—we danced and he pulled me to him hard, with passion. At some point we were even going to dance in a different room, but . . . it didn't feel appropriate.

Poldek and Maciek avoided me at first, and then Maciek said he

---

* Words written backward.

couldn't ignore me any longer. I danced not just with Zygu, but with everybody. And on so many occasions I was stolen right from under Zygu's nose when he was about to ask me to dance (Maciek, mirror, Zygo). They kept teasing us and I kept blushing. Just imagine, Rysiek said that I must be writing poems in Zygu's honor. Zygu's wonderful!

After the picnic I walked down the street with a whole group of boys and Maciek said, "Look, there are buds," and Zygu to this said, "Rena, spring!" I can feel its first waft . . . Of course there was a lot of teasing from Maciek, Poldek, Fredek and Julek, but no matter.

Today in fact (do you remember, March 16?) I am to compare today with this other March 16. Can you compare those two days at all? No! Or in fact yes! True, Mama's still not here, but I hope to see her soon (war should be over). And I love, love this beautiful, wise boy, the best boy at school. And it's mutual. Yes! Even though Zygu hasn't told me anything, he said, "There is something I won't tell you," and he wants to write it all down and give it to Irka to give it to me.

I now have a so-called social life and, to be honest, I'm quite popular. Anyway it's looking good. I go to parties now, enjoy picnics, like a regular 16-year-old girl would.

It's different with Nora. Her love for Nacek, which collapsed and I believe will be restored, but in the meantime I wanted to drag her into the youthful hum almost by force. But she wasn't well again today. I was so sorry, as I was the one trying to get her to come to today's picnic. She sat there, even though most boys were there, and later she read a book. I know she'll write an entry in her diary today and compare those two days one year apart. Even though, when we were saying goodbye today, she said, "This isn't what matters most in life," which is true and I say that too, but on the other hand what is more important than "this"? Yes, tell me, what's more important? I remember that I used to say I didn't care about those things, but that's not true. Perhaps my opinion will change one day, but for now it's simple: life is worth living for the person you love, for the person you dream about and think about during sleepless nights. Living not for fame or knowledge, not for learning—these are just intellectual concepts. Living the sensual life, "getting to the bloody core of life," snatching what's best, satisfying yourself until you're breathless.

Whatever they say about me when I die, I'll die like an animal, but I can live the way I want now. To be able to say, standing over one's grave:

> *I got what I could out of life*
> *a lot, but still not enough*
> *Today my wizened body lies in the grave*
> *I desert what others still crave*
> *To live, live, live in such a way!*
> *Everybody can in the grave decay*
> *Dying is easy, but to live is art, I say*

I've read Nora's diary once. I read she wouldn't write about her loves anymore, she wouldn't describe details, and it's all because if somebody were to read her diary, they could say, "This is some stupid, vain girl who only cares for flirtation in life."

Norka! You're so wrong! Firstly, why do you care about other people reading it? You're writing it for yourself. And secondly, is your dearest, intimate diary to be a political almanac or an almanac of your heart??? Somebody very harsh, with a stony heart, might say what you thought. Every normal human being should rather say, "This was written by a young, 16-year-old girl who loved so deeply . . ." That's what I think, Norka, and I hope you soon agree with me. I wouldn't go back to the old sentences, the old situation. I'm in love, which is my explanation for writing all this nonsense. You forgive a person in love, you forgive them everything, and apropos the sad party I escaped.

> *You don't know how life can be*
> *It's like a leaf trembling on the water*
> *You don't know what does matter*
> *Sometimes you win and sometimes it's me*
> *Sun can dry it, change its form*
> *When it suffers yet another storm*
> *The leaf will hide deeper in*
> *Though that will soon be a has-been*
> *The leaf will shimmer in good weather*
> *On the long river like a feather*

It will slide on the surface
Carrying our life with no purpose

Yes, yes, yes. Buluś, if you could only read this. Thank you, thank you so much. Not sure I'll write tomorrow. You will help me, Buluś and God.

MARCH 18, 1941, TUESDAY

We made arrangements today, he picked me up at 6 p.m. First we went to the Socialist Club, then to Irka's, then back home.

It's cold outside again.

Today it felt as if there was something hanging between us, something elusive, something unspoken. And I kept thinking this one thought, about an unfinished symphony . . . And I'm barely able to control myself. I'm boiling, I'm broiling, I can barely stop myself from . . . And I know it's a bit similar for him too.

Pity it isn't warm anymore . . .

It's strange and wild with Mama (Leszczyńska*), I don't know what's going to happen with her now, will she come and when? When? When???

Ah, I'm so shamelessly vulgar, Z is much gentler than me and even though he said, "I forget about everything when I look into your eyes," I put my hand under his arm and it was so nice. He made a little pout with his wonderful lips, so, so, so sweet, but it was as if . . . Zygu behaves like my guardian. There is indeed something elusive in the "unfinished symphony" . . . Will it ever be finished? Will it be soon? Mama, please tell me honestly, would you like it to end well and lovingly, please tell me? Anyway, Buluś and God, help me!

MARCH 19, 1941, WEDNESDAY

I'm feeling guilty. I'm so vulgar. I can feel something powerful swelling up inside of me. I need to confess to somebody or I'll go crazy. I can feel

---

* Renia and Ariana's mother was baptized on January 20, 1940, later changing her name to Mariana Leszczyńska after she secured false papers in Warsaw.

all my senses are churning, I'm aware of myself boiling. For example I know I suffered terribly yesterday. Ha! What a curse.

> *I feel I'll destroy the old foundations*
> *I feel they'll get smashed and crushed*
> *by my rampant temper and frustrations*
> *I feel so strong, so strong with love*
> *hot blood is boiling in my veins*
> *I am so drunk with closeness,*
> *hotheaded, dazed with desire flames*
> *my senses send me writhing*
> *they're tying me, entangling*
> *I know I'm like a beast*
> *My self-respect has decreased*
> *I despise, I degrade myself so much*
> *But still I understand that like a dog*
> *like a wounded lynx I don't budge*
> *my heart twitches, I howl inside, agog*
> *in no time I will jump up and go savage*
> *shake everything off and snort and bellow*
> *the red lips will be ravaged by my lips*
> *I'm in a frenzy, my urge and fear's not mellow*
> *I live now, I'm not gone*
> *and I want*
> *I can't go on . . .*

This is disgusting, repulsive, animalistic . . .

MARCH 21, 1941, FRIDAY

I gave myself a day off today. I didn't go to school; I had a headache. Yesterday I was supposed to see Z, but he didn't come. Today I was unwell, as I've been unwell for several months now, ill with Zygu, lazy with Zygu, daydreaming with Zygu, my unfinished symphony.

My dear Diary, do you know how much I love you? Very, very, very much. I feel that I need you, I open you on one bright sunny day, read for a while—and then I know. I remember everything and all those days live in me, together and separately.

Buluś has written that there would be war. Who knows? Will it interfere again with my life, this powerful, hated enemy?

Tomorrow is Saturday. I don't know what'll happen. I don't expect anything. I shook off some of this madness. It's gone. But it might come back. And it'll be back as soon as the wind brings spring again, when I see ... I'll get terminally ill with Zygu. Or maybe it won't be terminal? Those images I pasted there, I should paste here, if I could write what I wanted.

Let some quiet song
Play a loving tune
About you living in my heart
And me living in yours too
It would be nasty, not so smart
It would be sad, teary and dreadful
If you indeed lived in my heart
And I not in yours! That would be fearful
It would be even more unkind
if cruel fate decided
to let me sleep in the heart of mine
and you in yours, divided.
Good that it is not the case
Go away, terrible nightmare
I dream of hazel eyes, your face
You dream of blue ones, of my hair
A quiet sweet spring concert
Plays us a loving tune
About you blossoming in my heart
And me in yours too.

Ah, it's Saturday tomorrow, on the one hand this is a bit too daring. Buluś, love me! Help me, Buluś and God.

MARCH 22, 1941, SATURDAY

It was so good! Not only out in town (though that too!). I met him at the post office. I could see he was really happy to see me. It's nice of him that he didn't go to the picnic. Maciek kissed my hair and Z laughed and then kept calling me every now and then, saying, "Do you love him? Is your heart filled to the brim with love? 'Cause he loves you, don't you know that beggars can't be choosers?" I told him he was a total swine. Z kept kissing M. When I told him to stop already, Z said, "You can do it all day long, so I can do it too." My sweet, wonderful boy. Even though I kept saying I wouldn't go to the party, Z laughed under his breath and said that I would. What did I do? I told him the whole story with Irka and Felek. I'm so very sorry—this was somebody else's secret, but Z is discreet and anyway, I can't say "no" to him, that's the effect he has on me. I don't know about tomorrow, as we didn't make plans. I might meet him somewhere. You would be happy for me, Buluś . . . God, You will help me too.

MARCH 23, 1941

I don't know why, but I'm very sad today! Very, very, very sad. Sometimes I know the reason.

I met Zygu twice today. We went for a walk in the afternoon with sweet Felunia. And suddenly! I felt this emptiness in my heart and in my life . . . Later Zygu said he noticed it and asked why I was so sad? We went for a long walk and had a serious conversation. Z told me he was never like that before, but now he is sad and serious. When we were saying goodbye, Z said, "Maybe it's my influence on you? But tough, that's what I am like. Maciek might entertain you." He is stupid if he still thinks that I have any feelings for Maciek. But then he said, "You will be my solid support (something, something), I will be crushed." He doesn't know what it might be, but I suspect that Zygu is sad underneath this sweet burden. As am I.

We are supposed to go to a party tomorrow. I want to be in a good mood, even if it's fake. We made arrangements. And for the first time without my participation, but with his; he was eager. He reminded me about it when he was about to leave.

Zyguś! I would like to be joyful, because you're sad and you want this. But sometimes a "time of apathy" comes, as you call it, and one can't, one simply can't.

You like listening to music, you love music—and I like daydreaming, daydreaming while listening to music with you. I like to daydream and be happy when my dreams come true. But then, there are times like today. Today I am sad, even though half a dream is coming true.

I don't believe I have changed so much, that I only have expectations, no! Let's see what happens next.

I am to see him tomorrow morning, we are to go to the party, I am to be in a good mood.

Irka is traveling to see Felek, pretty much everybody is traveling to Lwów, and I'm staying with Zygu. We're staying! Spring! Seven days off! What for? To get bored? To be sad? No, to love!!! Mama, do you know it all, can you hear my heart beating with love for him and my long-distance longing for you? You will help me, Buluś and God . . . Great Lord God! What will tomorrow's party be like?

MARCH 24, 1941, MONDAY (PARTY NO. 3!)

So nice. Zygu picked me up (even though I was supposed to come later, but he got too impatient), he paid our entry fees, bought me a cake and water, and danced with me all the time. Maybe with a few exceptions. This party was different than other parties; this was a real "Zygu" party.

People treat us like a married couple. For example after a dance one boy doesn't take me back to my place, but says, "I need to give you back to Schwarzer." And then somebody else says, "Thanks, I brought your wife back." I even got outraged at some point. What is all this bargaining? Tusiek said, "I will bring her back to you untouched." He told me that, for a while, since "this" has started, Z has not been able to think straight. Eau de cologne.

Z and I bring couples in love together. We do it very subtly. Z, "Let's open a marriage bureau." He annoyed Irka with Felek so much that she had to go home, but it was a revenge for Irka annoying him, as she did to Felek with Fredziu, to Julek and the whole class.

Zygu asked me how he could make it up to me, all that swing dancing. I can't do swing dance and neither can he, so we suffer and keep apologizing to each other. Oh! How to make it up—I know how, and so does he. I told him he is provoking me with this alien military stuff.

We didn't make arrangements, because Julek was with us. Z is so good, so loving and understanding. It's so nice to have a "pretend husband." Tusiek was surprised that Zygu is allowed not to shave—how can I let him, how do I curl up against him? To which Z said that nobody complains about him.

Zygu was happy with the party and so was I. This was a real "Zygu" party. I send you kisses, Renia. Please help me, Buluś and God . . .

P.S. Studying this and that with Luśka. He danced with me several times, he was completely drunk and he hugged me tight, rambling on and on. I got scared . . . Bye, dear Diary, see you next time.

MARCH 28, 1941, FRIDAY

Today we went for a long, long walk. It was so good—we just walked down a half-dark street and talked, talked, talked. Now I couldn't say what he said, but I know he said a lot of pleasant and a lot of ambiguous things. He told me we would go to the Riviera together one day, somewhere far away from other people, somewhere with "azure sky"—to which I added, "And azure sea"—and he finished, "And azure eyes." Or, for example, that Mochnacki* is so passionate about mathematics, but "I prefer to be passionate about something else, don't I, Rena?" And then a lot about hearts. "Poor darling, I'm so very sorry for you—why didn't you come to me like you would to a doctor?" Etc. etc.

A long, friendly walk like this is perhaps even better than . . . But what do I know?

We've made arrangements for tomorrow; he'll come pick me up

---

* Mirosław Mochnacki (1904–1970)—expert in mathematical analysis, algebra, and calculus of variations. He taught mathematics at the Juliusz Słowacki Polish High School in Przemyśl starting in 1934.

around 4–5 p.m. Buluś, if you were here . . . I'm so happy and it's thanks to you. You will help me, Buluś and God. Bye, kisses, Rena.

MARCH 29, 1941, SATURDAY

Our arrangement didn't quite work out, but in the end we did meet. We went to the Socialist Club and then for a walk. The walk was the nicest part, a long walk, just the two of us. We walked arm in arm and talked and talked, and apart from that we also talked with our looks. Such a walk is for me the most wonderful symphony and can replace tens of other nice things.

> *This walk is a force and power*
> *This walk is immortality!**

  He said that at his wedding he would want Mendelssohn's "Wedding March" played. Fela pointed at me and Zygu also pointed at me. We talked about the future, about medicine, etc. etc. Z said he wouldn't want to have a son or children in general, because children between the age of 13 and 16 go through a period of rebellion and a lot of internal turmoil. I felt so good! His looks make me so warm. Not to mention that we walked arm in arm. Well, I say, such a walk is something powerful! About living in a dorm, he said, "I don't want to look at anybody there, I would rather look at you." We didn't arrange to meet. Aha, what antics with Maciek! Zygu was happy I didn't want to meet him. You will help me, Buluś and God . . .

APRIL 4, 1941, SATURDAY†

The entire week was bright, but for me it was empty. I feel emptiness today, and sadness, such sadness. But I found out that he came over to

---

* Reference to a line from Adam Mickiewicz's *Great Improvisation* from *Forefathers' Eve*, part 3: "This song is force and power / This song is immortality!" (translated by Louise Varese, published by Voyages, 1956).
† April 4, 1941, was a Friday.

mine, and that made me feel better. And tomorrow? Sunday, probably nothing will happen again. You will help me, Buluś and God . . .

APRIL 5, 1941, SUNDAY*

Residency—invitation. He kept saying, "Shush, Renia!" And when I asked, "What?" he didn't say anything.

Ah! Today! "It was wonderful, warm, loving." I saw him twice; we spent five hours together. We went to the movies. He held my hand tenderly, so tenderly, and kept yawning. He pulled a sweet face when we bumped into Maciek. But, you know, I found his photo with some girl. Z was sheepish. I was too polite to ask anything. But really, believe you me, sweetie pie, my poppet, that it was wonderful. The best thing was with the candy. Ah! Zygu, I can't even express how much I love you.

Z is supposedly angry at Irka for lying to us about Felek. And so am I. Today he said we would start going to the Castle—really??? You will help me, Buluś and God.

APRIL 6, 1941

It was so wonderful, so blissful and now it's gone like a dream, the fairy tale is over. Up until now I was still preoccupied with this Sunday, but now, you know, I'm choking with anger and I'm glad at the same time! Yes, I'm glad that I spoiled the good mood of his afternoon! I'm glad I won't show up tomorrow at break time. I will show him, just you wait.

The devil sent him and Irka, and, of all days, on the day when I was considering the issue of Irka and Zygo! I was just imagining the most fantastical images of Irka and Zygu in romantic poses, when I met them together in the evening. At first I wanted to run away, but we played a good trick with Nora—lucky that this building has two entrances! Ah! I got some satisfaction! Wait, you think that I'll watch you embracing Irka in my presence and at the same time watching my reaction? Go caress her, walk with her, call her even more tender names, but I'll play

* April 5, 1941, was a Saturday.

on your nerves, I'll play you Beethoven's Ninth Symphony so that you'll remember me, you prat, so that you realize what it means to vex a jealous woman in love. I know that Maciek annoys you. So I'll use Maciek to get on your nerves. "Your conscience can be absolutely clear that it is because of you that I don't study." Anyway, none of your business. Zygu! If you only knew that I'm on the verge of tears and how terribly I hate you right now. And with what pleasure I'll take revenge on you, even if it hurts you a lot. Now, God Almighty! I'm in despair, I don't know what I'm writing and I so badly want it to be tomorrow already!!! Ah, Bulczyk, if you knew my suffering and my hatred!! You will help me, Buluś and God.

APRIL 12, 1941, SATURDAY

This week was somewhat sweet and hazy and I felt like that too—somewhat hazy, I was in a so-so mood. Irka kept sneering at me, but she realized that nothing came of it and she almost erupted. Anyhow she is flirting with Z For what reasons—I don't know. And him? I don't know (he keeps badmouthing her in front of me). Do you remember?

On Sunday we made plans with Z to go to the movies and Irka knows about it, because I told her and she would like to worm her way in. I'm saying no so far, but I am furious. I'm trying with all my might not to show it, but I'm only partially successful. Irka actually told him that she's looking for love, that she's missing something. All very nice, I understand, but I would prefer she looked elsewhere and not at Z. Everybody knows about us now, including the students, the teachers, even Mrs. Polak who saw us from a distance, but not me.

Tomorrow we have an evening with my poetry reading. I'm not happy about it; I'm very embarrassed. And then there's a party. I'm not in the mood for a party. I don't know; I'm scared! I'm terribly scared of any party. No, I'm in no mood and I would rather go to the movies, but—with him, thank you very much for the rest. Anyway he can bend over backward. Do you know that today is a

holy day—holy day—holy day
not like any other day

In my despair I tried to find some oblivion in aphorisms and started writing on the subject.

What is love's worth
if you need to worry?
Bitterness, no mirth
it only carries
Each slope on earth
causes much misery
What is love's worth
if you have to worry

Do you know that everybody thinks that we have already . . . ha ha ha. And I could say something about it. I understand it myself, but, well, I'm still stupidly scared of love and tomorrow's party, but . . . You will help me, Buluś and God.

APRIL 13, 1941, SUNDAY

There was supposed to be a party. But! Wasn't this better than one hundred regular dancing parties? Better than swirling in circles in a crowded room? Not letting Maciek and Poldek keep me there after the cheering of "author, author" and instead going far away arm in arm with my wonderful Zyguś? Listening to his tender words, sitting in the cinema with him (and almost, almost, ah . . .) and returning home at 12? Well? Wasn't it better?

I really should stop worrying about silly things. After all I have firm evidence that Z loves me (*mein Liebchen was* . . .). Arianka stayed at the party. A wonderful, wonderful, wonderful evening. Let's hope that this week we finally . . . oh! Buluś, really. Z left the party because he was jealous of me.

APRIL 17, 1941, THURSDAY

Actually nothing happened today, neither today, nor yesterday. Life goes on as usual, i.e., we meet from time to time, walk arm in arm (I don't know how to walk differently anymore), we talk, hum and we are very happy together. I mean I find it ah, blissful, angelic, sweet. And he? Must be the same, otherwise he wouldn't be making plans about going to a party on the 1st "to belong to each other only," like Maciek has said.

I keep thinking all the time, recalling and dreaming, I daydream all the time at school. I can't learn anything, I can't talk about anything else than the moments when Z says, "Don't be scared, I'm with you," or "We had a tempestuous night," "It's only half past eleven." It's strange . . . Everybody thinks, nobody even doubts that we have already . . . But in fact we still haven't, though it's as if we have. Once it was raining and each word was said into hands, temples, with lips and heads, in whispers, ah! It gives me shivers. I don't know . . . I don't think . . . He wouldn't be so refined as to agitate me to the utmost! And why am I writing today? Because it's raining and everybody walks hunched, and there's commotion with Mom which I can't even understand and I'm feeling wishy-washy, but still quite safe, because . . . Nora tells me that I "should be happy." To be happy I need Mama and sun and (first child). I have those shivers, but it's not because of the cold. "Are my eyes misty?"* Ah! I'm such a little animal, well . . .

> *Sometimes those moments arrive*
> *especially in springtime, in May*
> *when thoughts like fine butterflies*
> *fly far out, in disarray*
> *They sway gently on trees*
> *with May tranquility elated*
> *highly thrilled and intoxicated*
> *look for the distant eyes these*
> *Eyes that are misty, filled with longing*
> *And then, as if a warning*
> *A voice breaks your thoughts with force*
> *Not ever reaching you, of course*
> *You are among the clouds in the sky*

---

* Possibly a reference to the 1931 waltz entitled "Mały pokoik" (Little room), with lyrics by Tadeusz Kończyc and music by Wiktor Krupiński.

clouds that are like a pink awning
strolling through green fields, don't deny
everywhere seeing those brown eyes
Eyes that are misty, filled with longing

APRIL 18, 1941, SATURDAY*

We didn't make arrangements for this post office party, but we met in the street (how great) and went there together. I danced a bit with Julek B. and once with Zygu. I felt faint, so we left.

Z was troubled today, but didn't want to tell me what it was about. Things got really nice during the walk. At first he was apathetic, but then perked up and we couldn't say goodbye by my gate.

I will report the broken finger at the polyclinic and I am to tell father that it was caused by son's sadism.

Rena, study! We've wasted some precious moments in front of the pharmacy. A very nice goodbye, aha! I'm sleepy, but I feel a bit cozy, i.e., nice, that I'll see him tomorrow at 6 p.m. Should I? You will help me, Buluś and God!

APRIL 19, 1941, SUNDAY†

I was waiting on the balcony, Zyguś came, tra la la!
We went for a long walk, then to the movies, tra la la!
My hand was so tiny
barely visible next to his
So Zyguś, oh so kindly
covered it protectively with his.
And since I don't feel pain
but have some moral distress
Zyguś promised to abstain
To never put me under duress.

---

* April 18, 1941, was a Friday.
† April 19, 1941, was a Saturday.

He won't be in the bad husband category
Like the one in the film or worse
He will read poems for my glory
He now lives and breathes verse.
Come, poetry, let me take you in my arms
Come, pet, forget all the strife
Eyes full of yawning, ringing alarm
I'll break away from the prose of life.

Zyguś, my husband. He has a silky beard—who would have thought? Smooth hands, nice, it's so good to stroke them lightly. There's a piece of candy, which Z'll bite first. That's why he "wouldn't be able to sleep by me." I didn't even understand the film; it was all about Zygu! Zygu! Zygu!

I'm so stupid, I was thinking of my situation—and Nora's, wondering if hers was perhaps better! But I love my beloved and we're together and I can touch him and talk to him. Just that, but that's a lot. I am to keep my fingers crossed for him and give him a mascot for his graduation exam. But he still needs to study, tough. Tomorrow at school. Bye, darling. Mama, if only you were here and could see it. You will help me, Buluś and God . . . You will, won't You?

APRIL 26, 1941, SATURDAY

Some Saturday it was. Two days he wasn't at school. Maciek tried some scheming! But what?! Silliness.

Irka started flirting with Waldek like crazy, so I told her that he had a crush on me. I did it like a real woman. After all I only like Waldek a bit and I don't really care about him. Same goes for Maciek, but still!

Today I saw him . . . And then I heard a snippet of a conversation between Julek and C.G., "I'm astonished with Zygu." I didn't know it, but I instinctively felt it was about Zygu's love, or rather Zygu's fondness for me. It unnerved me so much that I got a headache and was in a really bad mood. I do really feel that on every level I'm not worthy of Zygu, that's the truth . . . But who is? Nobody! There is no girl who has as many virtues as he does and who would love him as much as I do. Anyway it worried me. But in fact what do I care about Julek's astonishment? Let him, why not. Oh, I'm being silly and that's that. If Z wanted, he could find me, but it doesn't matter. I am the one who loves the most; all I want in return is a bit of fondness, not love as big as mine. I'm happy with that—just that and so much at the same time! In fact we made plans for today last Sunday. But not exact ones. Do I know about what'll happen? You will help me, Buluś and God. I doubt we will meet.

APRIL 27, 1941, SUNDAY

Tearful sky and a day somewhat somber
Somewhat rainy, slippery, scornful

Mama, on a day like today it would be good to have somebody, some-body close to my heart, dear, loved and loving. It could only be you. Mama, I'm so low. You know, sometimes I find excuses for Zygu. For ex-ample, he didn't approach me and I said it was just because he couldn't; he didn't come to see me and I said it was just because he was feeling shy (it's true that he is easily embarrassed!). But deep down in my heart I think that he . . . well, I don't know. And finally today Granny started talking about it. Yes, Granny has a fair point, but her approach is very old-fashioned. Poor, dear Granny made a clumsy attempt to help me, but instead only lacerated my already bleeding heart. It will take a while for it to heal. And will it heal at all? I know now that J and T have decided to interfere with our love. Ah! It's so nasty, this fighting and this day. I don't know why this day feels so dirty.

I don't know why today's so sad
So cloudy and so bad
Why are there so many cruel hours?
Is it because of my tears?
Everything is nondescript
It's so empty and so lonely
I would like to have somebody picked
To talk and to not feel lowly
I would like to be somebody's

Tiny, beloved child
To sit in mama's custody
By the old fireplace and smile . . .
to listen to stories, make drawings
to dream this very sweet dream
to not know how hard is longing
when a day like today gleams . . .

Not to know it can be so sad
Not to know it can be so bad
Why are there so many cruel hours?
Is it because of my tears?

APRIL 28, 1941

I saw Z today. Something was telling me to play offended, so I did, but then I melted completely as soon as he looked at me. It's good. Even though those idiots made me doubt, it's a trifle.

There was a dance party at Irka's today. I mean, it wasn't a dance party, but boys from our class brought a gramophone and we danced. It was very nice; I had a good time. And it was Irka who told me that Krzyś had a crush on me! Which surprised me a lot, so I started watching him and it's quite possible . . .

Major asked how many boys have I seduced already, was it half a dozen? I said only one, but it isn't true! Krzysiek is a very pretty, smart boy, but that doesn't mean anything. I have Zygu; I love Zygu. Well, he is a bit lucky too. Let's see what the next days bring . . . I am waiting, Z. Zyguś, it's time. You will help me, Buluś and God.

APRIL 29, 1941, TUESDAY

Tuesday! A lot of commotion at school today with Zygu, with Ewa, with the letter etc. Zyguś tried to explain himself, said it was only ten minutes. It made me want to laugh. When I told him that I danced yesterday, he was angry, furious. We haven't arranged to meet for a while now. You know how sensitive I am about it and then this terrible brat Arianka says,

"You haven't been out with Zygu for a while." So I told her he was busy studying, to which this old person trapped in a young person's body replies ironically, "Suppose so." Aha!

Nobody cares about me anymore in our circles. A friend from the trade college approached me today, asking if I wanted to go to a party, and if so he would get an invite for me. Do you get it? I'll ask Z if he wants to go, otherwise I'll say no. My wonderful, good, sweet, darling Z.

We were out in town with Irka and a teacher from school. Waldek walked me home, he really does . . . this and that. And I'm a typical girl, why do I mess with his head? It's instinctive.

Norka is down. We went to visit her. She is unwell after yesterday's dance party. She's in bed, crying, worrying. Three parties like that in a row could break her. Poor Norka, I so feel for her. Some of it is her own fault, because she removes herself, but how can she not, when she lost faith in her own happiness and popularity? I believe that it'll get better with time, that time will heal the wounds, but in the meantime I do know how hard it is for her. God, please make it all good for her again. I'll write if anything, but so far nothing . . . You will help me, Buluś and God.

APRIL 30, 1941, WEDNESDAY

I am the unhappiest of unhappy people. Why did all the troubles come tumbling onto my head in one day? Why those two postcards from Mom? Why won't I see her? Why did Zygu arrange to take Irka to a party? Why does he want to spite me (I'll tell you about it later)? You know, I am going to go anyway. I'll let myself be tortured. I can't just give up altogether.

> *Life is a battle*
> *The world a battlefield*
> *I'll fight even though*
> *I don't believe in victory*

Or perhaps I shouldn't go? You will help me, Buluś and God.
Oh, if you could only speak.

11 P.M.!

Glad I went. As it was, Z was in a so-so mood because of me. We danced a bit; I jived with Krzysiek and a bit more.

Maciek has his own girlfriend now. Poldek is in love too and I'm left with Z, even though he is not sure of me and I am not sure of him. Ah, so many worries and troubles, but even that has its charm. There were plenty of couples dancing together, but I don't know why ours felt somewhat unnatural. Perhaps because Zygu also danced with others. Anyway I'm terribly jealous, Z is too, a bit. We both suffer (or so I think). About Irka! Even about Irka, i.e., not just about her, but I am jealous when he shows her interest. He told me he wants Irka to come on Saturday. If she comes then he will come as well? Is that it? As he said, P. and M. are taken, my school backup won't come, so I don't know about the party. Perhaps I shouldn't go . . . We might meet tomorrow. Well, we'll see . . . Will we meet at all during those three days off? I would like that; I miss him.

Z remembers when we last . . . So he remembers too. I would really like to fall in love for a long time . . . Zyguś, I want to go on a date . . . Come on . . . You will help me, Buluś and God.

MAY 1, 1941, THURSDAY

> Mama it would be so lovely
> To rest in your arms and cry
> To cry away my sorrows
> even die.
> To die or to sleep
> With all the beauty of youth
> And join forever our souls in truth
> And join forever in the peace and bliss
> To sail quietly to a haven
> Without tears or parting . . .

Mama, you poor thing, my poor darling soul. Alone among strangers . . . Look, out the window I see a small boy hugging his mother, and I feel such sorrow, because I'd like to hug someone too, and complain, I'm so upset Mama, so very upset . . . Why, why did this bubble burst? Why does the first joy give me such sadness, so many tears. You know, I cried today, oh, cried for so long—from the heart . . . You know, I love him after all, and he . . . I have been waiting for so many months, yes, and I've thought about this spring dream as something holy, most wonderful. And he, oh God! How foul! So this is what his shyness and modesty are about!? Today at the march . . . but tell me, why was it like that? I'm not going to impose myself on you at all. No! I'm never going to take one more step, not even half, whatever for? No, Zygu, don't worry, even if I were to suffer, I will step aside. Oh no! I won't go to the party on Saturday or any other party; I won't even try to meet you. It's not true that you're doing this out of love. Or maybe out of jealousy? And today is the first of May. The first day of the month of love and I, who had so believed in May (we'd had an arrangement after all) for those three days, must cry today. One thing, one thing bothers me: what was all this, because I don't think it was nothing. Ah, I know. I know what it was like then, and I was sweet too. If I only impress him, then . . . No, I'm not saying I'm not in love, but I won't impose myself either.

Don't cry my injured heart
The arrow that wounds you won't kill
With yearning, your beating must start
Although I don't want this to happen
It will
You may now cry your helpless tears
But they won't make them pity you more
Then they'll rob you and double your fears
Since you didn't learn about people before . . .

The will-o'-the-wisp will deceive you
and bend you to its will
you chase them—they run away
colorful
I found a heart
on a boundary road

a gingerbread heart
fresh, hot and lovely
a heart-shaped work of art
clapping my hands with joy
across the fields I ran
before I left the boundary road
the heart was lost and gone
Bitterly then I cried
And sighed with grief so bad
Should I look for a new heart
Or seek the one I had
I don't know
But why am I grieving
Why did my tears even fall
Before I found a heart
I didn't have one at all
I found it, I lost it—it's over
I'll visit my common sense
And say: "Make things carefree again
As they'd been ever since . . ."
But there'll be a frown on my brow
Like clouds hanging over the land
Because I had that heart to heart
And felt its warmth in my hand
It smelled so alluring and sweet
I thought I felt its beat
And that's why I've been crying
That's why the sorrow and pain
For having found a heart at last
I lost it once again

Well, I'll see, I'm in love, and he . . . You will help me, Buluś and God.

MAY 3, 1941, SATURDAY

God! Only you know what torment I have suffered during these days, what torture, it can't be described or even retold, it has to be experienced to be understood, but it's better not to understand or experience it. I didn't go to that party, but at what cost! And he, I don't know, maybe he's having a good time, maybe he's dancing happily, maybe he never spared a thought for me? You will help me, Buluś and God.

MAY 8, 1941, THURSDAY

I'd like to tell you so much, so much—nothing. I'd like to speak to you, but soberly, about the state of my soul. You know, I'm missing Mom awfully; I feel that this emotion of mine is intensifying, growing mightier. And I can't say how much longer we'll be separated. I so need somebody really close, someone who would care for me, a friend—a mother . . . And today I saw her, she came in the night, she was ill, suffering. Walking away, she said: "Renuś, I will come on June 25," she said she'd come, so I'm waiting . . . I'm waiting for this symbolic dream to come true. So perhaps she will come, because Her soul was with me.

Norka interrupted my writing and I'm finishing in the evening and I won't write what I'd wanted, because on the way I met "Him." The lord and master of my heart and soul, the wizard whose one glance, one word or smile changes me into a different person. I succumb to the charm like one succumbs to supernatural poisonous raspberries, like one succumbs to the thorny, yet deliciously scented rose. So I take it and although it wounds me, although it draws blood from my heart, I feel I cannot give it up, because its thorns have grown into me, because if I remove them— I'll die . . .

I'd thought that it's already "pro forma," like Olga wrote. That it is the end, and the ground is falling away beneath my feet. But now I feel that no, not yet, it's not even reached its height yet, so why am I thinking of the end. Today's walk and everything, was it not close—yet so delicate like the aroma of perfume in the air that one senses intuitively. I feel that I love more than any of the girls I know. Olga is in love, raving, loves with a purpose, loves an ideal. And I love a hundredfold more, to me any trifle is an enormous bleeding wound, I'm in disquiet, distress, despair . . . I love him and just him, an embodied ideal that I found not accidentally, and that has become my ideal . . . I love, I love . . . There's so much studying now, there's no time . . . You will help me, Buluś and God.

I love because there is May
in chords of bloom on Earth
the world around is pink
the soul is full of mirth
I love because he is a wonder
And has the strength and power
He took the obstacles down
And climbed my heart's tall tower
I love because I've a will
To thunder with cascades of feeling
Because I won't stop any longer
The flood of the love and the sting
I now know the reason I love
a head that is held so high
and eyes and the lips oh the lips . . .
I love because it is worth a try!

MAY 10, 1941, SATURDAY

Long live May! I'm feeling it again. We went to the movies and sat closely entwined, brow flat against brow, and . . . you understand? Z, "Well, I'd let you go to war," "What will our young people be like?" "We'll be in Lwów together . . ." "Will you go to Lwów with me?" And he wanted photographs from me; he said he must take them along, because all he will have will be memories and photographs. "You see, I'm poor too," with all the bullying . . .

Z likes to study my poems, knows the order they're in and threatens that he's going to get them published. He's generally marvelous and I love him! So much it chokes me up . . .

We won't meet tomorrow, but in between the examinations we'll be "laughing." You will help me, Buluś and God.

YESTERDAY . . .

Every time it's so similar . . . every time lighter, closer, and now it feels like peace, blissful peace has been sown in me. What's left are memories, something intangible, which even yesterday I would have been able to grasp in one word, in a glance, in . . . Funny, darling, slightly teasing memories . . . (it was he who accustomed me to such views, thank you). He walked in my scarf and we haven't got a home yet, anyway everything's whirling in my head. What's it going to be like later?

MAY 13, 1941

And what's it going to be like then . . . ? Oh, May! How intoxicating this May is, but perhaps only to me? My whole life is swelling up in me, all 17 years of it. All the emotions pile up into one heap of dry leaves and this May too, it's like fuel poured on this heap . . . And it's growing, growing, just one spark and it will erupt, flames will burst high in the sky, it will heat up and go wild like my long-imprisoned, suppressed, curbed love. Let there be a blaze, heat, fervor. Let the heart, brain, mind, body catch fire, let there be only conflagration and heat—and desire for burning, red-hot lips, desire like today, like then . . . like always. Desire! Damn.

Have I lost my mind? Exams soon, there are only three days left until the end of term! And I have learned absolutely nothing, I'm wandering around, daydreaming, ruminating . . . I'm not studying for my exams at all. I just can't! Zygu's eyes are green, but his lips are the most beautiful. Such amazing lips!

> *The lights in the houses are all out*
> *And all the loudspeakers are now dumb*
> *The shops and stalls are closed again*
> *The hot day's gone . . .*
> *The footsteps stop their drum and chime*
> *And night of silence, night of dark*

upon the city makes its mark
the city finds its sleeping time
And why does May wound us all over
and tear new wounds in hearts unhealed?
why does it rouse and wake the lover
why does it burn in eyes, still filled
with April's yearning—why, at night
does May conquer our souls by might
when nights are bright with starry dust
although the mind may think "I shan't"
the lips will whisper "yet I must"
Why does this May with fields of green
keep getting mixed with dearest eyes I've seen
why does it swell my chest, and make me drunk and giddy
why, if this is such torture
do I still say I need it

Silly me, what do I care, this May won't be any good anyway.

MAY 18, 1941, SUNDAY

On Friday, after school, Zyguś walked me home. On Saturday there was a row with Irka, Zygu and Maciek. You know that I feel something for Maciek now, I can't say I detest him, but somehow it seems he's taking Zygu away from me. Sometimes I think him passable, but sometimes horrible, foul, capable of anything. And Z is under his influence.

The school year is over. It's passed more quickly than any other before it; it passed, it fell into oblivion, because it was brimful of love. And the school year is over—a pity . . . Admittedly this won't change the love, but still, it was something that connected us legitimately, something that we shared, which concerned us equally. Well, but it can't be said that only school connected us, well it did, but love most of all.

Irka told me that Z's mother said that Z is in love, that he is not looking well, that she doesn't know what's going on with him. She was also very keen to learn something about me, see my photograph etc. So finally, some real, tangible proof that Z is in love. And I'd thought about it so, so many times, about his mother. I like her, I love her for what she said, and I also love my darling Mama, the best one, the only. And I'm not preparing for the exam even a little; I don't know how it will go. I'll see you on the 4th, either happy or wet-eyed. Well, until the 4th, unless . . . but I doubt it. Rena. You will help me, Buluś and God.

I can hardly stand it. Dear Diary, I miss you so much. I get no sleep because I'm sitting two and a half exams: for Zygu, for myself and half for Arianka. I've never known I could be so worried on someone else's behalf. Zygu is awfully good to me, and then horribly jealous for no reason.

4 P.M.

No, I'm not writing down the date, what for, I wasn't supposed to write until the 4th. Z is sitting his exams and I am so nervous I don't sleep at night, I don't care a whit about my own exams—am not studying. And today, God, God! Why am I so sad today, why did I do that to Z when he came? I'm awfully angry. Not angry—sad. I'm not sure why? How stupid that I stuck around for three hours, waited for the result of the task. Those girls from the boardinghouse were screaming, "Ela!" What for? Because he walked me back, and Stefa from over the way was angry that Krzyś (her love) and Waldek whistled her "Chopsticks" under my windows. But why am I telling you all this? Probably to depict the tragic state of my soul. Examine yourself what else could have made me so—aha, perhaps that bad state of mind, I'm going through a phase when I have to admit that I'm awful, downright nasty, but perhaps it's the disappointment that I haven't done too well with my task?

> *I would go far away*
> *and leave the people behind*
> *Maybe a sunny May stillness*
> *will soothe me*
> *Maybe a subtle breeze*
> *Will cool my mind*
> *No, I can't clearly meet a gaze*
> *I can't seek out someone's eyes?*

Go far, fall asleep in a haze
let the time fly away
Leave above the earth
And follow a dream
Become a bright fragrant shade
a slender thought's stream
and like a daydream's mist
spread myself on the sky
caressing dreamily with smiles
to fade with a sigh
Oh to be a cloud of thought
pink and blue
pale milky-watery and orange in hue
taking the word and the gaze
to fly away
and to become fully one sweet dream of May . . .

10 P.M.

I've had the most wonderful May evening. Maybe the first romantic evening in May and in my life. We climbed up high on the hills, along paths. The San was flowing beneath our feet—powerful, glimmering, red in the sunset. And the red, slightly hazy sun was slowly descending from the sky. We talked a lot, pleasantly, and I know that our spirits were so connected that I'm not sure if any physical contact could have brought us closer. It's hard to remember what we talked about. I only know that when I mentioned something about his reputation, he replied, "So you wouldn't want a famous husband . . . ?" and then he said something else and got very confused (passport, you don't want to come to me, you can't even control yourself, much about eyes).

Good, lovely Zyguś, although he gets angry with me about being afraid of dogs, and says that he was minded to give me a wallop, but he is perfect in absolutely every respect.

I'm really at a loss for words, so just picture silence, greenery, May, sunset and fireworks, and the two of us, in love.

But Zygu is still testing me about Maciek; does he not believe me yet?

And that leaping heart? I don't believe in that power so much anymore, "is the binding of souls not worth the binding of bodies?" You will help me, Buluś and God.

Stupid idiot Belania! Those girls are shallow and trite after all! She asked me if I'm not getting bored with Zygu yet. She gets bored with students because one can't exchange two words with them—the countess walks away.

Despite everything I see that I am more profound than they are, I really don't switch loves like handkerchiefs, I'm unable to talk about it in a cold, cynical manner! It's repugnant, disgusting! To love truly, passionately, honestly, this is what I believe in, this only! I'm terrified of chemistry.

Today's walk was—oh, nothing worth mentioning. There was company, and I always feel worse then. I will tell you I was a little jealous, but Zygu was a hundred times worse when Maciek approached, because he really had more reason to be. Anyway, I found out how they study my poems (about that explosion, about blue), aha, that linking of hands and Mendelssohn's "Wedding March" again. And those two female neighbors that he boards with, sweet boy, tender, anyway there is something very cordial about him. The evenings and starry nights are pretty, but apart from that it's so dull, somehow empty and lonely in the world, one wants to have someone, say something. What? Why not . . . Zyguś. I'm mostly interested in poems now.

JUNE 4, 1941, WEDNESDAY

Done! I should be jumping up to the heavens! Everything went well, I passed everything, although I didn't really study too much. Well then, holidays ahead of me, three long months of holidays, and also ahead of me is emptiness. I don't know, I've got a constant feeling that something has evaded me, that something has ended. I'm in such a strange mood that I don't know what to do with myself.

Zygu was wonderful yesterday. He was so pleased when I let myself be stroked by him, but not by M! But there is something strange about this Z, something different from other boys. On the one hand that's very good, on the other—a bit bad . . . You know, I keep expecting events, I keep waiting, waiting for the dream to come true, and if it fades, then—I'll leave for Horodenka—only I know, I know for sure that I would yearn something fierce . . . Zyguś! You will help me, Buluś and God.

JUNE 10, 1941, TUESDAY!

Zygu is sitting his last examination tomorrow! To celebrate, I'm going to wear my new navy shoes.

Today we spoke about this and that, and everything. You know, I can't write down whole conversations anymore, never mind. One can't write it the way it is, anyway.

Z has a sore throat, he said I should recommend something for it or only say a word and it will get better. There was talk of Salcia and Krela. And that he's got a way of influencing me and many, many more nice things. "Well, what am I to do to you?" he said twice. I wanted to ask if we'd go to the movies tomorrow, but I did it so awkwardly that I couldn't manage to utter a word. Z thinks that God knows what I am to say to him? I said I'll say it tomorrow. All right, but what will I tell him, he thinks . . . yes, he thinks that. And I'd also really, really like to tell him. I love you, Zygu! But no, I can't, so what shall I tell him? What shall I tell him tomorrow? He was making such a sweet, darling face . . . Zygunio, I love you so much! I love you the most! That "And whatever you prefer!"—I let it slip and got very embarrassed, but he guessed, the most wonderful wonder. I love you. Good night kisses. Renia.

I'm off to daydream. I will look at rooms and think about how the two of us will live there. It's a dream, a fairy tale, but one can dream. You will help me, Buluś and God.

JUNE 11, 1941, WEDNESDAY

Zygu passed his final school exam today! He was so wonderful today! Very, very tender and very darling. I do want to tell him something after all. No! Honestly, today Zyguś was the way he's never been before. No more from me!

JUNE 17, 1941, TUESDAY

I haven't seen Zyguś in such a long, long time! I do see him, but he's preoccupied with his graduation all the time. Tomorrow is the graduation and . . . my birthday. I'm turning 17. We will talk tomorrow. Actually I already know that I won't be happy, because I won't see Zygu at all. Today I translated a little Heine—this feels like a relief, some of the thoughts there are so "mine," e.g.:

> *They both loved each other, though neither*
> *Would love to the other confess;*
> *They looked at each other so sternly,*
> *And suffered their loving no less.*

> *They parted at last and they met again*
> *Where dreams would linger and dwell;*
> *They died so long ago before,*
> *But neither of them could tell.**

Perhaps this thing of ours will, however, have a happier ending.

I have a wonderful collection of my poems. Irka and Nora made it for me, I'm grateful for it. One for Zygu, I'll write it in, but I haven't got a rough draft. So they will be a bit disappointed tomorrow, especially that my leg's swollen and I can't leave . . . tomorrow!?

JUNE 18, 1941, WEDNESDAY

Irka and Nora got me the most beautiful leather-bound diary. I am very grateful to Noruśka and Irka and love them very, very much. Only why did she write that maybe I will be a famous poet and Mrs. Zygmunt S., and if not . . . then this diary will only be a very painful memory. I'm not really contemplating my life too much today, maybe I can't do it now like I used to, and anyway—it's not worth it. Perhaps the biggest event today

---

* Song XXXIII from *The Book of Songs* (1827). Incipit: "*Sie liebten sich beide, doch keiner.*"

was that I met the S. family. It happened by chance, but I got very embarrassed, good thing it was dark. Z found out at school that it was my birthday. I'm 17. This is not so terrifying yet, but 18 is a nightmare. I don't know why this one year means so much. So I met them, precisely on my birthday, well . . . Mama, is that right? The second birthday without you. And you, are you thinking of me today? Why me . . . ? A new phase won't start tomorrow, no, the same one still.

JUNE 20, 1941, FRIDAY

Today. Yes today. I knew it, I felt it, that I'll only be able to tell you. We had another wonderful evening. Two of us alone, properly alone. The sun had set and the stars started to emerge, and the moon floated up, and we sat next to each other and talked. And it was so . . . When we left, it was dark; we couldn't find the way. We got lost, yes, we got doubly lost, or rather—only just found ourselves. It was all so sudden and unexpected and sweet and intimidating. I was at a loss for words and terribly mixed up. He said, "Renuśka, give me a kiss," and before I knew it, it happened . . . He wanted more later, but I couldn't, I was shaking all over.

Z said that he really liked this "intentional going astray," he said, "We can do this again now, or tomorrow." I feel so strange and nice. It was so light, elusive, ethereal, delicate. There was much, much more, but I'm only interested in that one thing—that he has become so close to me, the dearest person in the world, and I'm dizzy all the time . . . How did it happen. No more now, I need to think and dream . . . We'll meet tomorrow—Z and I, and you and I. And will tomorrow also be so good and sweet . . . ? You will help me, Buluś and God.

JUNE 21, 1941, SATURDAY[12]

I love those green eyes. First we wrote each other dedications on photographs. We used Latin grammar for this. It's a scandal, that's what Z said, that this scandal has been going on for six months already. We also went to the pines. And again it felt very good. We kissed for the second time, i.e., actually the first, because today it was reciprocal. It felt so nice too, but you know, it wasn't fiery or wild, but somehow delicate and careful, and almost fearful—as if we didn't want to extinguish something that was growing between us. Who would have thought we could talk so "scientifically"? You will help me, Buluś and God.

Zygu wants very much to go to a party on Monday, I don't, but it seems I have to—I really don't feel like it! I do not enjoy those stuffy, crowded dances. I prefer to be beneath the stars, beneath the moon in the evening's darkness, with my grown-up Zygunio.

JUNE 26, 1941

Do you remember, on 25th of May I wrote I had a dream. I dreamed that Mom said she would come on the 25th of June. Good Lord! I didn't know this was what it was going to be. I can't write. I'm weak with fear. War again, war between Russia and Germany.* The Germans were here, then they retreated. Horrible days in the basement. The city has been evacuated. You remember, dear Diary, what price I paid for a short moment, today we stayed too . . . Grant us, Lord God, that the same thing happens now as it did then. I begged you, Lord God, for my dream to come true and it did, you saved my mother, you gave me him and the thing I've been waiting for for such a long time, and now this war. Give me my Mama, save all of us who have stayed here and those who escaped the city this morning. Save us, save Zygu . . .

Today they woke me up, I ran outside and saw his silhouette. Oh, I remember that last Saturday evening well. Holy God Almighty, save us. I want to live so badly. I'm humbling myself before You and begging on behalf of us all. Save us. Tonight is going to be terrible. I'm scared, today was horrible too. I believe that You will hear me, that You won't leave me in this awful hour. You have saved me before, save me now.

Date . . . I don't even know, Saturday, a week ago . . . Why, why speak, why write? God, thank You for saving me.

But my heart is now so heavy
And old thoughts are torn in two

---

* The Third Reich attacked the Soviet Union on June 22, 1941.

But my heart is held in a leaden fist
And the scary thoughts are new

Now maybe I'll see Buluś! I don't know what's going to happen to us. Dido, I believe nothing bad is going to happen to him. I'm terrified. Almost the whole city is in ruins. A piece of shrapnel fell into our house. These have been horrific days. Why even try to describe them? Words are just words. They can't express what it feels like when your whole soul attaches itself to a whizzing bullet. When your whole will, your whole mind and all your senses cling to the flying missiles and beg, "Not this house!" You're selfish and you forget that the missile that misses you is going to hit someone else.

Dear Diary! How precious you are to me! How horrible were the moments when I hugged you to my heart!

And where is Zyguś? I don't know. I believe, fervently, that no harm has come to him. Where he is, I don't know. Good God, protect him from all evil. Zyguś, my only one, because of that farewell of ours this separation feels all the more bitter. We exchanged photographs and said that we might be separated by the war after all; you were making plans for the future, mine and yours, and I was telling you, "I don't know—there might be a war." All of this started four hours after the moment you blew me the last kiss up to the balcony. First, we heard a shot, then an alarm, and then a howl of destruction and death. I don't know where Irka and Nora are, either, where anyone is.

That's it for tonight; it's getting dark. God, save us all, Dido, Zygu. Make it so Mom comes and let there be no more misery, God . . . You will help me, Buluś and God.

JULY 1, 1941[13]

We're all alive and well. All of us, Norka, Irka, Zygu, my friends, my family. And today I want to speak with you as a free person still. Today I'm like everyone else . . . Tomorrow, along with other Jews, I'll have to start wearing a white armband. To you I will always remain the same Renia, a friend, but to others I will become someone inferior, I will become someone wearing a white armband with a blue star. I will be a *Jude*.

I'm not crying or complaining. I have resigned myself to my fate. It just feels so strange and sorrowful. My school vacation and my dates with Zygu are coming to an end. I don't know when I'll see him next. Everyone is working today. No news about Mama. God protect us all.

Goodbye, dear Diary. I'm writing this while I'm still independent and free. Tomorrow I'll be someone else—but only on the outside. And perhaps one day I'll greet you as someone else still. Grant me that, Lord God, I believe in You. You will help me, Buluś and God!

JULY 3, 1941, THURSDAY

Nothing new so far. We wear the armbands, listen to terrifying and consoling news and worry about being sealed off in a ghetto.

He visited me today! Do you hear? I thought I'd go mad with joy, and . . . confusion. He's working at the clinic, dressing wounds, so there's practice without theory. He's sweet and wonderful, as always. It's a shame he can't go to university now. He'd be an excellent doctor. But he will be one anyway, you'll see. We've arranged to meet tomorrow at the clinic. It seems a little strange, but why not? Even now that we're wearing these armbands—the thing is to be with him.

The border is supposed to open on the 7th, ah, I want Buluś to come so ardently, with my whole heart. Buluś, come. God, bring Mama, let her be with us for better and for worse. Buluś, come. Zygmunt's wonderful. You will help me, Buluś and God!

JULY 6, 1941, SUNDAY

Days pass . . . The other day I didn't see Zygu—it was my fault, yes, my fault. Today I had work (physical, of course), one gets bread for it, I also got potatoes, that is I have had a victory in the field of provisioning. I'm very tired, but less with work than with missing Mom and Zygu. I miss them so much, I'm dying of yearning. When? You will help me, Buluś and God!

Wedding photo of Bernard and
Róża (Rose) Spiegel, 1923.

Renia (right) and her cousin Lila,
approximately 1933.

Renia and Ariana (Elizabeth)
playing in the Dniester River in
Zaleszczyki, approximately 1935.

Renia in a boat in the
Dniester River in Zaleszczyki,
approximately 1936.

Renia, Róża (Rose), and Ariana
(Elizabeth) in the city of
Przemyśl, approximately 1937.

Ariana (Elizabeth), Róża (Rose), and
Renia in a vineyard in the region of
Zaleszczyki, 1935 or 1936.

Grandma Anna Finkel and
Ariana (Elizabeth) in Przemyśl,
approximately 1935.

Ariana (Elizabeth) and Grandfather
Markus Finkel, 1936.

Renia, Róża (Rose), and Ariana (Elizabeth)
near Dniester in Zaleszczyki, 1935.

Róża (Rose), Renia, and Ariana (Elizabeth) eating
ice cream, most likely in Przemyśl, 1935.

Ariana (Elizabeth), Renia, and Róża (Rose)
(all standing) in Zaleszczyki, 1936.

Róża (Rose) and Ariana
(Elizabeth) in Skole, 1936.

Ariana (Elizabeth), far left; Róża (Rose);
and Renia at the Lesieczniki grape farm in
the region of Zaleszczyki, 1937.

Róża (Rose) and Renia in Przemyśl,
around 1939, before the start of the war.

Ariana "The Polish Shirley
Temple," in Warsaw,
approximately 1936.

Norka and Renia, around
16 years old, 1940.

Norka and Renia in Przemyśl,
approximately 1940.

Ariana (Elizabeth) and Róża (Rose) in Warsaw at the
Hotel Europejski, where Rosa worked, likely 1943.

Wedding photo of Elizabeth and George Bellak,
New York City, 1965.

Andrew Bellak and Alexandra Renata Bellak, the
children of Ariana (Elizabeth), at Jones Beach, 1976.

Alexandra and Andrew at Alexandra's
25th birthday celebration, 1995.

JULY 11 OR 12, 1941, FRIDAY[14]

One loses track of time now. Today I finally saw him. It was, however, a meeting at a distance, and Maciek was there, so naturally nothing much happened.

Z's working at the polyclinic, changing dressings, stitching wounds and doing other horrible things; they call him doctor. He told me to come to the clinic and have him called, but I'm embarrassed again and I don't know whether I will go.

But what news I've had! I learned from Z's cousin that he took special care of my notebook with poems and did not let anyone touch it. Comical—I ran away with you and his photograph, and he with my notebook. He said this about me (just listen, isn't it about me?), "My woman is subtle."

Where Irka works, so does Z's cousin and many friends from his tenement; they all want to meet me, they know my name is Rena and that I'm "Zygu's woman." I'm horribly embarrassed, because I don't like such fuss, and most of all I don't like to be observed. I'll try to pop over there, but I doubt whether I can make a decent impression, usually I come across as either an uncouth barbarian or an idiot. But I shall see? Still, you will always remain my friend, and Z too. You will help me, Buluś and God.

JULY 15, 1941, WEDNESDAY*

Today was very eventful. Namely, in the morning I met Z, and how? I was wandering around the clinic, saw Maciek and he called for Z, who was already at home. We talked and walked for a long time (and because of Z, without armbands). Our walk almost had a tragic conclusion; a policeman approached Z, asked about his nationality and passport. Z said he was Polish and had no passport, and then they both disappeared. I heard it was to the police station, so I ran like mad there and back; hard to describe what I experienced then, the despair, the fear, the guilt etc.

---

* July 15, 1941, was a Tuesday.

145

Everything ended well. I saw Z in a doctor's coat (suits him so wonderfully) and rubber gloves.

This event, though it's very distressing, is another brick in the mansion of our love.

In the afternoon I went to the clinic, brave as you like, and met Z (with minor complications). We went for a long walk and it was very, very good. Oh yes, I gave him cigarettes and sweets, a fortune these days! That Z is the most wonderful, the most lovable of all. Tomorrow we are to see each other in M's garden. Z is to pick me up. So I'm waiting . . . for Z and for Mom (this is my whole life). Bye, good night and good day, Rena.

NEXT DAY, THURSDAY*

Yes, I did meet him. He came with Maciek. M left to see Julek, and Zygu and I went for a walk. It's good to write down the details, but today I'll try to relay a few fragments and think aloud a bit, that is on paper. I say fragments, because it is hard for me to describe a three-hour-long conversation. You know, it's no use writing at all, it should be filmed, and on color film too, so you could see how green his eyes and red his lips are, how unwell—but wonderful—he looks.

Fragments of the film: That he doesn't have anyone anywhere in Jarosław etc., thinks about his family, has no male friends either, and . . . female, "Ah, I knew this was what you meant" (well, despite everything I did not ask about the one in the photograph, but I will), later that he would certainly be able to keep me and that I wouldn't break free from him. Then that he wants to use me to learn how to make injections and that one day he'll do something about my nose and perhaps my height. He picked a fly out of my eye and do you know, it's even pleasant when flies fall into my eyes if it's Z who is taking them out. Later about the graduation exam and what "he will do with me," and at the end—that we can die together, holding hands, and share a grave. What do you think, it's very touching indeed, but sad. If there really was a shared grave like

---

* Given that the day for the previous entry was incorrect, the next day would have been Wednesday.

that, and us inside, joined in the last, but eternal embrace, and on it the words:

here lie those . . .
who were in love
who will not be moved
by any command
who will no longer be parted
who are joined together by death's hand

Yes, but not now, now one still has to live, has to strive, try, has to leave something to the world. One has to, for perhaps . . . one creates happiness, and then come the blessings of the world, of God and people, and one departs with the sense of a duty fulfilled. Z, you probably think otherwise—more wisely. But I think in this maternal way and because, as you say yourself, I am a little too calm. Yes, I know, I'm like a fat stretching cat. Why do I feel sorrow now, a strange, vague and unfounded sorrow— ah, yes, Dido. So, apart from that, I think about them all day long, and at night I also dream of them both, Mom and him. And I know that I would give them everything, and myself, and my soul, because I feel that I love those two beings the most, I feel they're closest and dearest to me. When I walk the distant streets with Zygu (such irony of fate, we're uncertain if we'll live, the city's destroyed, war, horrible uncertainty, white armbands), I'm happy, it feels good, and I'd like to grasp, to pin down "something," something that is, and is not—but is. I walk and look at wonderfully green eyes and listen to words, ironic at times (because we are having an ironic conversation), and that normal world that I know so much about . . . the horrors of war . . . seems a happy one to me. And this state is not only selfishness (selfishness, i.e., Zygu and I), for example: I laugh. Z says I'm laughing at him, although he knows that's not the case, and after a minute we speak at the same time. Z, "Laugh if it gives you pleasure, and whenever you can." Me, "I won't laugh, because it distresses you," and we both burst out laughing. In such a state of mind one wants everybody to be happy, wants things to work out beautifully between Nora and Julek B., Irka and Henek, Arianka and Rysiek, and every girl with her beloved; one wants all those loves to mature and turn into

exemplary, loving marriages. "It's madness to think like this today," do you think I don't know what you want to tell me, old friend. Yes, but lovers are always mad, because love is madness, and madness is life. So may it be good for all of us, may I soon kiss again, and may Zygu always remain the way he is now! If I could, I would sing some mighty hymn to praise God, love and the world, but I couldn't, so I hum in my heart!

> *Be merry, friend, and laugh*
> *embrace the passersby*
> *feel good enough to cry,*
> *"I'm living," that's enough!*
> *And a strange crowd crept out*
> *From cellars hot and damp*
> *A swarm of pale gaunt faces*
> *eyes shone like a lamp*
> *a starving swarm that faints and sways*
> *crept from the rubble, and see*
> *They all fell into a strange wild craze*
> *and laughed in a hysterical haze*
> *and . . . felt happy*
> *see the one who sat on a pile of rubble*
> *he has no kids, no wife, no home*
> *he poured the vodka in his mouth*
> *and puked his blood out in wild laughter*
> *he clung to every passerby*
> *and howled, "I live, that's what I'm after!"*

JULY 18, 1941, FRIDAY

A meeting. Again, another one similar to all the other ones, but still separately wonderful. Zygu almost kissed me in Maciek's presence, and Maciek—in Zygu's. I will point out that Z was very angry. He dismissed Arianka, dragged me upstairs (so beautiful in that white coat), and then we went for a walk.

As usual, we talked of the war, of medicine, compliments and eyes. I know we're both still waiting, this can be surmised from his various

allusions. I'm an awful coward. I try to overcome it, but it is very hard. Z is sulking that I don't trust the strength of his arms and his protective wings. We also spoke about the future. We always do, and we mean by it, although vaguely (at least I do), our shared future. I blurted out one very spiteful thing, i.e., that he wants to get rid of me with his nervous yawning. Then he drew me to himself so strongly, and so close, that . . . I don't know. But when I told him that my cousin was coming, well—he got very embarrassed. In the past we had a place but we didn't know how, and now we know how, but we haven't got a place; and I'm certain we are both waiting. You know, it's so idiotic, I am suffused with happy meetings, I string them on the gray thread of my life like wonderful, gleaming pearls, I string them all, equal, smooth, round, and sometimes they grow and strive, strive tirelessly toward that main one, the huge, most beautiful one. It's true what I told you, I'm incurably sick, and you know full well what with, Zygu, because you didn't ask me about it, only laughed, and how—divinely, charmingly. There is something wonderful that one can't write about, it's just what I feel and what I try to express with words in vain, because I'd distort it. Z adores children, he introduced me to this little, sweet thing he frightens with injections. I am grateful to God that Zygu exists and grateful to Zygu that our love exists, and grateful to love that she sets hearts on fire, grateful to hearts that they can love. And you see, everything comes down to this enchanted word: love. We are to see each other on Monday, "even if there's a downpour." Ah, if only Mom could arrive before Monday, oooh . . . You will help me, Buluś and God!

NEXT DAY, SATURDAY! (JULY 19, 1941)

Those accidental meetings are rather unpleasant. Was it not better only on Monday? How much better? I wouldn't have been in this mood, there would've been no tears and the heart wouldn't have ached so. I feel better now, because I'd vented a little before I told you—but earlier, a while ago, I was squirming in the sort of pain every loving and every jealous girl suffers. And I myself broke the string I was so joyfully filling with pearls. The "happy company" broke it, that Lidka who imposes herself on him with her sweetness, and his whole behavior, and Maciek saying that he wants to move to dentistry on her account (you don't know her and I don't know her, but she hasn't played any part in my life yet and I hope she doesn't) and my stupid, scandalous behavior.

Yes, I am stupid, I was punished for being so happy, for screaming happiness. It's better now and there's less bitterness in my writing, but I remember, remember how much it hurt. The whole fault lies with me and the jealousy, which I will try to eradicate. All this compensated me a little for Irka's desires and that she kissed Zygu's hand and that he is to feed her. God sent me this little creature as a consolation . . . I don't know when . . . I'll see you. Lida is horrible. You will help me, Buluś and God!

JULY 21, 1941

Already a month has passed since our memorable kiss. Zygu reminded me of this. He came by with Maciek. Maciek kissed my head by way of greeting, Zygu went red. Well, but when Maciek kissed my face, Z was furious, and rightly so. He tried to make up for it all, and at the same time hide his confusion, so he began hugging me, caressing me so warmly, that I felt extremely moved and . . . almost dazed. "How smooth her face is," he said—he remembered that once, at the house of that darling little Irusia he smelled my scent, i.e., perfume, Maciek recalled this. He held my hand tightly. When we spoke about that, er . . . book, and Maciek was talking about the accident that Z wanted to tell me about on Friday, Z said, "Maciek, stop, this is a 'flower of thought,' she can't listen to this," and took as many pains about it as . . . he only can.

Many more, many things I am unable to write about because I do not know how, I have to immortalize in my mind, preserve in my heart, so that I can draw on them in moments of sadness. I must surely know that Z loves me! And one has to ask God that things happen like "our friend" said they would: after the war, after school, with Zygu, my wonderful husband—it really took my breath away—he wrote in my diary like so: "1) Happiness is the contentment man feels when he can stop wanting even for a moment, and cherish what he has. 2) The sight of something beautiful in art or nature immediately awakens the memory of a beloved woman." How wonderful and true! I experience it in every moment, even in everyday life, in the fairy-tale life from books, and in the life of thought, i.e., in the land of dreams. Only memories and dreams live there. I love with all my heart. I'm choking on love like—he does . . . yes, for he also . . . We both want it, we make meaningful faces, and our lips tilt slightly of their own accord, M even made a remark. Buluś, come, hear me out, assess. I didn't make a date, I don't know, I'm still waiting . . . You will help me, Buluś and God!

JULY 22, 1941, TUESDAY

I went to the parish. I'm starting to get used to it. Z and I went for a walk. I was looking for a defense against Maciek in him. Irusia Hauser, that Irusia, is making huge progress with Fiunio. I wish her happiness and I'm very pleased. I get very confused there. Z is the loveliest, "Have I ever been angry with you?" But those eyes peer! Bye! Good night, I'm off to daydream, although I'm tired. Until the next time I meet Z, when? I'll see the one from my dreams. You will help me, Buluś and God.

JULY 28, 1941, FRIDAY*

I have already seen Zygu and had a sulk, and I missed him, "and so it goes." And in the meantime I live with no news of Mom. Apparently it's bad there. Poor Mama. Whatever I eat, I think of her, I share every bite with her in my thoughts, like I do every joy and sadness. Please, God, may it really happen, that I might share everything with her. Mama, I'm writing this to you! I'm writing as if the words scribbled here had some magical power and could summon you. May they sound out so that they can be heard by the Great Lord God in heaven and you, dearest, all the way there.

Yesterday I saw Jews being beaten. Some monstrous Ukrainian in a German uniform hit every one he met. He hit and kicked them, and we were helpless, so weak, so incapable. . . . We had to take it all in silence. And at that moment my only consolation was the thought of revenge, oh yes, revenge is sweet, but it should not be bloody. And I want to live until the moment when I can hold my head up high, when I'm an equal, free person in a free, democratic country! I want to be happy then with Zygu, with everyone who had gone through this hell of dishonor, slaughter and

---

* July 28, 1941, was a Monday.

humiliation. I want to be happy, I want my dreams to come true, and you will help me with this, God, because I believe in You, because You have never let me down!

Every morning whole troops of wounded Germans walk past. And . . . I'm sorry for them. I'm sorry for those young, tired boys, far away from their homeland, mother, wife, perhaps children. Someone says heart-felt prayers for them too, and someone weeps for them during sleepless nights. Such is the irony of fate . . .

I curse the hundreds, thousands, millions
when new recruits go to war
may they all meet their bullets
may neither of them come back to what they knew before.

May grenades' horrible hail
bring them all down one by one
may the whole cursed army fail
For the blood of fathers, brothers, sons!

Slowly he walks, harried and weak
a soldier, look, how young
wounded in hand, or in arm, hard to speak
his uniform hangs from his arm.

He walks, he limps and rests by the wall
He's sweating, he won't walk too far
His gaze is a helpless begging call
His eyes, oh how sad they are!

As if in his blackest depths
a complaint now burned with alarm
look, see how young I am
and how they did me harm.

I learned all life the hard way
I knew next to nothing before

my mother, my father, my house went away
I had to fight—but who for?

Now on my way back . . . and again
my eyes are flashing with grief
I cry and my heart's full of sorrow
I'm weak and I can't find relief.

This is the fate, it's the life
and who can explain to me why
I curse the thousands and millions
And for the one wounded, I cry?

AUGUST 6, 1941

Moods and thoughts, and words, all change . . . They change, flicker from wave to wave. I'm pleased, because my heart tells me Mom will come. There will be a message from her next week.

I'm sad when I hear that they are to send us, that there's to be a ghetto, that it's so bad. And apart from this my personal trifles make me lose the last dregs of spirit.

Lida is making disgusting passes at Zygu in my presence. He behaves very stupidly. He's awfully selfish, why doesn't he think about me? Why? But I am already making solemn promises to myself that without an invitation or an arranged meeting I will not go to the parish. With Lida it's not making a pass, it's something natural, and how unnatural! Irka did a vile thing. I'm angry with Zygu, but all my worries are consoled with one thought—Mom! You will help me, Buluś and God. Mama, Mama, will come??? When . . . Mom. When . . . Zygu.

AUGUST 11, 1941, SUNDAY*

I'm working. I have reasons to be pleased. I'm expecting Mom any day now. Each strike of the clock may bring her to me. I'm seeing Zygu, he's

---

* August 11, 1941, was a Monday.

sweet, good, darling. He proposed that we get a photograph taken together, the two of us. I have reasons to be pleased, and yet I yearn for "that night" . . .

> *Such a night happens once in a lifetime*
> *so in memories it can linger on*
> *so it can be dreamed about day- and nighttime*
> *and remembered as years are long gone*
> *Such a night—it's in dreams it begins*
> *In a girl's wishes*
> *Such a night turns a memory, it seems*
> *Like a smile, it perishes*
> *Yes, I remember the charms of the moon*
> *and holding the head I so missed*
> *and a bird's midnight tune*
> *and how you kissed*

I can't write any more, but every night I miss that night so, I miss it, I miss those lips . . . ah, that night lives in me. Those nights exist to awaken yearning, and then an unquenched thirst. Tomorrow? You will help me, Buluś and God

AUGUST 12, 1941, MONDAY*

It's a shame I talked about that dog. I feel better today than I have felt for days. Yes today. Zyguś was perhaps the loveliest! He gave me a photograph of himself and wrote: "To darling sweet lips." Zygmunt said, "I see my sweet lips, so I'm thinking of lips," and generally he says that "this" is an understood and certain thing, and "this" is precisely our love.

We walked far, avid for "only sensual delights," Z said that, and we sat down, I did not want to sit in his lap, I don't know why, but I can't. I sat next to him, with leaves stuck to my lips all over. Why? I imagine it's exactly because I was choking with . . . Z embraced me like he did then, and like then the scent dazed me. It was quiet again, the road empty and

---

* August 12, 1941, was a Tuesday.

the field, and the pond, and when he finished unsticking all the little leaves from my lips and when . . . two Germans came.

I can't describe everything, so I'll mention the "alley of love," i.e., Z and I'm off to daydream, live through everything all over again.

Z invited me, he said he had a nice little room, but what of it? And you know what I wrote him, the dearest darling? Z was awfully pleased, but that's not enough, with a whole slew of words I would not be able to say how close he is to me (and to reciprocate). Zygu, our every meeting is a priceless gift to me. Can one repay God for the sun and the sky, and life, can we speak of it? We are to have regular meetings on Thursdays. You will help me, Buluś and God.

AUGUST 15, 1941, FRIDAY

Z said that I absolutely should give you to Mom to read, I should not keep secrets from her. Mama! Come, and I'll open this diary to you, and my heart at the same time!

I'm ill. I have a fever and a sore throat. Yesterday I wanted to tell you that this makes me inordinately happy. Zygu came to visit, sat by me, and was, well—as always. He wanted to examine me. I was happy, but I always talk myself down. Yes, I told Norka and Irka about it, and talked myself into sadness.

Z came today too, he was sweet, but whenever he comes to me, the whole "esteemed company" gathers, and I'm upset, Zygu is too. Apart from them came Rena F., Lunka and Lidka, but more on that later. I will have a photograph, but I had to give him the one from the graduation anyway, he asked me.

Apart from my illness I don't really have anything on my conscience— but still, how many worries weigh down my heart. Mama, when will you come? I haven't heard anything about that, or from Lila . . .

You know, Z held you in his hands today, he wanted to read, I got very nervous, and in the end he asked, "Well, but when I become a doctor, will you let me read?" Zygu, do I know what will happen before you become one? But may God make it happen. That you are a doctor and that I can give it to you. I miss . . . You will help me, Buluś and God.

AUGUST 16, 1941

It's a normal, gray, wartime day. It's like those 63 days that have already passed, and like the days that are to come. It's a neurotic day, drizzly, cold, unfriendly ... What do I know? I reply, "I don't know" in advance to all the questions I desperately want to ask. Why is Mom not writing, why is there no sign from her? What has happened to her? Why do we live in fear of searches and arrests? Why can't we go for a walk, because "children" throw stones? And why, why, why? I'm overcome by some infectious fear, no, I feel no foreboding, but still—I am so afraid, so very afraid. Miraculous God, keep and save my one and only Mom.

> *Maybe one day the sun will shine again ...*
> *maybe one day we'll walk, me and you*
> *through a world that has awoken*
> *from a long winter's dream*
> *to have our students' rendezvous*
> *as the memory holds what's dear*
> *maybe one day yet, one day*
> *we will sit there on the bench*
> *forget and remember what we may*
> *maybe once more we'll get "lost"*
> *in an alley lined with pines*
> *with a scary premonition*
> *it may well have been "on our minds"*
> *maybe a green blade of grass*
> *when we face the final day*
> *and maybe for real this time*
> *a flash of sun—a golden ray?*

You will help me, Buluś and God.

9 IN THE EVENING!

Something's bursting within me, choking me! One wants more, endlessly more. Oh, how good it is to be kissing lovely red lips, how good to be caressed "like that," talk about the taste of kisses, about love. About obstacles to our love etc. All that hurt has already been erased, a kiss wiped away the reason why . . . why I cried on 1 May. Oh, how good is it to kiss . . . kiss . . . kiss. You will help me, Buluś and God.

AUGUST 25, 1941, MONDAY[15]

On Friday there was the 1st letter from Mama, then a 2nd, then 3rd, and then dread, a horrible fear for her life and ours, and everyone's. My heart's been so heavy since this morning and now and always I'm calling to God and placing our fates in His hands. He's the only one who's never disappointed me; He will hear my voice. I want Him to protect Mom and return her to me from far away. God, protect her and all of us from everything that is evil and protect my Zygu from the evil that can happen to him. I'm suffering today, but I thank You that in those horrible days of the turmoil of war You have sent me a bright ray of light. I'm writing down what I feel, and I feel gratitude, deep, sincere, immortal.

Zygu talked to me like nobody else apart from my mother . . . He said he felt sorry for me and that I deserve happiness in the future for the things I am suffering now, and know, Zygu, that it is for always! He said that the hearth and home is only needful in childhood, but I know he wanted to console me. Good, darling Zygu! I am not worthy of you even in part. You wanted to substitute my mother with those caresses and console me, that's what you said. Zyguś, my Mama will give me those maternal caresses, and these ones, they console me very much. You will help me, Buluś and God. God protect Mama and us all. God and my entreaties will help you, Mama.

AUGUST 27, 1941

War! War! No end in sight. I would like to write something, but I can't. I'm dreaming, dreaming, dreaming. All that's left are dreams, hope, and what . . . what's left to you, Zyguś, yes, and me too. Oh, to see my mother just for a moment. You will help me, Buluś and God.

AUGUST 28, 1941, THURSDAY

It's no use moaning, "Don't cry, don't cry, it won't do." It's what must be, it's necessary for us to walk with our heads lowered now, to run along streets, to shiver. For the meanest streetwalker to provoke and insult me in Zygu's presence and he can't help me, or I him. Trifles, really, but it is very, very hard. I've felt a little confused since Zygu's lecture about Nietzsche, Werne* and their ideology, about how he's for young marriages, "childless for now." You know, my attitude to those "serious" matters is awfully silly and childish. For example I completely do not understand that Rena who works with Zygu and says that I have "a unique face," but do you understand me? Well, yes, you know! No, this has nothing to do with her. What is it really that makes me feel indignant, or worried, or bored?

> *Rejoice, rejoice*
> *this is your feast*
> *oh gutter, cellar, tavern, inn*
> *the world is yours, we are your toys*
> *streetwalker with a nasty grin*
> *today you bully, yell, and curse*
> *you bring me low and make me worse*
> *you, flowing here on gutter's scum*
> *from what is lowest, rotten, vile*
> *the only homeland you have got*
> *is a pile of trash and a lustful smile*
> *Your day—remember*

---

* Renia possibly means Werner May, the author of *Deutscher National-Katechismus.*

you'll see the day
when I will spit, not turn away
you and "your" lover, vermin both,
will travel back to swamp and sloth
in which you brood, cavort and sway
And I will . . . no!
Although I hate
My contempt and disgust are too great
Your kin, your sins, you cursed one
Mean that to you no harm is done
Like snakes and worms that live in filth
Because they would not be killed—just despised

You will help me, Buluś and God.

SEPTEMBER 1, 1941

A year ago . . . Oh, a whole year has gone by. I've experienced so much good and bad. But perhaps more good. Maybe Mama will come soon after all. Today Z came and I felt some sort of thing when he said, "Well, talk as if we're married." With that Hala—a trifle and that thing, you know, with the one from the photograph, also a trifle. Generally every-thing is a trifle, apart from my mad love. Oh, God, how I love him, how much. Even though he thinks I'm the opposite of dynamite, still . . . ha ha ha! I gave him a photograph to whet the appetite. I haven't seen Maciek in a long time. Despite everything, I like Maciek. Why do I give away that I'm jealous? You will help me, Buluś and God. And you, Mama, come as soon as you can!

SEPTEMBER 10, 1941, SUNDAY*

And sometimes it's like it was today. And today it's—I don't know—today it seems to me that everything is stupid, love, and him, and life, and all the daily matters. Everything in reality that is stripped of its romantic

---

* September 10, 1941, was a Wednesday.

ornaments and flourishes is odious. No! Not odious, just genuine, just how it truly is. And on days like today it feels that this can be soothed by music, light, resonant . . . Yes, on those days all that's left is music and dreams. But not the dreams related to reality, those that are pink, but still connected to life, no! Detached, fragrant, colorful dreams—like poetry. Ah, I would like to know how to play beautifully. One can conjure the soul's every state with music—to only know how. Today I feel an aversion toward love, no, not for the first time. It is unfair, I know, but I don't understand that today, I can't believe in anything. Today it's good to listen and think . . .

> *My chiming song, keep sailing so*
> *Across the Danube's deep blue flow*
> *Through waves that glitter like a star*
> *Carry on, song . . . far*

So I'm thinking, and thinking, and dreaming, and mocking life's worries, gossip, jealousy and love, I don't know . . .

> *Life is some ugly, worthless stuff*
> *stripped of its charms, it's bare and rough*
> *so calculating, hard, and dry*
> *dirty and daft, though you may try*
> *it's lewd and boring and it's weird*
> *with stuff you cried at, hurt at, feared*
> *it's cruel, noisy, and it's mocking*
> *two-faced and empty and so shocking . . .*
> *J. Strauss**

> *My chiming song, keep sailing so*
> *across the Danube's deep blue flow*
> *through waves that glitter like a star*
> *Where tears and grief no longer are*
> *in a land of dreams*

---

* Poems inspired by the waltz "The Blue Danube", composed by Johann Strauss in 1867.

wind and the clouds swap poses
and there's a sea down below
of orange flowers and roses
and dusks and dawns are pale green
and the dreams are just like mists
colored . . . and nothing's felt or seen
but ethereal and full of shimmer
ever so light and unreal
fragrant and dreamy in feel
slow, dizzy, and lazy
careless and hazy
dreams
fragrant, bright and ever sweet
loveliest, when senses never meet . . .

SEPTEMBER 11, 1941, THURSDAY

4 in the afternoon. I need to leave the house. I am simply escaping Zygu. If this had happened, let's say, a month or two ago, I'd have cried my eyes out and screamed that he's foul! Not today—nothing at all, as if nothing's happened. It's strange . . . and yet I can't even say myself whether I'm at least a little sorry. I don't know if it's over, but this is exactly what I've been suspecting on the "subject." A woman senses it, oh, yes, she has a well-developed warning system. You know, I don't even hate "the other one," I will admit I find her somewhat attractive, like Natasha does Katya. But this whole thing is a little different, although I've also been hurt—but never humiliated! I'll see you again today, I'm going to Norka's. To my only Nora I've got left. I've also got you, Mama, and you, dear Diary, and it's almost like it used to be. Only there is no yearning left for something close . . . unknown . . . To be clearheaded about what I feel, I'd say this: I very much want to impress them with something, I very much want to take my revenge in the same way, but for the sake of revenge itself, for— pleasure. I used to despise this attitude and today I admit it's awful and when I perhaps become such an easy girl, it will only be your fault, Z, and my jealousy's, that sacred feelings, sacred rules and sacred love have been desecrated . . . You will help me, Buluś and God.

SEPTEMBER 14, 1941

But still—it's sad, so very sad, so utterly, so horribly . . . I didn't tell you that evening about him coming—what for, anyway? I didn't want to tell you anything because I felt that I loved him the most then. And now—I do not. I'm waiting. Waiting's tired me out. And I'm afraid of tomorrow and I want it to come already, and I feel aversion, and doubt. And sometimes I don't want to say anything, only think and be silent. And sometimes I want to be evil and hated, I want to spite everyone, I want to torment and hurt everyone—no, not everyone, not him, and not her either. But really I'm only sad, utterly, horribly sad . . . Sad, but I can't cry, I simply do not have the strength. So I look at the wild ivy, how raindrops stream down its leaves, and somehow it feels like I'm crying.

> *Springtime—fresh and green*
> *a wild vine climbs*
> *rises full of life*
> *onto the balcony glass.*
> *It reddens in the summer,*
> *pales with the autumn winds*
> *and hangs its head, in sorrow,*
> *sad for what now must pass.*
>
> *I like sun and the flowers in spring*
> *When I also feel a joyful thing*
> *when the laughter's in me and nearby*
> *When around me life can abound*
> *When the earth is all joyful all round*
> *like me!*
>
> *And when I am both angry and sad*
> *then I like a gray day, wet and bad,*
> *and a cloudy and tearful dark sky*
> *crying just like my heart, full of rain,*

quiet, full of tiresome pain
like me . . .

That's when I like a mist on a hill
and a sadness that wants yearning still
and the voids you can't calmly pass by
Polish verses, of autumn, of tears,
that are filled with the sadness and fears
like me.

No, I didn't mean to write that, but I'm very, very sad. Ah! What a rainy, nice day. You will help me, Buluś and God.

SEPTEMBER 18, 1941, THURSDAY

How good that I didn't write throughout this week. I didn't write or I would have blasphemed. I suffered, that's true, and a lot too—but now it's fine again, perhaps even better than it had been. Because every time there's a bit of a worry and some crying, and hours spent thinking, I am more convinced that I love my wonderful boy very, very much. And an apology—although one can't really talk of apologies if one were not angry—confirms this conviction too. So it will be even better than it had been, because Arianka is at Mama's and she's to bring her here, and maybe I'll finally see her. Ah, I've let it slip; it was supposed to be a surprise. Everything at once, oh God—really, how can I thank You? Now I believe in happy endings . . . I believe and trust You, for You have given me what I asked for. I love You. You will help me, Buluś and God.

SEPTEMBER 22, 1941, MONDAY

Now the dream has practically come true. It's the New Year* today and the dream has come true? Actually not completely, but in 99% it did. And I wish all dreams came true like this. It feels so strange. To think that

---

* The year 5702 of the Jewish calendar started that day.

Mama is so close, that she's in the same city, that she's thinking about me now, that she'd like to embrace me as much as I her . . . to think there's a horrible river, a river people have made horrible. A river which has been separating us for two years—and now again. Why, it's unthinkable that I can't see Mother when she's here so close, so close. Arianka, I'm so jealous, she is with her. And now she will leave again and I won't even kiss her. I won't say anything and again—but for how long—and again this question, when? But still, there's a weight off my heart that it's not so far, that You have brought her closer to me, Good Lord God. How good would it be if I could tell her everything, tell her about today and those past two years? You know, Mama, I am who I have always been, your reticent one, all "yours," but maybe I feel somehow more, well, I don't feel that good. All because of Z. I don't know why, I'm abashed by this thing I've dreamed of? Why do all those kisses only burn me up after he leaves? I start to feel everything, I writhe on the sofa, I don't sleep, my senses are stimulated to their limit. And when "this" happens, when it lasts two hours, then Z. doesn't have to threaten me with bromide injections etc. Why? I don't know . . . but I know, that is, I feel instinctively, that much has changed about Zygu, I can't say whether for better or for worse, because I "generally have no firm opinion about anything, damn it," but the changes are surely there. It even seems that, er, well, I don't know . . . In any case there is a distinct influence of that "freethinking and free-doing" woman. And I have a stupid, odious, irritating feeling, aah! I am an idiot of the highest order that I can even say something against the prettiest boy and besides, I know that I love him very, very much anyway—but still, I am horribly upset, and I think I already know why, namely! Because I am stupider and uglier than he is, and I stand lower in every respect. "What can I do apart from writing poems?" Well, but do not try to persuade me that you have to teach me everything, because you don't know everything yourself, you have no idea. Blind leading the blind. But I feel much better now, I love you so much now, dear Diary! Phew, what a relief. I'm not telling you the silly details; it's better this way. Although they're not so silly, they're sweet, but always, well . . . the secretiveness. It's much better now, oh, almost good. So good night, Mama mine, I can say this to you for the first time in two years. You won't hear me, but I know that you're thinking about me too and wishing me a good night. Mama, come to me. Come, my only Bunia. You're the only one who always loves me steadily and you don't laugh at me. Bye, Mama, sleep well; may you dream that everything I prayed for yesterday comes true. Today I wish for a favorable end of the war, for my parents to reconcile, Zyguś for me only and good things for everyone. You will help me, Buluś and God.

SEPTEMBER 29, 1941, MONDAY[16]

I'm on this side. You know, I'm here with Mama. Just think, I have finally found myself beyond the river and met with Mama. How did I get here? It's a secret. Know only that I've been through a lot and was very scared. I am still afraid of Wednesday. The dream has practically come true, I'm seeing Mom and I've got a letter from Zygu. I'm still waiting for something in politics and I know it will happen, like that other thing did. You will help me, Buluś and God.

OCTOBER 5, 1941

For Buluś (letter to Mother). I love you so, so much, and "I love the eyes that are green." Yours, Renia.

> *A ship sails for a haven after a gale*
> *A bird that's scared away returns to hide in its nest*
> *A child, in trust, chooses its mother's arms . . .*
> *to cry its grief away, and soothe the pain as it knows best.*

For Buluś:

> *When pain starts burning*
> *Or you feel the hearts' frosty chill*
> *When you feel ground to dust*
> *By the turning wheels of life*
> *Shelter under her wings*
> *She'll hear you out and understand she will*
> *You will feel good again and free from strife.*

There's sadness for those who are in grief and pain
Pity for those whose hearts were broken again
Shame on those who face both contempt and fear
But you're really unhappy without your mother dear
I suffocate in small rooms
And feel crowded in vast halls
They won't bring down the sadness
Even if it tumbles and falls
In life's vast, great expanse
The winds of life blow wild
They'll blow away all sorrows
For one sweet moment mild!
   6 duvet covers
   8 pillow slips
   2 small pillows
   3 sheets
   2 tablecloths

OCTOBER 9, 1941, THURSDAY

I haven't seen you for such a long, long time. I've missed you. I was unable to talk, to write. So many thoughts have gathered in my head, they have made it heavy, although this little head of mine is usually light and empty. And now I don't know where to start? So much has happened . . . So maybe I'll tell you briefly. I've dreamed through the dream. I was with Mama and it seemed so wonderful, so extraordinary, this thing which for others is so wonderful and natural. But then also my mother is different. She is a friend, a peer. And now I'm back on the other side, yearning and wanting again. But listen, my dearest Diary, listen and listen, because it seems to me that you're praying for me, that your prayers are being answered, you sweet little notebook that contains the depths of my soul. Mama writes me letters, so long, heartfelt and loving that I must cry. But that is nothing, I still believe! I believe in God, in you and in Mother. I believe it will be like Zyguś says. We'll survive this war somehow, and later . . . ah, will it really be like he says? Anyway, we'll both see, you and I, and either we'll be disappointed, or perhaps we will be happy after all, you and I. Because if I laugh, how could you be sad, you "little looking glass" of mine (this is what Buluś called you)?

> *My own diary can be just as cheerful*
> *Or nasty and mean as me*
> *After all, we went to school*
> *Together, and to dates, and a game*
> *to see . . .*
> *So it has just the same wild ideas*
> *the same laughter and yells and tears*
> *there's more bad and less good there to see*
> *because just like me, it's hard to bear*
> *sometimes shy, sometimes with a lewd stare*
> *sometimes trusty and the one faithful friend*
> *or a grump on whom you cannot depend*
> *my own diary is really just me*
> *But on days when I'm really in trouble*
> *it becomes my own soul's little double*
> *there inside—both in dreams and in verse*
> *in the yearning and each moment that hurts*
> *every word is as sad as can be*
> *where it's poor, and afraid, and it's shy,*
> *where it's sad with no tears left to cry,*
> *there my diary really is me.*

Yes, yes, this is what I'm like. I'm just one of millions of girls walking through this world—uglier than some, prettier than others, but still, different from all of them. Zyguś, he's also different from everyone, he's so good and wonderful, and subtle, and sensitive . . .

They came over with Maciek once, Zyguś got angry with me, because I behaved as if I didn't know him. I didn't do it on purpose; I didn't want to distress him. Poor Zyguś couldn't sleep. But he's no longer angry. Mama, why do you say I shouldn't drown in those green, deceptive eyes? Can you not see, I have already drowned, but those eyes are not deceptive?

I really like it when Z talks seriously about medicine, the future and so on. It makes me want to laugh a little, but it feels very good and blissful, as if Buluś was wishing me a good night. You know, I told him about that whole affair with RK, that I was distraught, that I went through hell. What for? Although I might tell him as much as possible, for now I've packed it into a separate suitcase and left in the "lumber room of the soul." In fact, it doesn't even hurt anymore, and I don't think about it.

Z became my guardian, he said he would take care of me. As a matter of fact Buluś asked them to, all three of them. But Z must tell Maciek that he doesn't need to do it. All in all, Zygmunt and Maciek are friends, real friends, but . . . but. It's good that I can write it all out. I feel the load in my heart and my head lightening. I can't describe "it all" with Zygu, and you know why, because now it's much more than when it could still be described. No descriptions, but it sinks deep into the heart and surrounds his image there with a beautifully warm, golden halo.

Mama, forgive me that I can't heed your words. You see, I can't, I can't do it any other way, it is always like this—whole heart, whole adoration, whole being. I really can't, not even from the outside. Maybe, maybe I will love somebody else in my life, but if so—it will be the same. It's this or nothing.

Zygu wants to read you and he said, "You'll see, we'll be reading it together when I'm a doctor and I will laugh and you will laugh." I hope he said it at an auspicious hour. I thought about how I've put in new pages which may last until the time when, when . . . well, anyway, it can be later or much earlier, and you will be my friend no matter what, even if you're scandalized and red with anger, so what of it?

Zygu wants me to remain what I am, Buluś would like that too—and me? I am very curious . . . anyway, let them be happy! But "everything in the world passes slowly." I love all three of you, each one differently, and you too. I think it will be like in my dreams, grant me that, Lord, and you, Buluś, give me your blessings. You will help me, Buluś and God.

OCTOBER 10, 1941, FRIDAY[17]

It's so sad at home. Today the piano was taken away, so the flat is empty; today Arianka went to Mama, so the soul is empty. It's cold and dark, and lonely, and somehow . . . aah, I'm left all alone and all I have is a letter from Buluś, or rather letters. I'll write a poem here. Actually I've put everything I feel and experience in the letter to Mama. And now I'm cold and my eyelids are drooping, and my fingers are numb. I'll go to bed, but not to sleep, no! I'll daydream a little, maybe I'll feel lighter. I'll think about being with Buluś, that the world is so good and warm and sunny, we open the windows and the lovely scent of the full carnations from Stawki enters the house. Or that it's a cloudy, rainy autumn and I've got a cozy room with a fireplace. It is this little house that Zyguś and I live in, working there in the evenings in the glow of the fire. And I write, write a lot and my legs aren't cold like now. And then I go to another room and our children are sleeping there, the wonderful angels, none sweeter. But it must be warm, must absolutely be warm, because my fingers are awfully cold.

It's stupid what I think about when I'm so alone and they leave, when the cold days will be full of yearning again. Buluś, but you'll come back soon. I'm off to daydream, after all God remembers about me, perhaps He will really make those dreams come true . . . Renia. You will help me, Buluś and God.

OCTOBER 17, 1941, FRIDAY

I'm alone again. I have already had a letter from Buluś, from Warsaw. Jarosia is away too. Bimba* is ill, Dido nervous and tormenting me especially—and I am alone. But am I really alone, no! I've got a whole guard of dreams, lovely, delicate, shy, and I've got you, and Zygu, and Nora.

Meetings with Zygu are so pleasant, ever more pleasant. He's even more wonderful than I thought, this "guardian" of mine.

Norka is teaching me English now. I'm learning eagerly, but I would learn French even more eagerly, and I will! Learn with all my might to speak French. After all, nobody can take knowledge away from me. I must learn, I promise myself that. All that I can. Maybe one day I will really go to the faraway France of my dreams—no, not I—we will go. Yes. "Z will be driving a Buick, and I'll be sleeping with my head on his shoulder. And then he'll enroll me in Collège de France. And he'll buy

---

* Renia's grandmother.

me the sort of bedroom I frequently travel to in my thoughts." Zyguś can dream aloud so beautifully, like a big child. And in the meantime Z. is preparing bloody revenge against me for those Sanok influences. I have some regrets perhaps, but he'll have his revenge. I can't help it that he's so tyrannical and firm, tough luck. His character is absolute. But I'd rather agree to everything than finish this, and that's that! Maybe we'll see each other tomorrow. You will help me, Buluś and God.

OCTOBER 25, 1941, SATURDAY

You're pretty now, handsome, bound . . . I've started missing you, being able to write. I want to write a lot, a lot, so many confused thoughts linger in my head. Zygu says he absolutely must read you, and I don't want to think about it, because then I'd write dishonestly (as it is, there are places where I'm not delighted with my honesty), I'd write for him then, and at the same time not for him, because this diary would not be genuine. Still, your sad pages are the sweetest, at least they're not so banal—he said, she said. But so it goes, when one's pleased, delighted with something, one's words get all confused in the enthusiasm and there are only cries of oh, ah, this and that!

And now, now I should study, after all I'm no longer at school, after all I need to do something for the future, after all I'm already 17! And it's just now that some lazy, awful apathy grips me, brr, I can't be bothered to do anything at all now . . . Now I stand at the window and watch the wild ivy getting wet, look at various people moving in the street and think about their worries and how they feel. Or I look at the women and think about which one has already had intercourse and what did she look like then? Yes, this one is old and wrinkled, but she used to be young and then . . . and this one, how strange, and that one . . . it's all laughable . . . poverty in its rags is laughable, people pinched with cold and hunger are laughable, and how laughable is the man afraid of the soldier, talking to him, smiling, standing at attention, bobbing . . . ? An old man in front of a youth. And prisoners? Those swaying, blackened skeletons, how funny the way they rock on those spindly legs, and how squeaky and quiet their voices—they're also laughable, laughable—it makes me feel faint. I go to the stove then, lean against it and daydream . . . Because what else is there to do? And even if there was, I can't be bothered about anything anyway . . . I somehow, strangely, can't be bothered about absolutely anything . . . Or maybe I can, yes! About dreams coming true . . . You will help me, Buluś and God.

OCTOBER 29, 1941, WEDNESDAY

All day yesterday and today I have wanted to talk to you. Yesterday I felt so bad, so sad and empty . . . I had this awful feeling of an "inability to act." I thought about learning mathematics and shorthand writing, and a language; I wanted to do it with all my soul, but at the same time I knew that I wouldn't raise a finger to do it, I knew my hands wouldn't obey and I myself would turn out to be powerless. Mama is right. Someone always has to give me directions, order me around, force me into things, even if I myself want them. And now Mama's far away again with Jarosia, and "the one for me," in Buluś's words, he can't, because he has no power over me, and generally it's not that . . . Now I'm sinking into some sort of stupor and what is it?—an aversion? I don't think so. I was thinking yesterday and I said this to Nora, "You know, Norka, I'm tired of life." This sentence coming out of a 17-year-old girl's mouth amuses me, and it's not accurate. It's not life I'm tired of, because after all I haven't really lived yet; I'm tired of anticipation, idleness, and maybe precisely the desire for life. Because not so long ago there was a time when I was intoxicated with sensual love, kisses, caresses, touches, and all this was enough for me, so much so that I forgot one can desire something more. Now? No! Now I have come to my senses. Have I rejected that? No! It's equally important as what is now.

> Don't look for solace only in the senses
> they burn bright as a flame, fade away just so
> If you look to your comfort in learning, then hence it's
> where your thirst will be quenched, where your soul did go

Yes, that soul's lying there, and not moving at all, though I myself often move away. I will give you an example, proof, or maybe not, not proof, well, judge for yourself. Yesterday at 5 p.m. I was supposed to go to Nora's for an English lesson. It took me ages to set out, I was putting it off (anyway, Nora couldn't have been at home yet). So I was all the more still, just watching the pretty, colorful, carefree film scenes. My dreams made up this film. And any moment would break the plot, so although the hands of the clock were rushing onward mercilessly, I didn't leave my chair, what for? It would be like leaving the cinema during a screening. Still, I went. I went, but . . . not to Nora's. I went, of all places, to Belania, to Helka, to Giza, those girls one meets most frequently, just those completely normal girls. I wanted to listen to their conversations, their thoughts, their plans; I went "for a bit of gossip." The whole "gang" wasn't there, only Belania. That was enough for me. Belania is, after all, the life and soul of the group, she's the cleverest and most intelligent of them all. I came, I sat down, I listened to some news, then I told her what I knew, and I asked, "All right, so what do you talk about every day?" "Food," says Belania. "What do you dream about?" "About once eating so much I can't stand up." Well, I knew everything then. Was I disappointed? Maybe not, to an extent I'd been prepared for it. I knew, and even agreed with Belania that it's best to have four "sweethearts," each of them of a different nationality. So I returned to my interrupted film. I really do prefer that to baked potatoes. It's good that there's something to tear me away from sorting out breakfast, lunch, dinner and breakfast again. I am glad, after all, to have my colorful, faraway film. Nora dreams too, but differently, in a more real, logical way. My fantasies are unrelated to everything, except, perhaps, my vivid, very vivid imagination. Maybe I never properly appreciated Nora. She is admirable. She's eager to learn and there's a readiness about her, but not just readiness—she does learn, she reads all she can (but never worthless books). Nora is a well-rounded person, the sort of girl you don't meet anymore. She says she's matured this year. I would say she's even more noble now, because "suffering ennobles one," and she's been through so much—she even "didn't dare to dream." And here, again, a difference between our dreams. Norka, she's so brave, after all she's got nobody, she's all alone (with that faraway "pretty boy"), and me, if I'd been alone, without Zygu? God forbid, maybe I'd break down, and maybe I'd do what she does . . . But no, I don't want to! I just don't have the strength. I would have to walk alone, and otherwise I can at least imagine that I'm supported by someone's arm, by "His" arm. Will the war end soon, God grant us that. Tomorrow I'll probably see Zygu, perhaps chat to you too. You will help me, Buluś and God.

NOVEMBER 3, 1941, MONDAY

Since we last saw each other I've often felt like sitting down with you and crying. I've felt so bad at times. Dido and Bimba are nervous and vent their whole anger on me, keep reminding me how they've deigned to let me stay with them etc. Parents would never say that to their own child, but they're not my parents after all. So sometimes (when I wake from my fantasies) I am terrified by what's happening around me. But this only lasts a moment and then I fall asleep again.

Buluś is there with Jarusia. They will come here to me. I'd like her to be with me, I want her to leave Warsaw (typhus), but I'm afraid of this stay. Buluś is so sensitive. She'd be very hurt by a statement like that. It hurts me too. I am strangely sensitive about it and I feel like great, great harm is done to me . . . In fact I don't cry often—but I always cry when it happens. I'd like to snuggle into something warm and nice then, and settle into a comfy armchair, and throw those worries into a roaring fireplace, and soar again. Such is my catlike nature that I need warmth (yes, Buluś, you know), much, much warmth, all the more for how little I've experienced it in life. Because apart from you and Jarosia nobody in the world can give it to me. Maybe you'll think—him? No, he gives a fire that explodes and dies down. I feel it, I feel it all, because I'm sensitive.

Guess who paid me a visit today? Ludwik! I've actually been thinking about him lately. Today he came over (by chance); we had a very lively two-hour conversation. He is perhaps prettier than last time and very handsome, dashingly stylish and well mannered, not especially educated and conceitedly vain. He talked of his victories and popularity, flirted with me from time to time and had the pleasant feeling that I was impressed. I was pleased with him etc. He probably noticed that I blushed when he came in, but that doesn't matter, because it's in my nature to blush and that's that. Well, but Ludwik doesn't know this. Anyway, it was nice to chat. I'd like to have some company already, ours, kindred.

I'm learning French now and reading books (quite good) and Nora and I are studying ancient history. Apart from that I do nothing, I don't listen to what people say, I prefer to listen to "birds in the bush" chirping.

When Ludwik was casting coquettish glances at me, I didn't react, don't think some other eyes have overwhelmed me, I've just got used to it. Ah, if only they could come as soon as possible!

Zygu hasn't come on Thursday or today. I wonder what is stopping him, but really I don't. Today I forgot myself that he was supposed to come. But on Saturday . . . I think he came, yes, wearing a winter coat, brr . . . He brought such a chill . . . So, Buluś, when will you come to your poor, lonely orphan and non-orphan? You will help me, Buluś and God. A fireplace is the pinnacle of my dreams? And how!!!

> *There's a blizzard raging outside*
> *All you see is a white cloud of snow*
> *All the world, all the people, each soul,*
> *Snow and wind are beginning to hide . . .*
>
> *Someone weaves all their dreams in a shawl*
> *Or remembers, and then smiles sweet and wide*
> *There's a fire cracking warmly inside*
> *You can wrap up in tales, stay, don't go*
>
> *This is my tiny little dream home*
> *where my soul always yearns to find rest*
> *a home full of pale yellowing memories*
> *a hearth full of motherly warmth*
>
> *A cold night, there's a big blizzard on*
> *In my home it is cozy and bright*
> *from old dreams, little lives being born*
> *I can put them to sleep, rocking light*
> *Fetch some wood so the fire's not gone*
> *And my worries can fade in the night*
>
> *This morning our grandma*
> *sat herself today*

reading a thick old notebook
she can't put away.
She's been reading squiggles
filling page after page,
nodding and then grumbling
"foolish, youthful age"
she's been turning pages
crossed out, scribbled on,
with faded hearts—which could be red
but the ink's all gone
from all long ago,
a time since so great . . .
Our grandma's been sitting,

reading date by date.
Sometimes she would smile,
take another look,
say again, "oh, the youth"
and smile at her book.
The grandkids wouldn't know it, but the book's not done
Among these old pages
A former grandma lives on
They won't know that from that page can waft, flow, or spurt
tears that don't turn bitter
griefs that do not hurt.

NOVEMBER 4, 1941, TUESDAY

I'm glad that's what I'm like
Little, round, and stout
because if I were slender
I'd fly up like on a cloud.
I'd fly up far away
Chasing dreams around
Then what force would there be
Pulling me back to ground?

Buluś . . . ? Zyguś . . . ? Life . . . ?

I like it when a wide road is rocking
Under the weight of the trucks
When a shrill street-side silence
Is pierced by a claxon's blast
As the steady rhythmic shocks
Shake a line and a house and a lamp
And the hum and the speed hang above us
Like a current rushing past
Till the trucks press the tarmac and shove its
lazy flow to each side till it spreads
And flows off the road and it sweats
In this frost

NOVEMBER 6, 1941, THURSDAY

I have such pangs of conscience, and I'm so upset! It's all because of Bimba, anyway the fault is entirely mine. I was actually only five minutes late—such a short time—and yet so long. It's been a whole week now. God, let me make it all right on Saturday. Will I, will we meet? I am to copy poems with Nora now. You will help me, Buluś and God.

NOVEMBER 7, 1941, FRIDAY[18]

Again a day came when all former worries faded. Ghetto! That word is ringing in our ears, it terrifies, it torments. We don't know what will happen to us, where we'll go and what they'll let us take. God, I believe in You, that wherever we'll be, You will not desert us. Last night everyone was packing, we were ordered to leave our apartments before 2 p.m. with 25 kilograms of possessions. Maybe there will be a ghetto, but it seems that we will definitely have to move out of the main streets either way. God, I know You heard me a moment ago, when I was petrified and my heart was fluttering so!

At 10:30 last night, suddenly the doorbell rang, and who was there? The police! I pressed my hands to my face then and I called You, oh

God, and You heard me. It was a policeman from our old village, from Torskie,* and he let himself be bribed. I reminded him of the good times, the friends, the revels, and somehow it worked. And now I'm asking You, oh Great One, I'm asking you—I, a speck of dust, I without father or mother here, a poor one . . . If those lonely, desolate voices have any power, then listen to my call, too!

Today I got a postcard from Mama. It touched and moved me strangely. Because in all the turmoil of the day I felt that I have someone who loves me, who cares about me. At the same time I felt the powerlessness of that love; my poor faraway Mama can't help me at all. Mama, I know what you're going through there, but know that I'm suffering here too and going through things that can make one's hair go white. But I believe in you and God. He has saved you from so many disasters, led you through so many dangers, because I was praying then and begging Him: save her, save my mother! He listened to me then, so He will help me, help us now too. Ah, if I only knew what's better?! For you to be with us, or over there with Jarosia? I don't know, I don't know, I don't know! "I'm sending Renusia a package"—so God has not forsaken me yet if someone out there is saying this, because the world is alien and cold, and this is heartfelt, like my prayers are heartfelt. My Beloved Mama, I never think you're hurting me, even if you said as much to me, I wouldn't believe you. Because your letters, postcards, your words exude love and concern, and something as warm as—I don't know. God, listen to my prayer, solve the puzzle You have given to people. I hope Zygu comes tomorrow, so that I'll have someone to complain to. Help us, God, and bless us.

NOVEMBER 8, 1941, SATURDAY

First and foremost thanks be to You, and secondly I shall deliberate over an issue brought up today by Zygu. I need to consider it carefully, mull it over and understand. This is how it started! It started with him saying that I'm childish, that I've got a child's mentality, that I have not matured psychically to the level of my 17 years. Actually at first he said that it's usually the boy who's not mature, doesn't think about the future or

---

* A village near Zaleszczyki, now part of Ukraine.

marriage, only the girl does. And in our "relationship" it is different, i.e., the opposite. But I don't think it is opposite at all—I do think seriously. So I told him he doesn't know me at all. Then Z took the offensive and accused me of being like a doll that he plays with and if he presses a button, it makes me react; he said I'm passive, that he didn't know this until our first "real" meeting. He kept adding that it's not an accusation and that I shouldn't consider it a reproach. Finally he said I'm like the North Sea, or the Arctic Ocean, or ice, that I have no initiative, in a word—I lack temperament! He said that his friends had already mentioned this to him (ridiculous, but I've known that since the beginning). He set, say, Rena K. (whom he apparently finds attractive) as an example, or rather didn't set her as an example but compared us, said that it's impossible to talk to me seriously about this, that it would be easier with Irka. He asked whether I have anything against him or if there's anything I don't like. I told him that yes, indeed, but I can say that to everyone else, but not him, and that he's right—there are many things he doesn't know, but I'm not to blame for that, at least not for all of it. Why? And how do I explain that I've gone through various periods ever since we first met. You know it best; you know them all, dear Diary. Wouldn't you agree, then, that I've been crazy for . . . love, that I sometimes clutched at the table so as not to fling my arms around him, that I had sleepless nights, tortured, tormented by the senses? But you see, this has passed somehow, at first it was hard to hold back, then it got easier, and then not at all. And then, back then, couldn't I have told you all that you blame me for today? Couldn't I have accused you of the same thing? Be fair, Zygu! It is possible that back then those old rules stood in my way, those great-grandma-ish opinions about love and a girl's attitude to it. But May came and I was, again, ready for . . . anything, and you were "passive" again. Then I waited for it impatiently, partly in desire, partly in curiosity. And then (on that first June night—it can't be called that), when you judged me, I judged you and . . . I was disappointed . . . Know that it was you who made me timid with your timid kiss. But it's true that I've unearthed this piece of information from the unconscious and only now too. Or maybe even when Belania asked me, "But the question is whether Zygu is a good kisser," and I said, "I don't know." But that doesn't mean I didn't love you then. I loved then and now, and always, only I had to cast off what overwhelmed me after you left, and anyway I am not reproaching you either, just telling the truth, to clarify misunderstandings, as you say yourself. But it needs to be said that you are not a good psychologist if you want to achieve a better result by what you said. In fact, in order to understand each other we'd need to talk seriously, unashamed by any-thing, we'd need to reach back into the past, etc. etc. And I can't bear to do that yet, maybe in 2–3 years, as you say, so perhaps you're right after all when you say I've got a childish mentality? That is the whole misfortune right there—you are usually right, and even when you're not, you some-how end up being right after all. And as for me, words are definitely not my forte, at most I can write everything down, and this happens only after you leave . . . Naturally you'll tell all this to Nora, as you'd guessed she will say I'm right. Ah, if Buluś were here too, she'd understand me. I could also show this . . . What had been written here absolutely does not stand anymore, so I erased it. I'm going to the Teich girl's tomorrow with the latest poems. Here's to feelings. You will help me, Buluś and God.

NOVEMBER 10, 1941, MONDAY

I got a package from Buluś. My darling Buluś and lovely Jarosia! I'll write them a thank-you card. We have reached an understanding with Zygu, it wasn't the way I interpreted it last time, after all. It was supposed to be friendly advice. So finally we're on the right track, although Zygu is to tell me many more things still. So now it's all right, but before it was—God have mercy! Zygu was irritable and sweaty with the effort; I was on the verge of tears. I wanted to say everything that I'd decided on dur-ing those past two nights and . . . I couldn't. The situation was so tragic that the phrase "break up" even came up. Now I'm smiling when writing this (even though I've got horrible menstrual cramps), but I really was worried and didn't know how to resolve the situation. I'm glad it ended well. I'm feeling strangely light, oh, good. I've got a very pleasant feeling, how—and I actually owe it to Zygu. By the way, nobody has ever taught me such a lesson before. Well, but he was right, I have to give him that. When things get better, we'll meet.

Open your hearts your souls out wide!
living is easier with less to hide
few things hurt more or bring more sorrow
than a grudge you choose to bear till tomorrow
until a thought you could nearly forget
awakes again, and brings more regret . . .

Maybe the bells should suddenly ring
and rouse a half-healed, half-buried sting
Open your hearts your souls out wide!
living is brighter with less to hide
Why choose the grudge, the guilt, the moping?
Open your hearts—to hearts wide open

NOVEMBER 14, 1941, FRIDAY

I should've written much more, really. But you know, back then . . . I couldn't, then I didn't want to, maybe I'll write more tomorrow. Know only that much has changed in life, in friendship, and in this (I don't know what to call it?), moods have changed, and maybe even . . . I did. Have I really changed? Or did I just pour out my feelings to myself and you? In any case I will write all the poems now, I've decided; at worst I won't show them to anyone. I was horribly angry yesterday at again being told I'm childish, so I announced to her that by now I have definitely matured and I do not want to hear it ever again. And tomorrow I'll tell you something interesting, something really interesting, you'll see. I was going to tell you today, but no . . . tomorrow. So you will help me, Buluś and God.

NOVEMBER 16, 1941, SUNDAY

We only met the day after tomorrow, because today is the day after to-morrow. And I haven't really wrapped up that issue. Zygu read all that I have written and . . . that's that. Now thanks to everything I've been through myself, and to what Zygu told me, I'm closer again to this life, the real one. Speaking out was necessary. Because if all those unspoken matters had accumulated, one day a flood could happen, destroying the bridge, yes, the bridge that connects us. And we've just built dams and reservoirs, and pools, precisely because we've been open with each other.

It's the same with Nora. Our long friendship has also had its stages. At times we would be close, cordial, and then we'd grow apart for long months even. And was that good? Was that heavy silence right? Why didn't she or I say to the other, "Listen, I don't like this, don't do this, that hurts me"? And there would've been an explanation, and it would've been fine. Why did we never, ever behave openly? We were friends after all! But it always somehow worked out that we found each other again. Because we were and are (it seems to me) made for each other, because we are kindred souls and I doubt, very much doubt whether we could find a third one who'd understand us (Irka—and Irka, I do not even want to mention her, that would be a profanation of our friendship). For now there's nobody like that in our circles. We are, in every respect, in the same situation and we can truly understand one another. And Nora is growing up now, growing through me, through my growth. And me? What do I know? And even if I do know, I can't write it down, because there's so, so, so much of it.

The thing with Rena K., although I was aware of it—or rather sensed it—after all I didn't know what it really was. And it was 1 mm more than I thought, or 1 mm less. But Maciek is to tell me all about it. I was only wrong about one thing, the first one

I can't write. My thoughts are just flying away somewhere far and I can't focus even for a moment. It could be called laziness, yes, outstanding laziness, e.g., I take people from my environment and I transport them somewhere into the spirit world, create thousands of contradictory situations and completely new persons, all of them talking, laughing and moving, like in life. Ah, if only one of those unreal, faraway dreams came true . . . But tough luck, it is those more real, vital dreams, those related to life, which rather ought to come true. Although tell me—a girl with ash-blond curls, blue eyes with dark eyebrows and eyelashes, red lips just so, lovely and sweet like my dream—is she not possible? I keep writing in snatches. Again. My senses have awoken, but not as strongly as before. Still, they've risen and they want to rebel. But no, the world is too sad for them to take off completely—and fly. Although "everything" also has its limits, this is what it was like in May.

It all took place one May
left that spring and did not stay
before it even began . . .
It melted away into nothing
There was no pleading, no gloom
but there is no need to feel pain
What once was may come back again
When the lilac again is in bloom . . .
When (grant this, God) the world around
can resound in green glorious May
May all be drowned in a flowery flood
and heart and body will blush with blood
and it will shiver in newfound might
in May each and every night

I can't write about it now because . . . Because I can't! How can I write about it when the world is cold and sad. We don't leave the house now, it is forbidden from 10 p.m. until 5 in the morning. At five the street looks almost funny, everyone rushes out of their houses and white armbands gleam everywhere outside.

Nora's house was searched.

I don't know when I'll see Buluś, maybe at least Jarosia will come. O God! Let us somehow survive this war. But it is true I'm awakening again, although it's not a torment to me anymore—a pleasure. Goodbye . . . how? You will help me, Buluś and God. As usual. It's actually not that I've been thinking for a long, long time about writing a poem, I'm just haunted by the thought of it, it's to be a description of one of my dreams, my "little beauty." "You're like a golden royal whim," I can't again, I know I can't now.

I was always shy and meek
never cheeky, always weak
as if always trying to seek
safe places from the hurtful world . . .

Goodbye . . . how? Here's to feelings. You will help me, my only Buluś and God.

NOVEMBER 24, 1941, MONDAY[19]

Buluś came on Friday and left today! Jarusia went with her (but will come back tomorrow) to take something. She was here for three days and this feeling is left:

> *with a flutter and a squeak*
> *rubbed soft down on sharp small beak*
> *left the whole bush rocking*

She came and moved the whole house, and left, and I don't know when we'll see each other again. Whenever Buluś comes, she talks to me and I feel then that she's the only person in the world who is truly most sympathetic to me. Buluś is actually against it. She doesn't like Zygu, maybe because she'd rather he were Aryan. She warned me not to take this relationship too seriously and says I won't be happy, because . . . etc. It's strange but after those lectures, I feel that I'm growing apart from him, that I just don't like him and am afraid of him. And then some other hazy figure appears, that old one, indistinct.

Sometimes Buluś is wrong, and she doesn't know him. But sometimes she's right! Because, listen, won't his assertive nature—which I find so attractive now—torment me one day? Won't he do whatever he pleases with me and with himself? Won't some Rena, Halina, Lidka poison my life? It would be all over then. Hope would be impossible. I'd only have one more home to look forward to: the grave.

And I, how would I behave? I think I would either be completely indifferent to everything, or horribly jealous, so much so it'd cause me physical pain, and then—no, I wouldn't argue or make jealous scenes, but I'd systematically, with full satisfaction and calculation, repay him in kind. This feeling has gripped me at times, *precisely* that. In fact, no, I still owe him. And when I'm able to do it with pleasure!

Why am I so angry, really? Is it because of what Buluś said? No, I do still want him to be my husband. And I said, "Maybe it's not the husband I want, but the children, yes, definitely, 'you're like a golden royal whim.'" Mama says you mustn't want anything that much, because you might not get it. I think perhaps God will listen to this heartfelt, girlish request. Yes, may it happen!

Jerschina might give me lessons. I'm nervous about it. Ticiu and Lila are living in the ghetto.

God, may my dreams keep coming true like that. I'll be so appreciative of it and I'll give thanks . . . You will help me, Buluś and God.

NOVEMBER 26, 1941, WEDNESDAY

After Buluś left, I dreamed I had an all-night argument with Zygu, I really did. I don't even know what I was angry about and why I felt hurt. It would seem it's because of those old issues and thanks to suggestion. Only due to that, only because of that. Jara, she hates him and keeps teasing me by wanting to provoke suspicion and jealousy, and only provokes anger directed at her. Because I am really not jealous. I mean I am, but only about the things I see, and if I don't see, then I'm not, I'm not angry or jealous at all. Close your eyes; that's all, that's all.

Z was very sweet and tender today and I was annoyed with myself for those unpleasant reproaches. Or maybe it's like Mama says, maybe I will be unhappy? That would be bad, it would mean not making the most of life. But am I ready to give up on my dream, even for such a price? Maybe . . . I don't know . . . I'll see . . . You will help me, Buluś and God!

NOVEMBER 29, 1941, SATURDAY

I wanted to write yesterday and this morning, but I couldn't get round to it somehow. I wanted, i.e., I planned two poems (about girls and school). But now we've seen each other and as always I won't start where I wanted.

I told Zygu that I always defer to him, that he's tyrannical. Why did I even tell him that? I think because of Mom's suggestion and that dream (the row about the swimsuit). Anyway, I've told you and Nora about this. No, not in a negative sense, on the contrary. You do remember, "Let them even be imperious, even commanding . . ." Yes, and I've told myself that, although I've given it a lot of thought. And Z, as usual, immediately started arguing and saying that he actually enjoyed the role of the "listener." It's ridiculous, no, it's even impossible. Either he doesn't realize or doesn't want to admit that he is the kind of person who exerts influence, imposes his will on others. But he doesn't think he's a tyrant because this word is completely negative. So a tyrant is someone who imposes his will on others regardless of whether he is right or not. So there, I'm changing my opinion about the word tyrant. It is negative. All right . . . I reject it. But what, then, do you call it when someone unknowingly exerts influence on others, who—also subconsciously—submit to it? Someone may not like this influence. There are people who would in fact break away from it, but it actually appeals to me and it's precisely what I like, maybe only that! It is not because, as he says, "I like it because it can't be changed"; it's not true. I liked it before I met him, and I remember that since I was about 14, heroes from books, movies and dreams had exactly this imperious quality, I won't say tyrannical, because I now consider this word to be negative! And we signed a contract, that is Z wrote it, so that I didn't change even a sentence later, it says, "I used to like and still like conduct which I used to call tyrannical, but do not call tyrannical anymore (due to the change in the definition of the word 'tyranny')." And? And nothing. That is Z all over, made demands of me, I'll try to satisfy and have already done so in part, while what I demand—actually, I demand nothing . . . I only said it. So Z remains as he was by mutual agreement. So why the whole discussion, when I feel good in this role and he wouldn't change his even if I wanted him to, and it seems this is what I'm looking for in the excess of words, what hurts me? Anyway, he'd like even me to impose my will. Or maybe what hurts me is this and I won't say anything else. I don't know, but there is something that hurts. There is some discontent—I don't know. Maybe the reason is that I can't accept him, that something is always in the way. Or maybe I lack interests. Yes, if I had other goals, it would be different. As it is, I think about it too much, I deliberate, I contemplate, it's the whole content of my life, and it's too early for that! Today, for example, I felt such a yearning for the school that adults talk about. And I'm due one more year of school, of learning. I would really, really like to go to a Russian school like that. I felt so free there and it felt good, and strangely I'd already realized this during the school year. I would like another year, yes, and then to go far away, to acquire life, learning, pleasures—but to return. To return and to make the dream come true. To return to him and for him! Yes, those are my most secret subconscious dreams. In anger or in spite, whether I love him or hate him I always think that and believe it will happen.

> *I think it could be really great*
> *To go to school again*
> *Come back to any previous grade*

I can't write now, I can't, all of me is preoccupied with that issue. If all men are selfish tyrants, he's also a selfish tyrant—because he is, after all, a man. Oh, life, life, stupid life.

> *Like a bird sprung free from a cage*
> *like a colt that was bridled too hard*
> *I would fly away from my nest*
> *and jump over fences and start*
> *crossing valley, river, and ditch*
> *I would run free and mad like the wind*
> *somewhere far where no eye can reach*
> *I would dance in a crazy whirlwind*
> *and sway as if in a haze*
> *I would drink down my bliss*
> *and thunder down my ways*
> *I would rumble and shake*
> *with laughter and freedom and joy*
> *and move from bloom to bloom*
> *flashing like a star, like a blast*
> *of dawn*
> *and at night*
> *I would fly back to my nest*

In any case, let Renuśka stop crying now. Because, really, Renuśka is a very poor girl, so poor and wronged. Rena is a teacher, there's a loving Rena, there's also such and such . . . but the one from the dreams, the loving one is the poorest and the saddest . . . Really? No! Not from the dreams at all, but the wretched Z's one. What is going on with me? And what will happen to me? You will help me, Buluś and God.

NOVEMBER 31, 1941, MONDAY*

A letter from Mom. She arrived safely, no adventures. The letter again mentioned "it." But it's lost all its power now: firstly, she's not with me; secondly, it feels good. It, and he, feels good. So apparently this is how it must be, that for this (some caresses and warmth), I'm committed and ready to sacrifice myself, that when it's cold and dark outside, there's goodness and light in my soul, and . . . I cannot renounce the dream. In the morning I thought I'll be unhappy in the evening and thought this:

> *I started to build*
> *A building tall and proud*
> *Wings and floors built from sighs aloud*
> *In my dreams, I was so skilled . . .*
> *In the dream-light, all looked bright*
> *Dark ebony, marble white*
> *Claws of columns there to hold*
> *A head of domes and towers bold*
> *Raised so high and held so strong*
> *Lasting solid, lasting long.*
>
> *If it came down quick! It wouldn't*
> *Cause me so much pain*
> *But look, the walls now crack with strain,*
> *Crumble, begin to fall,*
> *every fragment of my soul*
> *Melts and slips, goes slowly bad*
> *that's what's weary, that's what's sad.*
> *I started to build*
> *A building tall and proud*

---

* November has thirty days. On Monday, it was December 1, 1941.

Wings and floors built from sighs aloud
it melted, with my tears filled . . .

One must forgive the spring
all rains and storms and gales
the pranks one forgives and forgets
the clouds will be chased by sunshine
and roses and nightingales
and a bright day awaits as a gray dusk sets

You will help me, Buluś and God.

DECEMBER 8, 1941, TUESDAY* [20]

8th or whatever of December, 1941, Tuesday. Actually nothing happened today that was happy, or sad, or worthy of description. Just a normal December day. But I've decided to finally tell you what's going on in the world. Cannon shots are going on, muffled detonations from the south and the east. The Germans are fighting Russia at the long, huge Eastern front, a fight goes on along Italy with England in Africa, in Libya outside Tobruk, where a new front has been created. Hungarians from the Eastern front are riding toward the Heimat. Nobody really knows why. America is fighting Japan. And . . . so we've lived to see the second world war in this century. For me it's the first, but for others it's also more horrific than the previous one. Blood is flowing, cities are ruined, people are dying. There is horrible poverty among people, cases of typhus (Ticiu and Lila in the ghetto). God, make this terrible war end! Make it so that we survive and keep our health until a peace treaty! Everyone is praying now, everyone believes that only some higher power can protect us from evil—it's God!

In rowdy dancing,
in a wedding, a feast,
where the crowds make the floorboards creak

---

* December 8, 1941, was a Monday.

they don't ask for him, they don't call his name
God's name is silent and weak.
Drunken, they spout more vodka forth
They drink and shout, then the blood will spurt
"Come on, come on!" let the world all tumble
here's to you, if you drink too!
In drunken fun—pick anyone
life strife with a knife.
Let there be a gush
of blood. Let cheeks flush
with golden sweet champagne
let there be a screeching orgy again
of tinderbox moods of those with "no pain"
God is not needed
maybe the sad ones will silently pray
he is not with us
in laughter or play
in scenes or fights
in wine in glasses!
But when the unhappy hour comes
when the sky bleeds with fire and fear
they fall, and wish God was near!
when their lives waste away in sickness
when through poverty their bodies decay
when fear makes them dumb and hunger takes a toll
all they can ask is, "Won't God help at all?"
Then from barred windows of every jail
and from damp cellars you hear the wail,
You hear complaints from wide and far
Lord, won't you save us! Lord, but you are!
(You are the only one who can save)
If only our God forgot and forgave!
That's when they turn into your humble slave.
You're there again. In a loaf of black bread,
In clouds that darken over each head,
under each summer of heavy drought,

under each conscience guilty with doubt
in tears of comfort, in hope and need,
You're there again and called indeed.
And when the sun returns to the sky
And things get bright—from that day on
You won't be called
they will keep sinning, you will be gone . . .
as it was before

So it is. Jerschina came over. Actually I didn't know that I would care so little. Might be because I hate them. Forgive me, God! Zyguś is very good and lovely, and argumentative. Maciek came. We'll talk another time, when there's some news. You will help me, Buluś and God.

DECEMBER 11, 1941, THURSDAY

No! . . . war, who knows? Maybe in two years . . . But Zyguś, so wonderful, tender, sweet and good, and lovely, that he exceeded my dreams. I felt so good today. I would like to tell someone about the happy moments I'm experiencing within this misery. The way Zyguś was, it would be a sin not to love him like I love him . . . I've got many poems in my head, but I can't write. See you later . . . You will help me, Buluś and God, until dreams come true.

DECEMBER 15, 1941, MONDAY MORNING

Today I'd like to talk and write, and talk, and talk, and I don't even know where to start . . . I think with the fact that Nora doesn't understand me. Yes, she herself knows it and told me I am a step ahead. She's behind, where I was, well . . . more than a year ago, or a year. And I would gladly reach out to her, but she . . . why? She's hindering herself. I'd like it if you could understand me completely already. Why, Noruś, when I'm telling you something, I'm not complaining, I'm just saying, and you don't understand me and make it into an accusation yourself. However, we do understand each other in other matters, something always remains.

If only you knew, dear Diary, how many poems live in me, but I don't even know if and when I'll commit those thoughts to paper. And even Nora doesn't understand me anymore. Oh, I must have changed a lot. Well, perhaps I'm really not myself anymore, maybe I'm the lining of Zygmunt's soul. I've transformed awfully, but after all my old self is still there! And life, life is anticipation now. For do you know, there are moments in life without sad or happy experiences, without storms, without streams of happiness, and one doesn't count those moments later. And while they last, they plunge one into a blissful state of calm and indolence.

No, it's not because I wore a hat that I've become unfamiliar to Nora, not at all—but for some other reason, why, why has my sensuality faded? Because it has been replaced by a monotonous caress, an almost "marital" one. However, I realize now that I need it very much; I need this gentle, delicate tenderness as much as the outbursts. And do you understand now, Noruś, and perhaps it'll be: "How much one should prize you, only he who has lost you can tell,"* but you and I are similar, so I don't know . . . but maybe you'll need it too?

I've written an idiotic thing, I probably won't send it to her. And those poems crowd in so much, but I won't write either. Bye, dear Diary, until . . . I don't know. You will help me, Buluś and God.

DECEMBER 16, 1941, TUESDAY

Bulczyk's birthday is coming up, as is the date of writing the birthday letter, the traditional letter. Because I always send a letter, and only very, very rarely can give my wishes personally. And now what in the world can I send her? No, I can't send wishes, greetings—no. Buluś, what can I give you? I've been thinking about this all day. I will send you, then, a bright, silver, winter memory, a memory from a time when we didn't know we were happy. Only I don't know if I can re-create it so vividly as it was. No, I can't do it at all now. And such is the illness I am suffering from now. You will help me, Buluś and God.

---

* A paraphrase from Adam Mickiewicz's *Pan Tadeusz*.

Renia Spiegel

DECEMBER 20 1941, SATURDAY

For Bulczyk's birthday. Do you remember?

Horses galloped at a steady pace
A sleigh raced on just like a lightning flash
Snow and frost laid kisses on our face
Frosty hair, and snow-kissed winter blush
The wind blew panting, right across our eyes
Hooves struck up snow fountains from the ground
Riding in a sleigh felt so nice
With the bell's laughing sound!
Snow and pine cones fell on our heads
Which our passing there would shake and stir
Both of us went on, deep in our sleigh,
Wrapped up warm in a lovely coat of fur.
Silent trees around us stood in wonder
Morning silence shaken from its thoughts
We went riding, like a laughing thunder
With the bell's laughing sound!
Our tracks with fresh new snow are filled
The horses' silhouettes were drowned in fog
the driver and the sleigh, the wood, the field
all you heard still was the bell's sweet sound . . .

Know that when the dusk begins,
and the tower bell tolls for evening prayers
and the December day has spent
all its power—curled, and shriveled
in a ponderous hour—I will come to you
I'll come in yearning that flows
or in a sparkling star that glows
or in a silent holiday breath
or in a sigh instead?
I'll come . . .

In a gray winter's hour,
when the windows sparkle with ice,
I'll say one word, just one word,
frank like tears, but soothing and warm . . .

Yes, we'll be with her then, so that she's not lonely in that crowded, rumbling and empty capital. Bye, dear Diary, we'll go to her together . . . You will help me, Buluś and God.

DECEMBER 23, 1941, WEDNESDAY*

Nothing, days pass. They are all alike. Oppressed with thoughts, waiting, idleness . . . They pass, I sit at home and think, think, go crazy with thinking. I'm gaining weight. I'm as big as a barrel. Disgusting. I wrote a birthday letter to Mom. I've seen Jerschina; he has two sons. Well, is this even thinkable? We're making an album with Norka, i.e., Norka is making it, I'm helping and it brings me such delight, such pleasure, that I could spend whole days doing it. I wouldn't even want to see Z. Just keep making this beautiful album. And then . . . who knows, perhaps it can be published like this?

There is something I would like to say about Zygmunt. Something that worries me. Namely—I don't hate him, but I don't love him either. Maybe it's not true, maybe it's only temporary, and I did swear, did make solemn promises. And I did promise to last throughout the war, but I don't know how it happened and where it came from, but here it is. Can I deny it? I can't even tell him this either, that—what, I'm not attracted to him, I'm fed up with all "that," and I'm left, again, with poems, you, Mom, Nora, such ethereal beings. And you know that at times there's something and then all the shortcomings come to light and create something like aversion—weariness. Why? Whence? I don't know. Oh! If I hated, but not that, I don't hate, I'm indifferent to it. So why, why do I pray every night for the dream. I don't know either. I only know one thing: I need work, physical or intellectual, work away from home—an occupation! I've got many "poemy" thoughts in my head. You don't know that this question accidentally turned into a most genuine compliment.

---

* December 23, 1941, was a Tuesday.

I can wake the day
and spread around the shadow of the night
I can scatter blackest clouds
with golden flashes of light

I can stand around the deepest snow
and call forth Spring
and I know where treasures hidden lie
and where fairies dance and sing

I can find my way on city streets
in taxis, in trams I can ride
Light bulbs—I can light the spark inside
Wrap a village deep in muffling snow
Soothe the pain—I know
people who dwell in cities and towns

I can spread silvery cheer
wrap trees in warm moss, both far and near
I know where tiny dwarves reside
and blow forth bubbles with dreams inside
I can make starry skies appear
right in the middle of the day
And I know a magical world
of elves and princesses, castles in air
I know a whole world that isn't there

But that's something that I never knew
and I never thought of that before
Someone asked me with reproach, "And you,
you write poems, but can you do much more?"

The album is coming along beautifully, ah, it's come in handy, the way he is . . . no, no, I won't say. You will help me, Buluś and God.

DECEMBER 24, 1941

Ah, I feel like writing poems so much, I want to write and write forever.

> Windy, cold, and icy
> Wind is in a mood, not nice, he
> blows on since the dawn
> Gusts and gales, they swerve and sway
> People wonder at the wind, and they
> don't know what's going on
> Why's the wind so raving mad
> Was it crossed by some brave lad
> as it blew about?
> Maybe gnomes or dwarves awoke it
> with a woodland shout?
> or it had a dream in which
> a rival wind blew through, and each
> leaf in the woods blew out!
> It blows and wails and paces
> falters, picks up, races
> snow or no snow,
> sand or no,
> roofs get blown,
> branches caught
> Burned-out dust it raises up
> makes a mess and will not stop
> through the swamp and through the hollow
> where the streams flow, it must follow
> It sits on the windmills' wings
> and flings clouds through the sky
> then it jumped and swayed away
> shook around a pile of hay
> Messed a branch about
> and it flew right out.

DECEMBER 28, 1941, SUNDAY[21]

Or maybe because I didn't submit myself to Your protection. Think and believe, although it's hard to believe. Yesterday coats, furs, collars, oversleeves, hats, boots were being taken away on the street. And now there's a new regulation that under pain of death it is forbidden to have even a scrap of fur at home. I feel so sorry, actually for Dido the most of all of us. But then what is there to be sorry for—the furs or that warm, cordial relationship which dissipated and disappeared.

I didn't see Zygu for a week and I can admit I was pleased with this, it cured me of this persecution mania a little. But . . . but he came after a week, i.e., paid me an official visit (in a coat), and generally made the impression of slaving through some duty. That's not what's awful, he came because he had to, but he'd rather not come and it'd be a hundred times better if he hadn't. I'm not going into any details, but it's only my instinct which tells me that . . . well, you probably know.

Another thing, which abashes me slightly, is that he lies. I have never imagined a person I respect would lie. It's disgusting and I really do not understand it. They were all little, meaningless lies, so? So nothing. But this morning I choked on tears of anger. I know only one remedy for those miseries; perhaps I'll apply it! Yes, yes, but wait a bit. Oh, it hurts— so I love. You will help me, Buluś and God.

DECEMBER 30, 1941, TUESDAY

So it's been a year since I wrote: "Be gone, worries, tears and upheaval." And today, today it's completely different, today I'm a year older, a year more experienced, maybe a bit more mature, but not worth much more. There's not much more I can do.

I remember it was a variety show, it was fun, Rysiek was in excellent spirits. Today I met Rysiek too, how different than last year's. He's huddled, his fur's been plucked, he's disinfecting some sick people from typhus, but he still chats and tells his tall tales.

I saw Poldek, he was carting along some stiff.

I had a letter from Nora, so cordial and warm. Oh yes! Everything's revived in this area, everything fell into place, we've become closer and understood each other, and we're united in friendship. One year, how everything's changed, I don't know what the next one will bring? And how can I know what I will come to write next year? Next year and a year ago . . . And now I'm standing on the border and . . . I'm grateful to the one passing for listening to my pleas and I'm asking the new one to be favorable. Oh God, let all dreams come true like that! I saw Mama, there was something with Zygu and something started in politics. So this year, which will end today in an hour and a half,* will disappear and pluck one flower from my life. It was a year overflowing with love. Everything, tears, sighs, explosions of anger, jealousy, all this stemmed from that one emotion. And you, New Year being born, will you be sympathetic to Cupid hearts? You are young after all. You too know how to love. And if you want to be loved as well, for people to say goodbye to you with regret and not a sigh of relief, if you want your date to be entered in golden numbers into the world's history and in a flowery garland into people's hearts, become worthy of it. Bring a branch of peace into this howling, fighting world and quieten it like a rough sea with a magic wand. And let me still love the one I have fallen in love with, and let me be loved. Make it so that people who were separated by the war are joined in a blissful calm. And return parents to children and my Mama to me. Actually, it's a continuation of my dreams. Let them continue, each of them is a little part of the fireplace, of the "royal whim." You'll understand and I will too. And tomorrow I will greet you on a new page, although maybe only ugly things will happen tomorrow, but the Year will be New, it'll be full of hope for the long 12 months. So farewell, old year, with thanks and gratitude for those first love's kisses, for motherly caresses, for friendship, for everything good and bad. You will help me, Buluś and God.

JANUARY 1, 1942, THURSDAY

I promised, so I'm writing. It was a day like all the others, in the morning I went to Norka's, then I was at home, then I was sorting out a birthday gift for Zygu. And when I came home, I found Zygu there. He was very

---

* Probably: a day and a half.

debonair and pretty. His wish for me was to endure and survive. It was very ordinary; we sat at the table and talked.

Z left soon (angry that I didn't want to show him the previous New Year's Eve in the diary). But it's not true! I know that although by all appearances everything was all right, things were subdued somehow. It seems that Z had the best of intentions, but they slowly cooled down, and . . . I don't know, but I feel there's something. It can't go on like this! If we had decided to act openly, it must be done. The truth must be revealed! Because I know that all aversions, contemplations, inquiries, suspicions are just another form of love. Because there are no dreams in which he doesn't appear. And now my spirits have lifted, because maybe I've just convinced myself. And I'd felt sad, oh how sad. I was crying and thinking of Bulczyk. I wanted to write a letter, which would have been a cry of yearning! I feel so lonely, like I have nobody, nobody. There is only Buluś, but so far away. I've realized that mother and child are the closest beings after all. I understand that I am to Mom what my child would be to me. I feel like crying, I'm unutterably sad. God, make it so that it gets better now. I'm yearning for something warm . . . You will help me, Buluś and God.

JANUARY 5, 1942, MONDAY

The letter from Mother was warm. But I wrote nothing, I was waiting, always waiting for a warm embrace, a look, but only a cold, frosty wind blew. It chilled my heart, it brought tears to my eyes. I wanted to write a letter to Mama, but changed my mind. This letter would've been such a painful cry, it would've wounded a mother's heart. No, I'm lying to the world that I'm indifferent to it; it's not true! I am hurt, I am simply writhing in pain. I don't know, is it that unknown girl who won him over with her father's position and nationality? Or that he never mentioned a word about it, or that he practically stayed away for two weeks? What?— Everything!

I talked about this with Jarośka. We talked like two women friends. But there is a difference between us (not even of age), but of emotion, I love despite everything, she hates. But we agreed about one thing: I need entertainment, I need somebody, urgently; I've written to Norka about this already. If this doesn't heal the wound, it will make it scar over. And then . . . Who knows what happens then? Times are such now that one should think about something else, about life worries, but well, I can't. Maybe I am sinning. And do you know with what disgust I'm making an album of poems for his birthday? Because Maciek told me that he's asking for it. Well, but one has to be magnanimous when saying good-bye. Next time I will try not to fall so hard, treat it lightly, from hand to mouth, and not go into the depths. But this one has deeply affected me all year round. Just think, 365 days and not one when I didn't think of him, so few nights when I didn't dream. And now will all this dissipate in such a pedestrian way? Actually it should have already collapsed because of this a long time ago, after all he always had a roving eye for every skirt, excuse me, not every one—those who looked him in the eye. It is typical for him that he's attracted to girls who are attracted to him. In fact, he told me once that he reciprocates feelings excessively, apparently he reciprocates coquetry too. That I don't know, but surely, have I not experienced it myself? But in this album I'll write what I feel. I have to. Maybe he'll understand me.

HOW

A butterfly loves every flower
on the meadow, plain, and hill
lily and chamomile
plain bloom and bower
When it's not chasing scents
But yearns for nectar still

LEAVES

The leaves in May they shiver
play with the wind impatiently
Is it strange?
To me it is not strange at all
Through August nights
they burn
with a blissful might
of loving, maybe

in autumn they turn yellow
shriveled and pale
this must be envy
They're dead in the winter
and frozen right through
onto a snowy forest floor
they fall
they rustle, and don't sing
and instead of caressing, they sting
Is it strange? To me it's not strange at all

And I don't know, is he worth it or not? Rather yes. I had more joy than sadness after all. Goodbye . . .

I dreamed, a sweet
and wondrous dream
I moved my feet
in clouds, it seemed
a land of colors and scents
and bells
and bells
of laughter
which echoed after
repeated again
until it spread
wide and away
until a whisper
of a sunny golden laugh
what a day
then in a cloud of white
a flock of butterflies flew in
with a name across the sky, so bright
a name as sweet as my dream
and just as wonderful . . .
then the awakening
not as eventful

with a prod in the side
my eyes open wide
it's dark, day wakes
the shade's about to stop
a lovely dream
a springlike dream
but not worth the waking-up

A very sad and teary day. Noruś, I wanted to write to you today. Not—although I know this belongs in the past—"that I'm your friend for crying," but you see, this is how it works out, strangely. But have you ever thought about the meaning of those words? When someone is having a hard time, yes, a hard and sad time, when they need consolation, they turn to their closest person, to their mother—and I didn't have a mother here. I wanted to write about friendship, but I know that my mood has changed since the morning. And? And it's my lot to cry again. Oh God, but my heart is heavy! Words are only words and they say nothing. This burden won't be shifted either by a letter to Mother, or to you, dearest Noreńka, or even by poems; this burden was imposed by his words. So humiliating! Why did I ask about that? Noruś, just think, I've got a sword in my heart, when it's there, it hurts, it hurts very much, but when I try to remove it, it hurts even more. And the thought of our friendship seems to me such a quiet haven that I consider it sacred. Can you believe that he sensed it back then? But still, I am better. Can it be said that I have two faces? You will help me, Buluś and God.

JANUARY 19, 1942, MONDAY

Birthday! Dear Diary! Mama! Noreńka! I feel so good! I feel so light. It was his birthday today. I gave him a collection of poems (granted, it is rather pretty and I almost fell in love with it when making it) and he was so happy! I didn't know it would please him so much. He was touched. I asked him what he'd like me to wish him. He said for us to survive this war without splitting up. Do I want that, too? What a question, do I? I don't want us to ever split up at all. As Z put it, the poems connect us. How good that he understands this. Poems are something extraordinary and unique, they connect souls and ennoble, elevate love. God, thank You and may my dreams come true . . . You will help me, Buluś and God.

JANUARY 24, 1942, THURSDAY*

I feel so good! We understood that we've understood each other completely. And I opened your depths, dear Diary! Are you angry? I opened them to someone close and very loved! I gave all that's deepest, most precious, most honest—all the worries and thoughts enclosed in poems. "When we are like water lilies," Zygunio. The way you are honestly makes me feel at a loss for words, it's better to lie down, close one's eyes and dream. Only Jarośka keeps ruining the image for me with her comments, "He looks like a real Yid in that hat." Let her talk, maybe she's right, I'm unable to see it, and even if

The heart will take no orders gladly,
it is wiser than you are[†]

Generally I've been wanting to write something, but I've not known what all day.

First, "he" was on
a golden throne
a castle, horses, knights
a wings, like on a ghost
a true crowned prince—like most
sweet dreams on sweetest nights
He runs, jumps, flies
the dragon dies
and golden horseshoes gleam
and gleaming so

---

* January 24, 1942, was a Saturday.
† An allusion to the verse of a song by Julian Tuwim (lyrics) and Henryk Wars (music) performed by Hanka Ordonówna in Mieczysław Krawicz's film *The Masked Spy* (1933).

he jumped to glow
onto the silver screen
Again, it was "him"
a girl's true dream
He captured towns and hearts
so lovely and unique
He tore down walls
scored hockey goals
The suit showed off his physique
Then new ones made a start
heroes from books
the soldier and the guard
with airplanes and with rank
And it was due to them
your heart sank
And then, a—who?
A figure on the street
Someone with lips so sweet
Someone with eyes bright and deep
Someone you dream of and would keep
Someone like a daydream in May
who won't disappear or fade away
Again, it was "him"
a girl's true dream
a star of some repute
He tore down walls
and scored hockey goals

A talent beyond dispute
His suit was well-tailored and clean
and he vanished on a bright silver screen

And sometimes it's exactly like it was with this poem. First it gained speed, winged out and stopped, and I'm struggling, struggling, struggling and I can't finish. But maybe I will finish it . . .

He sulked and lay in wait
then with one leap
he gushed a stream sharp and deep
He spread dark wings
and in a flash
he scrawled a streak of poems
across a page at a dash
Each feeling and each thought
he pressed through signs of black
He moved in narrow scribbles
which gleamed behind his back
He spat verse after verse
and coughed up rhyme, and then
he brought forth inky tears
from a poor old fountain pen
Then he stood
his back against the script
on a clear blank page, as dark
as a stubborn mountain goat
as an arrow through a tree bark
he clammed up with a frown
and looked around in fear
and the ending of this poem
will never draw near

Maybe I will finish it after all. You will help me, Buluś and God.

JANUARY 26, 1942, MONDAY

Today was such a strange day. My poor darling Noruśka. She came over this morning at a run and said, crying, "My grandpa is dead." And ran off. My heart gave such a squeeze and hurt so much. Later I was anxious about her, I thought they rounded her up to sweep snow. I know how sensitive she is and what it means to her. And when I was wondering whether the poor thing isn't freezing somewhere and what she's doing, I felt how dear this little friend of mine is to me. Her diary is a story of our friendship. It could be entitled "How a friendship strengthened." Oh, but it must be said that she should be given the more noble position, the one of more respect. And now we're so close that I feel her pain like my own. I would like her to come to us. Her most recent letter was something so warm that one really has to be very cordial to be able to write it. It is so terrible, Irka lost her grandma, Norka—her grandpa. Oh God, preserve the lives of everyone else and stop this war. Buluś hasn't written. Ticiu hasn't written. Oh, this whole family of ours is also a body torn to shreds. Will it come alive? Will it ever come together? I've come to doubt the term "family home"—I can only have my own now. Oh, make it happen, God. The grandparents are to us all that's protection and care, and everything. Oh good, darling, saint Bimba! It's somehow warm and sunny with them in this freezing weather. I'm experiencing moments which are rare in life. I'm 17 and when I look into his eyes I forget everything that's sad in the world. And I'd inscribe them in my heart in golden letters. Because I'm at that age and in that state when words, glances, caresses give joy. When I'm happy at the mere sight of my sweetheart. And now perhaps the poems have introduced this clarity. Mama, write how you're doing! Your silence is such a burden. I say "good night" to the young and happy, "good night" to the sad and worried, "good night" to you, my far-away Mama, and you, my sad dear friend. Good night . . . You will help me, Buluś and God.

> *May this night bring relief*
> *some sweet respite*
> *to those in pain*
> *and grief*
> *a hopeful, joyful*
> *sprite*
> *to those in happy love*
> *May its cool hands lie*
> *across the temples burning*
> *with heat of day*
> *To the world*
> *may it bring all the help*
> *it might*

and may it knock on doors
to hearts barred shut
good night . . .

JANUARY 29, 1942, THURSDAY

Well . . . She hasn't written, no. It weighs so heavy on me. And, as is my wont, I immediately start imagining—and I don't want to think. I am so sad. Z stirred such concern in me too. He says I'd like to live lightly, that I don't care much about anything. Does even he not notice this mask I put on (with difficulty), or maybe, maybe it's true, maybe always trying to "mock the world" I now mock unwittingly? But I can't say I think like that about my only Mama, my dearest, and about our affairs, which are a difficult, oppressing experience to me. My whole youth has been like this. You know. I have never lacked for anything materially—but morally, sometimes. And I couldn't show it, and I didn't want to care much about anything, and it's stayed this way. And now, Buluś, write and visit. Such are my most ardent wishes. You will help me, Buluś and God.

JANUARY 30, 1942, FRIDAY

No, there's been no letter, not a word . . . only my head is thumping, why? And I'm thinking of writing a novella. No content, no so-so moods, no more. And in response to you, Buluś.

If I was just like you are now
I would have all the boys in tow
I'd be surrounded by many a lad
and let them kiss!
let them go mad!
I wouldn't mind, I wouldn't care
the young girl's shame would not be there
I'd fling my arms wide open, then
I would deny it all again
I'd kick back those who are a drag
Then I would show a lot of leg

And hike my dress up high enough
To let the blinding light shine through
With so much grace
who could ever face
so much temptation and resist?
The righteous ones would not be missed
The chaste old souls could let tongues fly
against my body, till they die
against my lips, and all my hair
I'd keep all boys so sweet right there
I'd make them choke on bliss—and how!
if I was just like you are now . . .
But I am not, and that is why
I'll love no other, even if I try
my love is young, ashamed, aware,
and so unhappy, so full of care . . .

I'm happy with what I've written about myself—I'll refresh it a bit. You will help me, Buluś and God.

FEBRUARY 6, 1942, FRIDAY

Such an ordinary Friday. Because you don't know that on Fridays too, and, well, generally always, every day. I've had a letter from Buluś, Jerschina brought it. I've studied nothing for him. I am so sorry, so ashamed—horribly. And I really want to learn now. I want to, so much, I think about it. Mama, forgive me, please, forgive me, you've experienced this too once, after all—I . . . I can't.

Zygmunt wanted to come more often, I agreed. But this is something I've experienced since the very first stages of love—I don't like to see him that often. It is as if I'm worried that it'll become commonplace, that I'll get bored, run out of energy (but it's not so, right, Noruś?). So why blubber? Because it was the way it was today? After all, yesterday and earlier, and before that, it was different. So it has to be said how it was. Was or wasn't. It got me very excited and caused pleasurable unsettling shudders. Everything was sweet: kisses, glances and words, and all that wasn't so ethereal, yes, that too. And today it was like that at first too—not at the end. Because really, who's to blame that I started thinking about the honest and clear way Z has of telling things. I told him things too and perhaps it was this telling of mine that humiliated me so much internally. "Renuśka! You're so silly!" Mama would say. Because you didn't experience another love before this one? Because your dream was so undreamed? Because that first kiss, as Z says, was like freshly picked cherries? Yes, because of that! Because when he (after all quite honestly and in good faith) told me about all those flings of his, the casual flirting and little romances, I couldn't impress him with anything like that, if it could impress him at all? Or maybe not that . . . I must touch my heart like this, bit by bit, to see where it hurts. Maybe the impassioned speech about that first Jadzia, no, not that either, and not the fact that those experiences were much more romantic than ours, or perhaps the comparison? Yes, yes . . . you compared me loving you to yourself loving her. I was nothing, nothing at all in your life; you didn't even pay attention to me. But what do I really want? I've always known this after all, I didn't even (at times) demand reciprocity. Still, why are you surprised that I was "consumed by reticence"? Why, I was embarrassed, humiliation was ravaging my eyes anyway. Whatever I said and did always seemed too much to me. You were free to do anything, but girls have their own special "blessed" rules. And why, Z, why did "it" happen? It was not because you found me attractive ("Because I didn't even try to make interesting conversation"), not because I found you, is that it? Or perhaps the row with the variety show and the contest? Perhaps that was unimportant—quite unimportant? Those rivals I conquered, that didn't make me happy (or did it?) (I know now—the variety show). After all each one of them could have done it. I knew all this, but never, ever, suspected that hearing it in such a nice, "accessible form" would cause me such pain, well, not as much pain as a spasm. You could only love her, although later no longer. And there was no name for our relationship—it was something between a friendship and exactly that—and then it took on a more distinct character. But I can phrase it differently. To me, you were immediately more than a friend (although I hated you at times), maybe precisely because of this. Maybe I would have withdrawn and closed the front if . . . ? Oh there's always been an "if," and that's why I stayed and would stay. But even today I'm sorry I was wet behind the ears, a novice, a goose; I'm sorry that I can't say, "At least I know I didn't live tediously." But one promise will be kept, even if I loved most ardently—like today. Now it feels better, it feels good, now I will leaf through the old, those disarmingly naïve pages. You will help me, Buluś and God.

> Let us then sing
> let us then sing
> until the dream
> of youth lives on
> till it can thrill and thrive and spring
> let us then fill
> the sky with song!

FEBRUARY 8, 1942, SUNDAY

I'd like to start a story. A story of our love. Written completely independently. But one has to, it's hard maybe, when . . . I don't know. You will help me, Buluś and God.

FEBRUARY 16, 1942, MONDAY

Tomorrow I'm going to Noruśka's. For the whole day. We'll talk to our hearts' content. We'll settle everything and build, at least theoretically, our future company. We have to do it. At all costs, we need to. I went to Irka's, she's paid me a return visit. And again a spiderweb of relationships is starting to be spun. But I don't want this web to wrap itself so much that spiders suffocate me. I need to see my own one, we must meet.

It is disgusting, this life, which starts with staring at his lips and ends with looking at his fingernails. I try with all my might to remove myself from this influence. But it's very hard, because I dream of throwing my arms around him. If I had some occupation, or someone else, I wouldn't think so much about it. It's strangely amusing that I always know it in advance.

Yesterday I told Jarośka the story of my revenge. Jarośka says, "Stupid, you are making up stories!" And today, today there's some truth to it after all.

Sometimes one has rivals; that's the way it is. In some cases their very name can make one see red. What am I if she's my rival?! I never thought of it, but he, apparently, did. No. It's nothing. It will heal, that is certain. Either it will heal, or break forever! Perhaps only for some time. Because I find it hard to renounce the dream. The dream I've brought to perfection, cultivated in my most secret thoughts. Endure moods—already? No, I've given it the wrong name. It was a good mood, but I immediately know, feel it at once and change, ah, adjust myself. And I'm angry! But it's best to hide a bad mood in the best mood.

We wrote portraits of each other. Zygu was more open, so I wrote an even more "adoring" addition. How strange it is that I always prefer to say more, that I like to give as good as I get? I know a frame changes a lot, it's like a stage set in the theater. Bye, good night. You will help me, Buluś and God.

FEBRUARY 18, 1942, WEDNESDAY

Why did such a nice day end like this? Why did this particular day, filled with friendly conversation with Norka and light, radiant plans from our world, close up and hunch down, like—me? Why am I not brightened by that day of March 16 and the beautiful dream of being together, being in the mountains, only for each other? Why is my own, my beloved, worse than all the others? Why is he so odious!? Odious, yes! This is not a cry of an effusive girl, no! I fully realize that all the letters of that word are odious little worms, which comprise an odious whole. How shallow, low and mundane it all is: circles, gossip, circles, gossip, circles . . . to infinity. Mama, my only, my dearest, take me away from this stifling disgusting atmosphere in which I'm suffocating. And Jarośka, she's making my life impossible too! You see, I wanted to give love wings. I put all my soul into it, but the wings broke off and it fell, earthed, turned gray. Well, why am I surprised? It all boils down to this. Or perhaps we never, never really understood each other? And I am in such need of warm words. Oh, Mama. And I'm reading a book about love. Great, pure, although "earthly," and I think that such a love can exist only in books, or maybe . . . Maybe great, beautiful love exists out there? Maybe one can receive what one gives? But not here, I have knocked at the wrong heart, I was wrong, oh, how horribly, horribly wrong I was . . . You will help me, Buluś and God.

FEBRUARY 24, 1942, TUESDAY

Me. I make myself laugh. I got fatter like some old, pudgy, chubby auntie. I have a triple chin. What is there to write about? I'm alive again. Plenty of errands to run. Plenty of things shared with Noruśka. And you know what? We might have an official celebration of our friendship anniversary. February 16, 1942.*

Today started just like any other day lately. He told me I've been nasty recently and this and that. And everything was kept at a distance etc. etc. Until we looked at our bet (and counted the poems). Zygmunt took the photo away from me, the one that entered the arena of our lives so many times before. He wanted to keep it, I begged him, I asked, I started crying. Nothing. Zygmunt was relentless, though I cannot say he was uncaring, on the contrary. Jarośka makes me cringe with embarrassment. As a gesture of peace I will let Zyguś have a copy. But I resisted with all my might, even his caresses and looks didn't tempt me—no! And why? Zygmunt asked me this and I couldn't, I didn't know how to explain. After all, this photo is part of a dream. The great, golden dream I carry with me through life, a dream that is stuck in me, that lives, that pulsates. So I said—whatever it takes. The price is peace and quiet, an incomplete album entry, perhaps even tension in our relationship or even a breakup . . .

But this dream is unbelievable, nothing will make me withdraw, nobody will wake me up to reality. I think that one day it will be in the album and I will tell one little poppet, "You know what . . . it's not my tears flowing. A dream cannot be conjured up before it is realized." So Zygu might be cross, even though I thought he reached out. Zyguś, I love you so much; whatever I did, you should forgive me. But when I thought that it might not happen on Thursday or on Saturday or . . . ever, it broke my heart, I felt such longing . . . again. You will help me, Buluś and God.

---

* It should be March 16, 1942.

FEBRUARY 28, 1942, SATURDAY

It was good and it was bad and then good again. Those feelings spill over in me. But I wrote a letter to Mama, a long letter, which gave me some relief. Oh, if I could only get away from here. It feels like every person I meet is my enemy. Perhaps it's those stories.

Zyguś is so sweet, but I am not able to dance, I am languid, nasty, terrible. I don't want anything else but . . . to go to Mama. Go there and have some respite for a while. I am so awful for saying all those things about him in a moment of weakness. It's wrong, it's low and it's true. Mama, I'm so unhappy . . . You will help me, Buluś and God.

MARCH 6, 1942, FRIDAY

This week has been very eventful. It was Irka's birthday. We spent the day with Nora; it was very pleasant. We had some pictures taken with Nora and Jarośka (they will probably be terrible, by the way). There might be some photos taken on Sunday and Mama wrote and sent two parcels and this and that.

I haven't seen Zygmunt all week long. Yes, and now I will have a ner-vous attack, I will vent my anger, I will explode! Yes, because I don't care that he goes on his little visits. I understand—and he even told me this himself—that he likes company. But he is too embarrassed to go with me; he is simply embarrassed and ill at ease. He actually told me this, i.e., he didn't want to go with me and said he would go on his own. Whatever, I will absolutely spare him the displeasure of my company, he might even be embarrassed in the street too. Well, tough. It is difficult to describe how bitter I am, I can taste the bile in my mouth. And just think, just think how I felt when Lidzia asked sweetly: "Why didn't you come with Zygu?" New disappointments all the time.

Letters to Mama are the only things that calm me down the most. I don't mention anything about "the issue," but I do say, rightly, that I would like to get away from here, to find a different world—I know it wouldn't be better, but it attracts me because it would be new. I have had enough of this tête-à-tête. And it's all because this roast is lacking gravy.

"I'm angry, because I turned my heart inside out like an old pocket and shook all the crumbs out. I know, I know I'm a stupid cow, you don't need to tell me." This is what I wrote for Binka. Do you remember "open your hearts"? I'm angry with this poem now, I contradict it; it convinced me only temporarily and now I negate it with all my might. I was biased. Indeed, "open your hearts—to hearts wide open" is the right thing. But only to the ones that are wide open. And if there is no sweet secret left there, it will be empty.

> *Purple light trickles out thin*
> *illuminating a ruby red urn*
> *showing some visions within*
> *enchanted specters that churn*
> *You can see some deep trances*
> *hidden in the ruby tone*
> *resting foreheads, sending glances*
> *You can see the crown of glimmers*
> *Mystery queen deep in fantasies*
> *on her throne of twilight dimmer . . .*
> *Then somebody opened the canopies*
> *Letting the light inside*
> *into the dark secret*
> *looking for something that hides*
> *Checking dressers, corners in sequence*
> *Peeking into a vase*
> *Looking, rummaging with both hands*
> *To conclude, "Empty, she's an empty place."*

A secret stops being itself when somebody finds it out. My heart is empty, because I said it all.

> *I will never be angry, my darling*
> *when your cheeks go bright red*
> *when you find a question alarming*
> *when you say softly, "It's a secret."*
> *You'll put a finger on your lips*

Your hair will fall onto your brow
Your eyes'll look up and eclipse
Filled with mystery, surprise, disavow.
I know you would like to say
I know you would like to call
it's tough, so tough, but hey
You want to know it all?
It's boring and it is fruitless
Yes, I'd like to hear about it
but I won't be angry, my sweetness
because then it would be unfit
it wouldn't be your secret sweet . . .

So he is embarrassed. Well, till tomorrow. You will help me, Buluś and God.

(ON SATURDAY)

The wound has not healed, how could it have? Irka was there and Waldek and Zygmunt. And it was nice. Quite nice. I'm sending kisses . . . You will help me, Buluś and God.

MARCH 11, 1942, TUESDAY*

Again he reached out to me and he was like he used to be. And again I rejected him. I can't say I wasn't tempted. Indeed I was, but the wound has not healed just yet and I think it'll never heal. This anger will resurface elsewhere, while it's all about me wanting to get the other part of the portrait back. Why? Because now the most intimate issues—not of the heart, but of the soul—lay shamelessly on paper and bare their teeth; they are in somebody else's hands. And it's not about him possibly showing it to somebody else, now or later, when "this" is not there anymore, or about him reading it himself, or not. It's about the fact that another "I" exists, lives. That I'm split in two, that I expelled something and that it now ex-

---

* March 11, 1942, was a Wednesday.

ists. It doesn't mean I'm stupid. It rather means that I love this idiot who doesn't love me back, that I believe, strongly believe in a dream which will never come true, which is just a phantasm. And I feel so very sorry for myself that I'd like to curl up in some corner and cry. I feel so sorry for you, stupid girl, because I can see how much suffering you have ahead of you—it won't end anytime soon.

So, so many worries are piling in front of me. I'm glad that Mama is coming, I'll tell her. But I'm afraid she might not understand me, she might tell me to laugh it off, to stop caring, while I still feel the love, I love so much. The slightest whiff is enough to give me heartache and it goes on and on, until I tell Nora or you. But . . . Nothing . . . Is it true that . . .

> *Yes, exactly this!*
> *I think spring is not a bliss*
> *It doesn't fit my mood*
> *I'll revolt, I will be booed*
> *I'll defy those hard constraints*
> *grab my old, leaky umbrella*
> *put on black galoshes, no complaints*
> *my scarf and autumn jacket.*
> *I'll sniffle, oh how yucky.*
> *And in all this gear*
> *I'll walk through town all mucky*
> *saying for all to hear,*
> *"What foul, autumnal weather."*
> *I'll bump into some moron.*
> *Passersby at the end of their tether*
> *will stare at this rubber phantom*
> *speaking now of autumn.*
> *"It's autumn where I am, really,*
> *I promise you, you have my word,*
> *I bring autumn to the fore pretty freely*
> *as spring is not in step with my mood!"*
> *Nobody seems to get it.*
> *Nobody says I'm right.*
> *So bored, tired, unhappy*

I stay at home, I hide.
I draw the curtains, shut doors
Put lots of wood in the stove
guarding myself from the spring
Rubbing my hands in the alcove
until snowdrifts are here again.
I will return to the autumn
unless it changes from the very bottom!

I really wouldn't want it to be nice and for thousands of "couples" to come out into the streets. I am selfish, terribly selfish, but, really, what for? I don't need it; it just yanks at my heart. Sometimes I get rebellious. I want to raise my head (after all spring is coming) and fight. Yes, fight against my love, against him and against my own helplessness and my own stupidity. I want to forget everything and write a novel. I'll start soon because I feel that everything has to find an outlet. Bye, good night . . . You will help me, Buluś and God.

MARCH 12, 1942

There is no way to express this. No way at all. I only think about my parents who, even though they are alive, made me an orphan. Why don't I have my own place today, why am I at the mercy of people who, at any moment, can say, "Go away! We don't have to feed you"? That's what Granny told me today. "Go away!" Why didn't she say that earlier? Why did she let me live with them? Why didn't my parents send me to go into service somewhere or even better, why didn't they kill us both when they split? And now I have to think about it. I have to think about a way to leave this life in a quiet, unnoticed way. To remove myself. Everybody would be happy then, my parents wouldn't need to think about what to do with me, Granny and Grandpa would have plenty of food for themselves, they wouldn't have somebody else's bastards to take care of and I . . . I'd be the happiest of them all. But I know it won't come to that. I don't have the courage. Why, why do I tell myself this, I don't know. I only know that the hope of tomorrow keeps me together. But if tomorrow is . . . I'll try.

Bye, dear Diary, I love everybody, but my raw nerve, my only goal in life was home. It's not my fault that I don't have a home; it's everybody else's fault, but not mine, but it's not them who suffer because of that, but me, only me. So I suffer without any fault on my part. Bye. You will help me, Buluś and God.

We'll compose a living poem
we'll drown it in a happy flood
by all it will be softly spoken
among spring, by all young
it'll be made of hot professes
with bloody laments of affection
adorned with our sweet caresses
linked and framed by our lips' attention
It will pulsate with our blood
taste of our kissing, our tears
smell just like jasmine or lilac
be sweet as old song in our ears
it will be fresh like a fierce river
whoever reads it, he will say,
"I know it, it could be my verse . . ."

MARCH 16, 1942*

The third year of the war. But Renia! What do we care about the war today! We celebrated the second anniversary of our friendship, just like we planned.

You didn't let me finish at yours, so I have to start from the beginning. The old-fashioned clock's hands moved just a few hours forward, but so much has changed in that time. The morning was wonderful, it was as good as one can only imagine, it was familiar, delightful and at the same time unusual. We triumphed over Irka, we felt we were heading for something better, we felt we had a great day to celebrate! It's been a while since I was in such a good mood . . . And it was all gone the mo-

---

* This entry has been written by Renia's friend Nora.

ment Zygu appeared. He brought with him something alien, something stiff, he pushed me into the state I am in now.

I'd like to write something cheerful, to thank you, Renia, for all your efforts to make this day a pleasant one, but I can't. In the morning I radiated joy, now I sit here, cold, hunched over a page from your diary, completely broken, and I can't even think of anything anymore. It is all Zygo's doing. He made me feel like some small, stupid, unimportant person who at best can smile idiotically, or rather laugh, and nothing more. Renia, don't hold it against me that I spoiled this day filled with warmth, sweetness, delight. We need to remember one thing: satisfaction is never creative. I'm grateful to Zygu for bringing me back to my senses (I'm sure absolutely unintentionally). I sobered up, I don't know for how long, because there is somebody else who can affect my state of mind again.

We could actually start our novel now, the mood couldn't be more appropriate, but there's one problem, Renia, I'm simply not able to. I don't have even the slightest bit of a writing talent. You have so much more imagination. To you writing comes easily, you have panache. And my knowledge is way too limited to undertake the writing of even the smallest novel. Renia, start writing on your own, I might join you or not, that remains to be seen.

But now I'm thinking of something new, Mila's idea. "Organize a day of truth," she told us and "Put it all on the table." Yes! We need to fulfill this plan. It might change my attitude to Zygu, it might even bring me closer to you two.

It's strange, after all we don't need any new circumstances, because I don't think we could be any closer to each other than we are now. Because, Renia, we are very close, but I am distant from you and Zygu. I always feel it when you are together and I would really like that to change. So chin up, all must end well. We have achieved so much, Renia, we'll achieve this as well. Vivat March 16! Vivat our dear friendship! "Be gone, worries, tears and upheaval . . ."

MARCH 17, 1942, TUESDAY

I didn't write yesterday because you were at Norka's. Pity. I felt so good. And all that joy, this blissful calm, I transferred onto the pages of Nora's diary. I felt like this even in the afternoon. We were together, the four of us, and I thought we were so close. Shame that you, Nora, didn't feel the same way . . . (ah, you don't know anything about Julek). Strange that I wrote so little about Julek. I'll write some more now, since he became my . . . let me say it . . . my "brother-in-law."

In fact I like Julek a lot, especially that he disappointed me in a nice way. I expected him to be rather experienced, to like girls, to be idle, a pleasure-seeker, superficial, talented and very smart. And now I see that there is something very straightforward about him, that there's nothing artificial about him, nothing unnatural. He's very good and not at all bigheaded. So I'm glad that Norka said the words, "I love." Admittedly she said it as a question, "Do I?" but she's loved him without being aware of it for a long while. And I wish her all the best in love. I'm waiting impatiently for it to happen.

Yesterday I felt that everything we dreamed about came true. We won over her, this awful cow, we have our shared "baby" (the album), we have our friendship and . . . we take photos. Yes, this (for those in the know) means a lot too. And then, i.e., yesterday, when we were finally alone, it was sweet and it smelled of spring. Zygmunt said that we would never argue again. But I replied it was not possible. True, I knew it and I admitted that I was angry and when I'm angry I invent outrageous things about him and I have already forgotten what it was about and I felt bad about it, until this wound stung again. Until I remembered that he was embarrassed to go with me to Irka's. And today this story with the photo unnerved me again.

And you know what, today I looked at him terribly unfavorably. Krela was indeed right when she said he was vulgar—I could die of embarrassment. But Norka made it all disappear, she presented it somewhat humorously and gently and as a result one could be sympathetic. Good, dear Nora, it's so nice of her. I'm curious about the photo and what he says. I'm sure we look like Antek and Margośka.* You will help me, Buluś and God.

---

* It might be a reference to Antek from Władysław Stanisław Reymont's *The Peasants* and the title character from Józef Birkenmajer's *Opowiadania Margośki* [Margośka's tales].

MARCH 19, 1942, THURSDAY

Sweet Thursday, which tastes of kisses and tears! I have expressed my worries and now I feel better. And Zyguś was also so good and loving. But something still bothers me. I don't know what it is. Some conversations leave me with an unpleasant feeling. But I still love him very, very much, even though I don't find him as beautiful as I used to. I like this tender atmosphere, full of caresses, warmth—I would give everything for it. Yes, my Dear Mama, I long for, I crave what I didn't have, because you were far away. You will help me, Buluś and God. Good night . . .

MARCH 21, 1942, SATURDAY

Irka is supposed to come. It's all trifling; she is meanness incarnate. Mila called it as it is . . .

But today's a special day for me, because Norka . . . I tremble with curiosity and contentment. Finally, phew! I can breathe now.

> *I am so very sorry*
> *for spring, for love, for myself*
> *I'd like to drown in sky expanses*
> *in blueness, following my gaze*
> *or into the unknown take my chances*
> *I feel so lonely, oh so poorly*
> *I know that by all I'm forgone*
> *I struggle in my helplessness, sincerely*
> *my heart'll stay here even when I'm gone*
>
> *I will do nothing, my dear madam*
> *'cause I can't fight against myself*
> *though I do know, though I do want*
> *though I push for it, I say it myself*
> *Stay, I'm dying with you*
> *I know this is not true*
> *Mock me, why don't you?*

I will not die, I'm not in line
I'll keep on living, I'm not yet due.

I'll finish later.

We've won. Or rather Nora has won. She pushed for it and today it (didn't happen) but manifested itself. We felt we had each other and that we have them.

Julek went with Nora, Zygmunt stayed with me. She was somewhat deflated, disappointed and lonely. I could see she wanted to make me jealous and then show me pity (like she once did), but she trapped herself. To a large extent it was Zygmunt's doing. I was so grateful to him for it. I could kiss him to death. Zyguśka, I feel such an urge now that I haven't felt for a long time. By the way you were in a bad mood.

The best thing is that now I feel sorry for Irka, I'm torn with regrets when I think about her almost crying when she was leaving. I'm very, very sorry, but it has to be that way, such is life. If she went away smiling, I would be the one crying now. Buluś, now you can laugh. Bye, I'm sending kisses to you . . . and not to you. You will help me, Buluś and God.

MARCH 23, 1942, MONDAY

Thank You, Lord! Many thanks that I'm not alone now, hungry and locked away in prison, but at home with my dear ones—that I can appreciate. I can still remember the face in the helmet and again I'm terribly scared, so terribly scared like I was then and I badly want to cry. It was really a miracle, an extraordinary miracle—thank You, God Almighty and my Dear Mama who prays for me somewhere far away. Compared to this, everything else is trivial and pale, a walk, kisses, photos. So what that Z, so what that I was worried that I didn't like him anymore, that he seemed ridiculous, that in my thoughts I turned his face in my hands. But that's not even funny, how can I even say that, what a terrible cow? In the face of his tenderness I have forced myself to get over it somehow and then I didn't need to force myself at all, which was the best. I'm glad today is over . . . and it's a pity too. Because I crave something again. You will help me, Buluś and God.

MARCH 25, 1942, WEDNESDAY

It's so ironic. They are closing our quarter (I won't be able to see Norka); they are moving people out of town; there are persecutions, unlawfulness. And on top of that—there's spring, kisses, sweet caresses, which make me forget about the whole world. Bye. You will help me, Buluś and God.

MARCH 28, 1942

Somebody stays at home, because they must. Somebody has a mirror on the desk and looks into it and can see that they gained weight. Thoughts rush through somebody's head like water through a mill wheel. I've been interrupted and haven't finished, bye. You will help me, Buluś and God.

THE FOLLOWING DAY

It's a pity I didn't write yesterday. Spring longing engulfed me yesterday. Zyguś is so good to me, so tender, so affectionate—like never before. Even in company I feel good about it, i.e., I have felt good about it, it's not the case anymore, no, it isn't. I simply can't stand all those "hunters." There are plenty of them; I'm surrounded as if I were in a cage. Some try their openness and honesty, others bad-mouth me behind my back, others still try through a brother or a cousin, still others . . . eh, it's not worth writing about.

Shame we didn't take any photos. Did you know? And what did you think? Nasty world. No, not the world, just our little world. And anyway why is Z. telling me all this, it seriously puts me off our relationship and at the same time gives me a kick, I start "feeling" that I am on earth. "If the sun only shines for the bourgeoisie, we will put the sun out."* That's right! Yes, yes, this is what I've learned.

Julek disgusts me. I feel bad about not telling Nora, but I can't. She seems so happy, so self-contented. How could I destroy it with one word?!

---

* Leon Trotsky's words.

No, I won't do it, I can't. And anyway nobody is perfect. Nobody. I don't even know what is better. But when Z was telling me this, I was glad; I was glad that he exists at all, that we exist, and our miss.* I felt that what we had was somewhat bigger than what she had. That Z is more permanent. But nothing's certain. Nothing at all. I'm going through a strange period, I want to write poems and I can't—I really don't have the energy.

> *Hello, listen, hi*
> *you funny passersby*
> *you dreamers, rhymists*
> *and incurable fantasists*
> *walking the earth*
> *always looking up*
> *what do you search for*
> *among the stars high up?*
> *Who do you sigh to*
> *on a silver moonlit night?*
> *There is life down here*
> *It rumbles ahead with might*
> *it bubbles over, boils, brews*
> *First the wave needs to be pacified*
> *You must not follow paths untrue*
> *on the map of the endless sky, its guide*
> *Stop staring at expanses*
> *with your daydreaming eyes*
> *unless you want to take your chances*
> *be jostled and well chastised*
> *Gather your powers don't think twice*
> *look what's here, take a look around you*
> *or else you'll pay the price*
> *and plenty of bruises will come through!*

---

* This term appears several times throughout the diary, but its meaning is never clear. It might be Renia and Zygmunt's inside joke, a metaphor for their love/relationship.

Yes, that is true, but it's so nice among the clouds and so ugly down on the earth—there is no point in it. Now for something for the club, a little gossip.

> *D'you want to?*
> *We will climb the mountains*
> *I used to say, "I do"*
> *But now I ask you*
> *D'you want to? Can you?*
> *You crave it? Know it?*
> *That is all my affection*
> *It's just one big question.*
> *Do you know . . .*
> *Yes, yes, our affection*
> *is another question*
> *What do you want?*
> *Yes, yes, our affection*
> *is really a question.*
> *How dare you!*

I will ponder on things in bed. You will help me, Buluś and God.

APRIL 7, 1942, TUESDAY

That's that . . . We fell out and . . . I've decided to stay angry. But Norka came to persuade me. And she did. I'm easily persuaded. And in fact I'm happy that Norka talked to Zygu. I've wished for it for a long time. I'm also glad she is coming to the picnic tomorrow and that she loves her Julek, that she's going through this spring with such a "flourish." I keep thinking of my spring last year. Let Noreńka be happy, she deserves it. Everybody needs to experience the first spring. Our "springs" are so similar, just like the two of us are. But there is also a different "something," as you know.

I'll fight Irka with . . . every available weapon. I had this silly, indifferent feeling and now—it doesn't matter . . . You will help me, Buluś and God.

APRIL 9, 1942, THURSDAY[22]

All's well already, all's well. Things are good . . . and that's good. My adorable, adorable Zyguś! My dear, dear Nora! I'm so glad you got to know each other. Zyguś, your soul is as delicate as a sprig of mimosa. It dwindles with every gust of wind. It dies. I'll never be different. I'll always be a dreamer and that is that. I still soar high, I still live in the realm of dreams. Buluś, today, even though I don't love you any less, I have a grievance, and it is not the first time. I feel so good with him now, I would like to cling to him, hold him tight and . . . already. Mine, mine, only mine! Good, better than me. Bye, Zyguś . . . You will help me, Buluś and God.

APRIL 10, 1942, FRIDAY

This morning I thought a lot about our yesterday's conversation. The sun was so bright and (it seemed) loving. I sensed the spring and I can tell that this was my first proper spring day. Today I wasn't annoyed with "couples"; actually it's been like that for a few days now. Today even kissing couples could evoke only friendly and warm feelings. But even today, yes, still, in the morning, I was planning to go far away, high up, deep inside and, as I've planned for a while, I wanted to take Zygmunt with me. I think the beginning went like this:

> *What do you say? Give me your hand*
> *Let's go away, let's leave this land*

Yes, this was the beginning for sure, I wrote it down exactly as it was, but later I gave up on it, I wanted to travel on my own, but then I thought we were walking together. Something like that came out of this jumble of thoughts:

> *I ride on each dragonfly*
> *I gallop on the bright sunrays*

I climb every cloud that goes by
I make circles all day.
The old wind knows me well
It warmly shakes my hand
And asks, "Are we going, pray, tell,
my fare dodger, oh so grand?
"Where to?" A snowdrop wants to know
which grows by the big bush of blackthorn
"Far, my friend, so far I want to go
where the sky kisses the earth at morn."
Worldly news won't catch me there
Even if they speed like light
But if you want to track my flight
Look for me, but there, not here!

Yes, but that's not all. In the morning I felt this rush, I wanted to write a poem made of pure absurdities.

Everything is twisted
Everything is wrong!
The earth is too slow unassisted
Giving birth to days too short
The sun creeps in too quickly
Into the sunset's dying might
The moon is looking sickly
Against stars in the sky so bright
Silence is too loud
Distance is too near
Spring unusually dowdy
sorrow is too drear . . .
But if you want . . .
we will get the world going
we'll move the sun to the sky's crust
the moon will be glowing
If you want, then you simply must!
The hum of silence must be quelled

Close distances—pushed away
Spring must be less dowdy, sorrows curtailed
No, let's get rid of the sorrows, if we may!

I've finished and I feel good! Today Z solved me like you solve a riddle. It's true that I run away from this world only because I'm not in a good frame of mind. He said that this is not a regular romanticism, but it's more something like symbolism. This is the escape from the oppressive life, which I don't know how to enjoy, which I don't love. He was terrified that this might be quite abnormal and that I might drag him with me. Yes, he is right, 100 percent right (as usual), because I wanted to do it. But now I see that I had no right, that I must not do it! I can't hijack a person who passionately loves life, who knows how to seize it and lets life seize him, just because I feel bad here. No, I don't feel bad, I feel unwell. Yes, he needs to stay here, play, have fun and . . . nothing. And I? I'll try to fall in love with life, with the "earthly" spring and people. Falling in love with life is my new task. Adjusting to its requirements, becoming a regular romantic (if I must) to a high degree. The other option is what I thought of so many times, shedding all those dreams, never writing poems again, never analyzing anything—and instead becoming a regular "earthly" 17-year-old girl, learning to dance, going to parties, enjoying it and everything else. Becoming like, you know . . . like Rena, but this other one, like I wrote. Then there would be no issue of developing a complex; I wouldn't even know that something like it exists and I'd ask, "What's that?" I know it'd be good, but that means dying and being reborn. Perhaps I can become the first one. I'll try, anyway.

Anyhow I'm full of good intentions and cordiality, I reach out. Let's see how the world receives me, no, not the world, our little world. But let me admit here that I'm only doing it under Zygmunt's influence and because of him; otherwise I'd never do that. Aha! Just in case I wanted to defect (it might happen), just look at me, Zygu, like you did today and . . . all will be well. See you soon.

Until spring betrays you
until it gives you pain
until false thoughts hurt you

get some hugs while you can.
Until you buckle under
the heavy weight of the moments, years
laugh out loudly, don't ponder
love the world, give it cheers.

7:30 A.M.

You will help me, Buluś and God.

APRIL 11, 1942, SATURDAY

I've missed Zygu, I've missed him so much. All night long I kept think-ing about it and the day seemed to go on forever. All day long I waited to see him. I was as excited as I haven't been for a while. And I was in such bad luck! I barely had him to myself for a moment. But I'm very con-tented, very happy! Zyguś, darling, you were so, so sweet and good, I was really touched. I can appreciate your behavior. My dear, good, wonderful boy! I'd like you to always be like that. That would make me happy. And what I'd like the most in the world is to have you by me now. I'd like to be with you, because this is no relaxation, it's a torment of waiting and longing, but! I'll just imagine in detail that we are together! Yes! Help me, Buluś and God.

APRIL 13, 1942, MONDAY

A sweet day. There were parcels from Mama, and in those parcels there was candy, sweet candy. But . . . It wasn't the only reason it was sweet. Somebody's lips were much sweeter. Whose? You can figure it out. I don't feel like writing it, what for? I would spoil "it" with words. "It" needs to be experienced to be understood. You can envy me, all of you who have never experienced spring, the second one with a subtle fragrance of April fields or love so hot, though earthly, which sometimes travels across my skin like shivers. Ah. You will help me, Buluś and God!

APRIL 16, 1942

Can you hear me? I call you over the world
The wind catches my every word
I command it to carry them across
This is my song, my response
My spring mating song!
I shout, I gush
taking air into my lungs
this chuckling rush
Listen to the wind when it comes
Listen to the hum, the chirp, the whisper
I call you, Mum, I summon
It's a cheerful call, the song's my whimper
It'll land by your feet, Mama
It might've seen blood on its way
It might've been scared by some graves
It might've met a cloud of gray agony
Or maybe hot tears in waves
And now any sound it doesn't deliver
It is pale, it curls up and shivers.
It was dawn
fragrant and vivid
in the orchard
wind
shook blooms
off the trees
We just sat there
daydreaming, in oblivion
forgetting the world that looms
Sweet gazes
and sweet verses
(d'you remember my blushing face?)
so very shy and cautious
the first ones, the very first

I loved, I dreamed, I longed.
All was quiet, bright and fresh
snow of apple blossom on the ground
we just sat there in the flesh
pale with happiness
white with flowers.
Sun took mercy on us
and covered us with dew
Not true, that didn't happen!
But it might happen anew.

You will help me, Buluś and God.

APRIL 20, 1942, MONDAY

Today is the Führer's birthday. And more. I want to scream with all my might. And I keep thinking of the words, "vodka is cold and lips are hot!"* And . . . No, I can't say this; Zyguś is right, can you express just how much? No, there are no words to describe it.

How can you be in love for 18 months? What an idiotic question! Only now you can really love. I am . . . Well, I lost my mind, I think. But no, everything is real, pulsating, seething with life and love and youth. I feel as though I were riding a chariot or racing into the wind and rain. And about Zygu, about my most wonderful one in the world, I can't write. I can't catch my breath, I can't find words. I might dissolve in my own tenderness, my affection. Today I was really ready to strangle him, but what would I do then? Zyguśka, I'm really writing this for you and you only! I've opened my heart to you and you're so very dear to me! I'm happy, happy and light and . . . Dreams! Stupid, mad, wonderful dreams! Everything.

I'll jump onto the windowsill
No, higher still

---

* Quote from a popular waltz entitled "Gwiżdżę na wszystko" (I Don't Care About Anything), with lyrics by Krzysztof Lipczyński and music by Jan Markowski, performed by Mieczysław Fogg.

Onto the roof I'll go
Climb a very tall tower
I'll strike a blow
Hit the bell's clapper on the hour
I will shout, I'll bellow
In a voice that is not mellow
The clapper ding-dongs
Bell-like, d'you hear?
Joy, bliss, life all along
Crazy love in the air
Which can't wait to be in the world
Quivering soul's a-ringing
I'm sweet 18 years old
It's all brimming
It's way too much to hold in
Perhaps then I will tell you
Perhaps I will begin
And it will be true
As if everybody knew
As if the whole world knew
What it doesn't in fact know
That in the spring breeze that cuts through
In every bit of sun aglow
Your little miss is on her way to you

You will help me, Buluś and God.

BEYOND TODAY. TOMORROW

I'm scared. I'm really scared for myself. I kept thinking in the night to write, write, write, but I couldn't write. Because I know my thoughts were focused. Just think, spring and the dreamy stuff that used to wander over the moon and the stars and in the world, was now combined into one strong embrace! And now it's not enough to imagine ♥, now I want to have him with me. It'd be best for me then, as it is I'm only well. But yesterday, I won't forget it, Zyguś, yesterday it was spring!

> *I'm just shocked that flowers*
> *don't sprout at your feet*
> *you, my bird, angel empowered*
> *you, May, paradise, you spring sweet*

I stifle this scream in me. I would run out to the fields, spread my arms wide and scream like crazy. May! Paradise! Spring! Spriiing! And then . . . One more embrace like this. Which would contain everything. God! I'm so terrible!

I've received postcards from Mom and Ticiu. Sad cards, horrible! And I, their child, feel so bright and singsong?! This is a terrible sin. Forgive me. Because I . . .

> *I don't care*
> *in the attic, in the cellar*
> *on the Aryan side, there, there*
> *as a ghetto wretched dweller*
> *my heart warmed with a flame like this*
> *makes the world a happy place*
> *my heart warmed with a gaze like this*
> *I'll go to the bottom of the sea with grace*
> *I can even wear an armband*
> *and not just one*
> *but bands abundance.*

No, this is still not what I want to write.

> *Listen to my news*
> *Wait, I will tell you something*
> *At night spring rain oozed*
> *And out of my head violets are sprouting.*
> *Don't know how it came about*
> *but when I was woken up*
> *the world was pink somehow*
> *And my head . . . green like a buttercup!*
> *I saw countless gloomy faces*

heard sighs full of black despair
and the lament, "what's with her
this girl! She whistles and leaps, oh dear
like a street urchin.
Incredible, something new is occurring here!"

Aunts, cousins and distant relations
Discuss how to bring the sinner back
Such disgrace for the family, such sensation
the whole clan is under attack!

I know, I should cower, make a sad face
I should hunker down a bit more
lament the world and the human race
busy darning old stockings, what a chore.
I should sigh over hard times
over endless human stupidity
I should worry
But why should I? What pity?
I promised myself long ago,
to chuck worries and sadness out.
Begone, what's distressing and full of sorrow
There's only space for love in my heart.

My buttonhole is adorned
With a pretty blossom
I paint hearts all over the world
I draw hearts all over the heavenly parts
Write your name in each of the hearts

I am to do physical work. You will help me, Buluś and God.

APRIL 24, 1942, FRIDAY

You were at Z's place. Zyguś knows you! Oh, paradise! Oh, May! Oh, springtime! Enough already . . . You will help me, Buluś and God.

APRIL 26, 1942, MONDAY*

I don't know where to start! I need to collect my thoughts and myself; I need to force myself to express everything. In fact this exclamation about paradise, May and springtime was the final one. At first I felt terrible. I wanted to tear you apart, burn you, crush you for giving my secrets away. How could you? After all, you promised me in the beginning to stay faithful! By what right did you reveal your pages so shamelessly? When I thought that somebody had forced (well, yes, forced) their way into my personal, most intimate realm, no, I didn't feel emptiness, but a terrible, burning shame. I don't anymore and I stopped feeling it soon after. You know, I thought he could understand me more than anybody else. In fact I thought he was the only person who could understand me. He knows me terribly well, scarily well. And he's good, loving, understanding and . . . Didn't he kiss me today like a father, a husband, a mother?

Ah, I don't feel like writing at all. I have some terribly sweet dreams to think through. But I have to write to make my soul lighter and brighter, to make everything clear. True, I'm not describing the details now, but I can't. (Zygmunt, after all you wanted me to grow up one day.) My writing's honest, that's true, it's fiercely heartfelt, but . . . (so there is a but) I think I lost a little, just a tiny bit of trust in you. In the past I entrusted you with my thoughts, those thoughts I didn't even think yet, but today I don't want to, I can't . . . Not that it's your fault, my dear Diary, it's not you, it's me and . . . no, it's just me. I'll forget about it now. I want to forget, I want to give you a verbal hug and say, "Thank you, my dear friend, for letting Zygu have a glance at my soul."

We came to an understanding today. I know we have understood each other for a long time now, but those words were not gathered together. I also know that I'm looking for a job and I know why I need this job. After all I'm me and I know why I'm doing something. But think, Zygu knows it too! This is outrageous and wonderful at the same time. And how does he know it? As I said, he knows me terribly well. Ah! Do you know that in fact this was the first time?! So did it come true? Do you know that Zygmunt's

---

* April 26, 1942, was a Sunday.

cousin came; she lives with them and I am to meet her? But I've saved the sweetest, the dearest bit for the very end. Do you know that we talked with Z about children today? About my, or rather, about our children? When he mentioned it I was very upset that he read it here (you spilled the beans again), but it was true. Zyguś was so loving when he asked me, "Boy or girl?" I almost went crazy with happiness. So now our secret has a third accomplice. This is so dear. I can't even . . . Even now I feel strange. Norka understands everything, but I know she doesn't want it as much as I do, that she finds it a bit surprising, because she's a modern woman. I, too, am not a thousand years old, but if the price of modernity is relinquishing a dream, I would go centuries back . . . Just to tenderly stroke my beloved child's head. And Zyguś understands it. Zyguś is a wonderful, good husband, the best. I'm still a bit shy writing about it, but it'll happen soon, very soon. You will help me, Buluś and God.

APRIL 30, 1942, THURSDAY

What do I have to tell you? Ah, there was something. It's almost May. But this May is not fragrant, green and fresh. I laugh my head off when I think that this bad weather is my doing. Indeed it's quite autumnal. I can feel this devilish temptation. So I won't say yes or no. But knowing that it might have happened because I wanted it so much pleases me, amuses me, delights me! Well, I don't need this wet weather for anything, but it also isn't in my way. And it serves to spite so many people. Ah, sometimes, like today, I'm tempted to be a malicious goblin. Yes, because Z said today that the little world consists of all people, while the world is I and Nora. He said it as ironically as he could. Well, because this is how it is. Aha! "But I'm sensing something." What? Something unpleasant must have happened to Z. Tough. I imagine he feels like a woman who has given herself away. I have also given myself away spiritually, i.e., I have given you away and now I'm not ashamed of anything (perhaps that's why I stopped blushing), but from time to time something flashes to remind me that it's happened, that it's done. I'll always be left with something, because I have thoughts even more secret than the biggest secrets, more secret $+ - \infty$. What Z showed me today about Brilliant People was very wise—that there are people who are proud but also sensitive, weak and touchy and that is what makes them bighearted. He's really got it spot-on. Even though I still sighed with relief when Z told me he would never read you again.

It's so nice to run a pen on a page. I'd like to write everything. That's why I create such a mess. But I'm still a bit worried that Z might have made me believe that I am somehow different. Will I not get manic, like Klim Samgin?* No! I will try to be normal (if I'm not already; and "average" too). Ah, excuse me! Perhaps all girls write diaries, ponder over everything, analyze everything? How do I know this isn't the case? My God, they do think after all. What do they think about? Perhaps they dream just like me?

Do you know, Z's mother said he doesn't look well when he comes back from my place, because he doesn't have an erotic outlet. I like that very much. Do you know why? Because it's serious and grown-up. This is not child's play, this is not about drawing hearts and staring at the moon. I can say that "an animal has awoken in me"! And again I get lost in myself or I annoy myself with my own thoughts, with what I say. I either exaggerate or there is more than I think.

No, today my writing's quite sober. It's horrible and cold. I can't smell the fragrance of daffodils or lilac. Not now, now there is nothing. But I know that as soon as I go to bed, it'll come; no, not today. Today I'll daydream; I'll imagine things. No, I'm taking it too far (or at least I think I do today).

It's natural that it's so incredibly nice to lie next to Z. Today we lay on the sofa. In fact all closeness is delicious and I constantly feel the need for such closeness. Yes, yes . . .

Anyway, I'm looking for a job, I don't have it yet; I don't know where I'll work. I don't want it to be at the Castle. But when I think that Z has read the diary, I can't believe it sometimes. But still . . . I'm generally sleepy, but I know that I'd happily drop all my complexes and shyness and analyzing and (oh no, not my dreams, I'm sorry, no, my angels!) and I'd give a big sigh like somebody who's removed uncomfortable clothes or shoes with some difficulty. In fact Z doesn't care that much about

---

* Protagonist of Maxim Gorky's series of novels *The Life of Klim Samgin,* describing the life of Russian intelligentsia at the turn of nineteenth and twentieth centuries. Its Polish translation (by Karolina Beylin) was published in the years 1929–1930.

children, how can he? I haven't met a person yet who would want to ponder on this subject. The other day I thought that he did. But he didn't even mention it. I know that if he'd talked about it, I would have been moved and happy. Ah, I'm such an idiot. I really am abnormal. It needs to be said. Bye, Zyguś, bye, Diary, bye, Mama . . . You will help me, Buluś and God.

MAY 2, 1942, SATURDAY

I feel heavenly in my blue shoes. Zyguś made them for me! What deliciousness! I'm touched when I think that he had me in mind while making them. And I'm so glad that it takes my breath away. I generally like everything and then this commotion with the clogs and all the fuss . . .

I'll write a letter to Buluś in a moment and tomorrow I'll invite Noruśka over for the whole day. Tra la la. Waltz and love and . . . May! Do you know it's May already today? It doesn't look like it behind the window, but you can sense it and you can kiss its sweet lips. Ah, how we caressed each other today! How delightfully! I simply can't write, because I float up in the air with euphoria.

Maciek came later and this and that, and Z, my love, was angry because of it and he said something (I stopped writing, I was taking a bath). You know, I haven't felt so great for a long time, I can barely keep my heart in, it wants to jump out. When Z told me today that it's May, I felt completely different, more love-like. But I calmed down a bit and I have to say that . . . well, despite everything I was a bit jealous of Maciek today. I was in such bliss today that I stroked Maciek. (Don't be angry, I'm trying to explain myself.) Well, whatever. Whenever something unpleasant happens to me, it's enough to look at those azure shoes and think that he's made them for me and . . . I feel somewhat azure-like too, i.e., heavenly. My life's filled with "this" again.

Aha, this cousin, Zośka, came today. I was terribly embarrassed because I felt she came to have a look at me and she did it with a curiosity that only women have. I don't know what to say about her, because I don't know her. But it seems she's quite like Zygu has described her . . . I don't care at all.

May has its own rights, especially for me. Zyguś is May-like too. This year he's more mine, not so mysterious, but affectionate and sweet. I think he loves me a bit more, while I love him the same, always the same, with all my might. "You cannot love less or more—you can only love" (*Anna Karenina*). It's the beginning of May.

> *Welcome, May . . . love*
> *illuminate our whole family**
> *you will only come visit in May*
> *but you will never cease to exist*

Bye, Zyguś . . . You will help me, Buluś and God.

Today is Sunday. But I can't wait any longer and so I write. I wrote a letter to my dear Mama. And I told her everything. And, in the spirit of honesty I also revealed what I didn't write down. I felt my joy was great—limitless, but somewhat stifled. And when I was writing the letter, I thought that I could hug her and show her my blue shoes and tell her that all is well; or perhaps it's this longing that I tend to always feel in May, this call of fields, trees in bloom, singing woods. Shame. If not for him, I wouldn't have even known it was May. But perhaps if Buluś were here, she wouldn't understand me. But Zyguś does understand me. I love her and I am writing to her. My wonderful Zyguś! I can feel this warm, heartfelt wave flooding my heart. In a moment I'll imagine myself hugging you, in your embraces and . . . much, much more.

Zosia L. came today. She's a lovely, very well-educated girl. Nora and I like her a lot. One can simply rely on her. I talked about Zyguś. Do you know his father asked if we were engaged? I like that very much, I like playing a pretend married couple. I like our "marriage." Indeed, you know, there's something very charming about those shoes, too. You have to feel it. How he brought them! Ah, he was such a darling. Can I write about it? No, there are no words for it, you can never tell how much. Why the mind? Why? And about May?

---

* First two lines refer to Rajnold Suchodolski's "Śpiew" (Singing), written during the November Uprising: "Welcome, May dawn / illuminate our Polish land."

It tosses, it wants to break free
It's locked away, sort of
May . . . May, crazy as can be
so green and so in love!
It jolts, it jerks, it lurches
"It's stifling, let me go
out in the fields, where sun marches"
It looks around feebly, but no
It punches hard with its fists
It fights with tears too
It calls for help, it twists
And opposite, is that true?
Another grave of the same kind
Among those walls so somber
A hundred Mays cry out
Asking to be freed to wander
in fields, in meadows, in the sun

You will help me, Buluś and God.

MAY 6, 1942, TUESDAY*

Norka's somewhat low-spirited. I think I've found a job; I might get it tomorrow. But no, I didn't want to write about that.

Today I was engulfed by this laziness, this delightful feeling. I wanted to laugh, to cry, but first and foremost to write. I didn't have time, I couldn't. But this May is more beautiful than the one last year. I mean, it's completely different. When I think about how close we are to each other, how honest with each other, I feel very moved. Just think, you can say what you think. I think "My dearest" and I say it. I want to kiss him, so I kiss him. I can tell him about my joys—and my pains, too. And he understands. Isn't that beautiful? Ah, it's so good. So good.

Today I fantasized, like before, that we are on a train. I sit in the corner, leaning against Z's shoulder, embracing him tighter and tighter. The

---

* May 6, 1942, was a Wednesday.

train rumbles and speeds somewhere . . . Where? I don't know. I shout out the name of some station—I don't care which one. We travel together; we leave the old world, its worries and regrets behind, we move toward a new, better one. That's why I always imagine us traveling. To make even one single step in life, you need to travel. So it's a pity that when I think "stay" (or even when I say it), he doesn't stay and then I miss him . . . We both miss each other. But this is the most beautiful longing, the most wonderful, because it's not hopeless. I would be embarrassed to write heresies. I'm sleepy. I send you such big kisses. You will help me, Buluś and God.

MAY 8, 1942, THURSDAY*

Ah! I love our miss so much! I love her, herself and her manifestations. Now I don't need to be told it's May. I can feel it in every muscle and every drop of my blood. I can feel something swelling in me, something growing to the absolute limit. It's nothing else but this love of mine, which became so "marriage-like," so bright and simple, direct, honest. It really is like that. Not only does it have its spiritual side, but also . . . the very tangible one too. Well, what shall I say, after all I'm not embarrassed in front of people—I simply feel that I can't get away from Zygu, that it gets more and more difficult to part with him. I never have enough caresses, I could bite him to death . . . you know, I can't . . . The memory itself has exhausted me. I don't know what happened to me. Just think, I am contented now that I'm not "flat as a board." I don't know what I need it all for, but I feel my own body. In fact this is the first time in my life that I am experiencing this feeling. I feel that my legs exist, I feel it all too well, I (cover your ears) would like to . . . well . . . I wanted to sgel ym neewteb mih ezeeuqs.† That's monstrous. No! Not at all, in fact it's pleasant! Why should I be shocked with something that seems to be delightful? Zygu's not so innocent either. It was him who stirred me up today so much I trembled, and then, then he gave me one more kiss and left as if nothing had happened, left me alone with my burning heart, my trembling soul, with my pressing thoughts and my simply sick, "nervy" imagination! No, it can't be like that! I don't write

* May 8, 1942, was a Friday.
† Words written backward.

poems anymore! I'm going through a period of not writing. And I don't want to force myself. But if I could, I would write! Rebellion! I'm rebelling; can you hear me? I don't want to lie there half the night with my eyes wide open; I want Zygu as close as is possible . . .

Phew, I got it out of my system. But even if I filled this diary to the last page, I wouldn't extinguish all of this fire raging in me. That other May was so very different, so much more subtle and romantic. This one, this one is wild, but it's this one, the untamed, wild one, the earthly one that's the most true and most delectable! How do I know?! Do I? I can't stop writing. Just like I couldn't part with Zygu. So much, so much . . . love overflows in me.

> *Tittle-tattle*
> *What a chatter*
> *about love, spring, May, some other matter*
> *About color red and green*
> *in somebody's eyes shimmering*
> *About the morning dawn's hue*
> *Listen, Renuś, it's all for you.*

You will help me, Buluś and God.

MAY 9, 1942, SATURDAY

This morning was so sunny, like a proper spring. The sun woke me up and as soon as I opened my eyes, I thought about seeing Z. And the sheer thought made me so happy that I wanted to see him then and there. I got dressed an hour too early . . . Doesn't matter. Finally we were walking together, holding hands like "two well-behaved children." No, it really was sweet and when I write this, I don't want to write the rest. Because when I started ruminating, a thought came to me that he's a bit patronizing, that he kindly allows me to love him (I didn't say he doesn't love me, I didn't say that at all), but sometimes he looks at me as if he wanted to say, "Let the child have fun." And when he notices that I'm all . . . well, springlike, then I have a feeling he thinks himself better and wiser. For example yesterday he said, "I will give you one more kiss and off you go." And it came to me that this is something a girl usually says. But whatever, let's assume that I love him like a boy loves a girl. And anyway, when I said that our miss is so direct, why didn't he want to look me in the eye? Perhaps it's only on my side? Ah! I must shake it off. I must! This stumbling is terrible. I know what it did to Anna Karenina and Anna Fülop.

I felt so fantastic in the morning and he said, like he hasn't for a long time, he said, so sweetly and brightly, "Bye, poppet." Aha, this was the so-called (self-) confidence that the sun shone for me! It must be because of the war, but the war'll surely end soon. Zygmunt says there'll be an offensive from the West, in France. He said that a long time ago, but he's convinced it'll happen now. Well, let's see if he could be a diplomat. Springlike bye-byes . . . You will help me, Buluś and God.

MAY 9, 1942, SATURDAY

The spring appearance materialized. But I know what I wanted to write about. Something's bothering me. It was terribly delightful. We started talking about a complex and again I felt small, unimportant, helpless. I felt very sad. Good that Zyguś put it down to unusual times.

I'm sad about not seeing anybody, I'd like to invite Norka for the whole day, but I can't and it's not up to me. I feel she's angry at me.

The job's not working out either. I have to go there the day after tomorrow and I'm very scared.

Zyguś is lovely, but . . . Listen, Rena (just between the two of us), aren't you by any chance jealous of this Zosia? No, why would you think that?! But something's the matter. Perhaps I'm envious of her self-confidence or the fact that she has him all the time, always, all day long and I'm left with such emptiness, like now . . . I got so attached. His condescension is still apparent, even more so now. "You are already thinking of a little house" and in general he says, "More and more." And he thinks that I . . . He doesn't even imagine how bad this longing can be, this longing for the person closest to one's heart. One can pine like that, I pine like that— but not all the time. And then I feel bad. I have decided to get it under control, not to say it. Not to say that I miss him so much, so as not to make him look down on me the way he does. Whatever happens, not to say it all. It is annoying, even to me, that he knows. But he knows how to mitigate it. He's so becoming when he says that we're children after all.

I wrote it all down, but I don't feel relieved. Maybe a bit. I'm still so-so. I can't even daydream, like I did in the morning. And it was so good to daydream in the morning! I'll write after work, which scares me so much. I believe in You. Surely You will lend me a helping hand. You will help me, Buluś and God.

I have been also thinking about the insignificance of life in the face of eternity. It calms me down. I didn't write down the date, as I was supposed to write tomorrow. But I have a terrible urge to write today, or to speak to somebody.

This morning I did some thinking and I wrote a letter to Mom, but neither calmed me down, on the contrary. I feel like it's terribly cold and stifling at the same time.

Today I thought about working incognito in the countryside, for example as a farmer, about experiencing only physical labor and not thinking at all. About feeling the work in my bones and muscles, about understanding the carefree calm in peasants' life. What am I supposed to do? Something torments me all the time. Recently I've been tormented by the idea of Zygu loving me more than I love him and I was feeling guilty about it. Now I think that I love him more and somehow more fiercely than he loves me. And so on, and so forth. And life's so simple. I just complicate it terribly. You will help me, Buluś and God.

10 p.m. I need to write again. Earlier I worried unnecessarily, now I have a reason. Ghetto again. Oh, God! How much can we take? Who knows where we'll live and how? You have to pay through the nose for everything. We used to sit here in this room with Zyguś and caress, hug each other, and now it's all getting ruined again. But I believe, I feel that nothing bad will happen. Lord, listen to my pleas that I bring to You every day.

I went to Nora's, on my way back I bumped into Julek and Lidka. They were walking together. This really unnerved me; I was disgusted and sickened. It was so insincere. I don't know whether to tell Nora. I think I will. I'm glad it's Monday tomorrow, I want to share my worries with Z. I can't live without it.

I will give you all the flowers
Just love me, my dear child

Nightingales' musical shower
Will meet you by your hut
My tears' stream will emanate
Meadows in bloom by the forest
And my deep sighs will create
Nightingales' nightly chorus

Bye, Zyguś, bye, Mama, I'm so scared of this job. Lord God, help me tomorrow and always . . . You will help me, Buluś and God.

MAY 11, 1942, MONDAY

Thank You, Miraculous God. The job isn't so terrible. I spent the day with Nora today. We talked all day long. We understood each other, we always understand each other easily. But her attitude to love is different, light, while mine is serious. She says that will make me unhappy. Perhaps, but I know I can't do it any other way. About the complex too. Yes, Nora, if we learn to dance and if we dance well, all will be well! After this conversation, I was exhausted and had a headache.

One shouldn't think or talk about it, Z is right. Z, my heart, has read you. I'm angry! This truly is the end. But we need to talk about this issue; it isn't our fault, but spring's. And this ghetto, this situation, this war . . . Bye, I will be working and I won't write often. You will help me, Buluś and God.

MAY 12, 1942, TUESDAY[23]

Recently when I feel bad, I write, and when I feel good, I write. I must write. Listen! Listen to me and understand. Some kind of fever has taken over the city. The specter of the ghetto, already forgotten by everybody, has returned. And it's even more dreadful than before, because it knocks on the doors of petrified hearts and it's ruthless, it doesn't want to go away. Yesterday it scared me too, but today—no. Nothing can touch me today. I'm glad I'm crying now, when nobody can see me. I shouted today, "Oh, God, I want the moment to come when they take me away!"

No, I don't want that! Lord, forgive me. But my soul was so embittered that I felt like maybe that would be for the best. Mama writes to us saying that children are being taken away into forced labor. She told me to pack. She wants to be with us and at the same time she wants . . . ah! They are splitting for good. Mom wants to send Ticiu an official letter asking for divorce. And us . . . well, what's the point of writing about it—it makes me blubber terribly and turn on my waterworks. In this terrible whirlwind of the war we have neither mother nor father. The turmoil of life has taken us to some terrible crossroads. We are left on our own. They'll never patch it up. Mama will remarry and I will never, ever again come to the door of my parents' home. My mother . . . Her husband will be a stranger, a foreigner. And father, oh! He wrote to me that he was not sure if he would ever see me again! Ticiu, you are an unlucky Jew, just like me, locked away in the ghetto. Holy God, can You save me? Can You save them? All of them. Oh, please, work a miracle!

Such a heavy mood at home. Bimba is stressed, overworked and exasperated. She torments herself. She suffers because of children, because of her husband and relatives. One can't even laugh in the house because of that. And they keep reminding me that I'm at their mercy.

Life is so miserable. Miserable, ugly, evil, but my heart still fills with sorrow, when I think . . . will I die? What awaits us in the future? Oh, God Almighty! So many times, I've asked You and You've listened to me—please bring an end to our misery. I feel better now; it's so good to have a cry. What hurts the most is them. Indeed a long time ago already, indeed always, but . . . still. People say now that food's the most important thing. I've had a good, filling dinner—and I feel so terrible. I'm not hungry, but I'm hungry for somebody's caring protection.

And Zyguś? Yes, that might be why I don't want to say goodbye to life. Mama, don't hold it against me. I know it would be a terrible blow to you, but you are going to have your own life now. You might even have more children. And my grandparents are old and tired, they deserve a better old age. Sometimes I just want to ask why we were forced onto them? But now I am so exhausted. I didn't really count on us having a home together in the future; I just had this timid, naïve dream. I'm not really disappointed, I just looked around at the world and it scared me with its emptiness. Nobody! Is there really nobody close? And Mama, so dear, is always so far away, and will be with some man who is a stranger to me.

I'm not crying anymore. The man I will be with will be a stranger to her. Life brings people together and then separates them.

> *With passion they squabbled and scuffled*
> *feathers got ruffled*
> *they tore their little nest*
> *to pieces and still didn't rest*
> *down was scattered around*
> *quill, blades of grass and chaff,*
> *hay too in all this riffraff*
> *they told each other words that were sorest*
> *and flew into the forest*
> *to look and roam*
> *for new homes*
> *forgetting, both of the birds*
> *about their two chicks*
> *left on their own in the sticks*

MAY 15, 1942, FRIDAY

Today is a memorable day. I've received the first money I earned. I'm very proud of it and I don't know what to spend it on. I'd like to send it to Ticiu. I'll see.

Imagine, he came today. I was so happy. So, so much. It was my dream to see him today and he came. My beautiful Kokośka, my Zyguś. He's the sweetest. My daddy. He was my shoulder to cry on for a bit. Oh, he understands me so well, like nobody else in the world. And, you know, indeed he understood, as I knew he would. He told me that he can't worship me all the time like some goddess, that he's not a perpetuum mobile and this and that. And I think sometimes, for example today, that I am indefatigable and that this miss doesn't show herself in her entirety at all. Great Lord God, You know how much I like hugging him, snuggling next to him, being cuddled by him. It's so lovely, so delightful, so sweet. Everything is easier and cozier when I'm with him. Bye-bye, dear Diary, so many new sensations, good ones, I think, thanks to you, who "leads me into the unknown." You will help me, Buluś and God.

SATURDAY

For you I waited
in the evening with bated
breath, with the door ajar
by brightly shining stars
their color was the sweetest
and the flowers' caress was the deepest
their fragrant grace
gave the coziest embrace
May breeze whispered to the moon
that my beloved will be here soon.
The evening's hum was gone
its wings slid across the nightly sky
the flowers and stars withered in front of my eyes
You didn't come, unfortunately.

Sorrowful is the last gaze
into the distant haze
sorrowful is longing
for love and bonding
and somebody's extended hand
to say goodbye in the end
Sorrowful is such a long, futile wait
like today at the gate.

Everything was so pretty
flowers and all the sweeties
goodbyes and handshakes
like the words of a banal song
out the window as if wrong.
A platform, noisy and busy
then the rattling and wheezing
of an arriving train
a window open again
in a carriage
a heart broken in the chest

tears barely swallowed at best
and the train and me and YOU . . .
Golden oranges were beautiful
as were words of farewell
and pleading looks and a sigh
The most beautiful was this one word,
an ordinary word—goodbye.

I'm so very sad. You help me, Buluś and God.

MAY 18, 1942, MONDAY

"The world is so lovely and I'm feeling good"—this is what I wrote to Buluś. Oh, so so good! Today made up for the Saturday waiting. It was so delightful, so May-like, so springlike! May is such a wonderful month! Zyguś is divine and love's beautiful! It's hard to part. And those caresses . . . Ooooh, I might see him tomorrow.

It's nice at work. Norka has a problem with Julek. I feel very sorry for her. Z'll see her tomorrow. Bye-bye, dear Diary. I send you kisses, just like I kiss and hug Zygu. You will help me, Buluś and God.

MAY 19, 1942, TUESDAY

My Mama has written a letter. So heartfelt, so lovely. I'm feeling so good and I'm so moved. She says she loves Zyguś. Oh, it's so so so good, Mama. She has called me from afar in such a sincere way, with such warmth. I need to respond to this cry of the mother's heart. She told me about her worries and joys, about her hopes. Poor her. Lord God, please protect her and carry my blessing to her. Sleep well, Dear Mama. God is looking after us.

Noreńka came today. She's in a terrible state. Irka and Lida are getting back to themselves. I can't write about it, it's disgusting. When my be- loved Zyguś mentioned him, I felt sick. Of course it's fear. He sometimes jokes about it too. But, you know, we talked about Julek's "involvement" (it's all because of the involvement) and then I thought that Z, as lovely, close and real as he is, is also afraid of it. He's afraid of words. He either doesn't want to say too much or is evasive. And I still blush. For example today, couldn't he say to this stranger, a soldier, *"Das ist meine Braut"*?* I'd say it for sure. But there's something else here; this is an emergency.

In the meantime I fall even more deeply in love with him. If I can, I'll rekindle the relationships with my girlfriends, otherwise I'll become a recluse.

I feel very sorry for Nora, it must be so hard for her to see us together. But truth be told, "The replenished understand not the pain of the starving." And perhaps I don't feel as sorry for her as I'd like to. I don't know why, but I do think it's her fault too. Well, what matters is that Mama stays safe and I and Zyguś remain in love and . . . I can't, I'm blushing, this morning was so wonderful. Good night. You will help me, Buluś and God.

MAY 20, 1942, WEDNESDAY

I'm so selfish, it's unbelievable! I have to write every single day. Even if it's just a few words. I have to repeat that I love him, because I don't know where it ends and where it starts. Yesterday I was a little bit angry. But think, Z came to pick me up from my job at the factory and we walked holding hands. Orchards are in bloom, May is shining with its blue skies and I'm shining, too, with joy. That's how I feel, I really feel like his little daughter and I like it oh so much!

Zośka works for the regiment. I told Malka about miss, but only in general terms. She's a very nice, sweet girl. I was really happy. Bye-bye, we might talk soon . . . You will help me, Buluś and God.

MAY 21, 1942, THURSDAY

Oh, the dream, the dream, the dream of youth! I'm tired, so very tired. It's a wonderful May night. So fragrant. The sky's navy blue, but I'm not allowed to get too emotional, because when I think of . . . Grrr . . .

Zyguś was terribly amused today, he was laughing and ready for jokes. Sometimes I think he jests on purpose, because he's embarrassed of

---

* This is my fiancée (German).

himself. But I get embarrassed when he reminds me that I . . . well. He said that he was quite serious about it; that he'd like to put me to bed, to take me with him (it was on the platform). Why does he say those things? Well, let him, I actually like it very much. Let him say it, let him kiss me, let him love me, love me, love me! After all! Is it true? Ah, how lovely Klaus* is, really, how about it? I think it would be the height of happiness. I'm so silly. But still I want and that is that . . .

> *You tell me that you love me terribly*
> *that you miss me unbearably*
> *I know it isn't very modest of me*
> *but I want it and that is that*

You will help me, Buluś and God.

MAY 23, 1942, SATURDAY

Always on Saturdays. It would have been easier if I wrote several days ago. Now I don't know what to write, where to start? Something has been bothering me terribly the last few days. I talked to Nora and in the end I told her that this other trait of Zygmunt is bothering me. This and that. But still, once, not so long ago, I asked Jarośka why the whole world was against us, why they all thought it funny, stupid, absurd? Not Mama, not anymore. And I'd like to give her a big hug for it. But Nora too, even her. I know that she is thinking about what it's going to be like when my romance ends. She's accusing me of taking it too seriously and (does she have a clearheaded view of it?) she makes my heart ache. I know that she's not sure, she doubts whether Z really loves me. I know it; I can feel it. And it pains me; it bothers me perhaps. Those tiny, unimportant details . . .

Because you should know that I am jealous, terribly, insanely jealous. And I think it's this jealousy and not my complex (which is gone now) that makes me hate. It annoys me. Constantly, it annoys me constantly.

And Zyguś sometimes says something without realizing it and it hurts

---

* It is not clear who Renia is referring to here.

me so badly. Sometimes, when it bothers me too much, I think about running away. To run away, to run away as far as possible, to be away from him but also to not see it all, to not suffer this agony. But there are times when I know that it is not possible. When I hold him tightly, when he's near, so very near, I feel that I wouldn't be able to part with him for all the treasures in the world. That would mean giving up my soul, the most important part of my life.

Nora, you are wrong. You're different, but I'd be left with nothing.

Studying, nature—that's all good when love is fulfilled or when you've never experienced it. One thing perhaps—poetry. Poems would flow in a wide stream like tears, like longing, like despair and suffering.

I knew that Zygmunt's parents were part of the hostile atmosphere surrounding us, but I wasn't aware how much against it they were and how important it was. Because of his late returns? What else? And what if Irka . . . What then? But I do know, because I take a bit of him away from them. Who ever heard of such a young boy getting so seriously involved? I understand and I don't resent them for it, but I'm a bit sorry about it, yes and no. It can be something very important or not important at all.

I love Zyguś the most in the world. He is my dearest and he is most mine. I don't want to bother him with my issues, but I know that nobody in the world understands me like he does. It's always so that when your heart aches, you can feel this pain in all your limbs. Which is why my worries hurt me more then.

When Z is good to me, everything is good and bright and full of sunshine. It's May, 23rd of May—such a shame the month is about to pass. The nights are filled with stars. They're so intoxicating and I dream so much, I dream, I dream. You will help me, Buluś and God.

MAY 24, 1942, SUNDAY

A morning like today can happen only when you're young, when you're in love and when you're loved back. Oh, my God, it was so amazing! We were so close and . . . no, nothing can change that. The world's so cruel! I always knew it too. But it's sweet that Z has various adventures and that he tells me about them . . . In any case I like to know. I'll come up with something. But why would I care that they are evil, insincere, jealous, when Z is the best and the sweetest? After all I am not in love with them, but with him. And I know that my dream will come true, like all my dreams, because it is fate. And it'll be so, if we persevere, we'll survive and we'll be a happy couple. And I won't be stupid anymore; I'll just smile when looking at silly things. Oh, Mama, my Mama! You and Zyguś, please love me! You will help me, Buluś and God.

MAY 25, 1942, MONDAY

He picked me up from the factory at noon. And it was (oh, Dido is so annoying!) wonderful. All young, all May—that should be enough for you and anyway:

> *When I hear those words so sweet*
> *those dear words, oh, my Good Angel*
> *each is a precious treasure at my feet*
> *each says more than many pages.*
> *But if I wanted to say*
> *how wonderful is this night in May*
> *words would become meaningless*
> *words would be laughable, I guess.*

It is a wonderful May night now! With a smiling moon. Oh, if only Z were with me. I place my invisible hands on Mama's temples and on Ticiu's. Good Lord God, take care of them and of us. You will help me, Buluś and God.

MAY 26, 1942, TUESDAY

I'm writing by the light of the moon—literally. The story unfolds. I know, or rather I feel that it's all Zośka's fault. And I know why she does it—it's not about the other girl, but about the change, about separating me from him and . . . Not tomorrow, on Thursday. I can't even tell whom I hate more—her or them. It's been like that from the very beginning, grrr. You will help me, Buluś and God!

MAY 28, 1942, THURSDAY

I love Z very much. He is so athletic and I'm so impressed. I can take cover by him, I can simply cuddle against him—it's so great, so snuggly and . . .

But let's start from the beginning. After all it wasn't a nice day today.

First thing in the morning—the meeting, going beetroot red and then discussing work; then the conversation with Zyguś. Then there was Maciek and finally this disgusting plot, which evolved into something of a horrible size and nothing of it. Because this whole adventure with Z is rather pleasant. But also strange, oh, so strange! I didn't realize it could be like that.

Z says that I am languid and inflexible, and this and that, and he constantly probes me about the reasons why I don't like dancing. And I don't like dancing because I don't know how to dance. And when I feel like today, when I feel so strange, it's like a shiver, like I don't know what, and I'm against it. Hell, am I the biggest swine on planet Earth? Oh, it's so good to get it off my chest, I feel relieved. I'm glad he feels comfortable mentioning me so openly, but at the same time it hurts, I feel like I'm stuck at a lower level and I can't soar. But then I forgot about everything in the world. When I hugged him, when I clung to him with my whole body . . .

The most difficult part is always saying goodbye. Somehow I love him with my whole body and having him close is like having a personification of spring by me. And spring can be intoxicating! Is it true that women are dangerous in springtime? Yes, wild females. But not me, I only like the most innocent caresses which then make me go into a strange state and if it wasn't 9 p.m. I would probably go wild just like them, but . . . Well, girl, don't go crazy—ah, I'm taken and that is that. You will help me, Buluś and God.

JUNE 2, 1942, TUESDAY

Probably—but it's difficult to write. You know, now I know what the word ecstasy means. I almost understand it. It's indescribable; it's the best thing two loving creatures can achieve. For the first time, I felt this longing to become one, to be one body and . . . well . . . to feel more, I could say. To bite and kiss and squeeze until blood shows. (And then there's this other symptom.) And Zyguś talked about a house and a car and about being the best for me.

Lord God, I'm so grateful to You for this affection and love and happiness! I'm writing these words differently, whispering them in my mind so I don't scare them away or blow them out. To write a poem, but a bloodthirsty one, a springtime one. Mama is on her own, even H is not there. I don't want to think about anything, I just want to desire so badly, so passionately like . . . you know. You will help me, Buluś and God.

JUNE 6, 1942, SATURDAY

Days and moods have shimmered. Not many days have passed, but many thoughts have flown through my mind. One morning I woke up and I thought that something had happened. Two aerials stuck out of the roof opposite, piercing the blue sky. I could only see those aerials and the snippet of the sky between them and nothing more. Why am I writing about it? Because I want to show you that it wasn't some symbol that brought this thought. I simply woke up from a dream, which told me not to believe in my great, cherished fantasy. Why? I don't know. I just felt grown-up and found this fantasy childish, stupid and unfeasible. So this is how it is when you look at the world dispassionately—two aerials and the sky. And me, so wise, I could smile with derision, but I have no energy and no courage for it . . . So my belief lessened now, but it came back and is increasing bit by bit. I still pray with the same zeal as before. Not now. What I want the most is the dream. I want the desire, yes, because I desire with every tiny bit of my body, my thoughts, my imagination. Even the most innocent book stirs me up, as does the closeness of other people, and us. Ah, I struggle with such horrible dreams, disgusting dreams. And I . . . and you. A swaying ship, I'm running, gaining speed . . . and . . . and . . . should I jump?! I would jump if . . . I'd jump a thousand times if he existed forever.

I haven't seen Zyguś today, he's overworked, tired and weak. And it's good, it's very lucky, because right now I'm brimming with energy. My greed for life makes me fierce. I'd like to use my power in an honorable battle. You will help me, Buluś and God.

JUNE 7, 1942, SUNDAY[24]

I'm at peace. Nora and I went for a long walk deep into the quarter and we talked. She was the first person I told. I realized that burden was what was tormenting me. We browsed through the sweet album and I felt good and most of all—at peace.

Zygmunt was there too, he was there and then left, I shouldn't have written it down.

We also talked about Waldek. It's strange. Sometimes I wonder if I'm not in l . . . e with him. I could choke on this word. And only half an hour ago my heart throbbed with fear.

Wherever I look, there is bloodshed. Such terrible pogroms. There is killing, murdering. God Almighty, for the umpteenth time I humble myself in front of You, help us, save us! Lord God, let us live, I beg You, I want to live! I've experienced so little of life, nothing. I don't want to die. I'm scared of death. It's all so stupid, so petty, so unimportant, so small. Today I worry about being ugly; tomorrow I might stop thinking forever. Yes, yes, war is terrible, savage, bloody. I feel I've become like that because of it.

> *Think, tomorrow we might not be*
> *A cold, steel knife*
> *Will slide between us, you see*
> *But today there is still time for life*
> *Tomorrow sun might eclipse*
> *Gun bullets might crack and rip*
> *And howl—pavements awash*
> *With blood, with dirty, stinking slag*
> *Pigwash*
> *Today you are alive*
> *There is still time to survive*

Let's blend our blood
When the song still moves ahead
The song of the wild and furious flood
Brought by the living dead

Listen, my every muscle trembles
My body fumbles for your closeness
It's supposed to be a choking game, this is
Not enough eternity for all the kisses.

I was interrupted. But this thought absorbs me. Is it worth making an effort? No! I'm telling you, something'll come up. What? Don't know. But it will. Or perhaps already has. Can't get it out of my head. Now is the time to think of other things. Lord God, forgive me, save me and protect me. Great One, end this war now. You will help me, Buluś and God. I believe in you!

JUNE 9, 1942, TUESDAY

I'm ill and slightly grumpy. I fear so much for Jarośka. She's coughing, she needs to be taken to the doctor's (her lungs are so weak). Granny refuses. I tell her that she should do it, Granny thinks that "should" is a relative thing to say. So what now? She's a young child. Ah, Granny herself never goes to the doctor, she has this rule, but should it apply to a young child whose whole life is ahead of her? Maybe she should simply be helped, saved? Perhaps she's really ill?

These are ordinary and stupid words—but tell me, do you understand the despair they contain? This child is really poorly. Bimba nags her terribly, but she never holds back. This situation's not her fault after all, it was others who did it to her, why is Bimba so unfair?

I really felt like crying today. Granny thinks I should revive my poetry writing ambition. I yelled, "Granny, you don't understand!" Mom wanted to turn me into a writer, but can one be "turned into" a writer? Oh, these people don't understand anything. And I'm being told this now, when I'm trying to stop myself from writing verses. Because I don't want to write when I have something to write about and I want to, but when I can, when I have to. They don't know how much it hurts. And the killing goes on, the murdering. Zyguś is the only breath of spring and sunshine. You will help me, Buluś and God.

JUNE 14, 1942, SUNDAY

It's dark, I can't write. Panic in the city. We fear a pogrom; we fear deportations. Oh God Almighty! Help us! Take care of us; give us Your blessing. We will persevere, Zyguś and I, please let us, let us survive the war. Take care of all, of mothers and children. Amen. You will help me, Buluś and God.

JUNE 15, 1942, MONDAY

I'm restless and drunk. I spent the whole day in a terrible fright. I was tired, exhausted, in despair. And I've longed so badly . . . I long. Just think, two days and two nights. Dark nights, thick with darkness, just think, I burned so badly, I longed so badly.

In the daytime I was choking with the heavy, threatening atmosphere of the dead city. Oh, days are so hard. Nerves are engaged, they jerk with tension, senses are engaged too, dying with longing.

Was Zyguś sweet? I don't know if he was particularly sweet, but he was somehow deliciously manly. And at the end I felt that he was first and foremost a man. It was the second time I felt it. I compared it to a book. I surprised myself that I could. I want to laugh out loud, ha ha ha, laugh myself sick. This feeling is worthy of gods and people in ecstasy. One would like to let go. No! No! We'll persevere, won't we? Yes. My wonderful springtime head, we'll persevere!

He was delightful and when I'm with him, I feel so small, like a child, I feel safe. It's completely dark now. I'm writing in the darkness, but I still know what I'm writing.

The conversation about lips was not pleasant, but it didn't spoil anything. Nothing and nobody could spoil this.

God Almighty, please let it go on, keep on saving us. Only You can protect us and my faith is so powerfully strong. You will help me, Buluś and God!

I devise you, my amorous tremble
I devise you with my thoughts alone
A bloody spring fruit you resemble
My body embraced by hips, I groan
My chest billows restlessly, I moan
Veins pulsate angrily, with danger
with a holy act, holy pain, holy anger
blessed be the sense that feels.
I will grab you, smother, crush you, peel
Take you between my hips
Oh! I will be generous and giving
I will be happy, I will be living.
I will absorb you, I will writhe and adore,
I will kiss you like a lithe whore
A real one, real and alight.

The pinnacle of crudeness! I will smack my own face for it, but I'll still write it. In the evening! I haven't written down a prayer. I wrote about silliness and I was thinking about it. Forgive me, Lord. Who will I raise my hands to, if You abandon me? Whom will I trust? Holy God, please protect me, put Your hand on the heads of those who believe, who need Your protection.

My Dear Mama, today, in this terrible, horrible moment, you're with strangers and perhaps it's better this way, perhaps you're safer . . . but if you were (God forbid) . . . if we were . . . I don't want to say it. And again, for the umpteenth time when children cuddle up to their mothers, you're far away. All of the important, dangerous, crucial moments in life divide us. And you, my Dear Mama, pray for us, pray for us wherever you are. There is one God. He will listen to you, pray for your orphaned children. Our God is the only one, people died saying these words, believing and I am still alive, alive and faithful.

You will help me, Buluś and God.

JUNE 18, 1942, THURSDAY

Today is my big day. I turn 18 on the 18th. I'm an adult now, but I don't know much. There has been plenty of sadness and worry in my life already, plenty of joy and love too. But I don't know much; I don't even know what I should know. Right now I'm feeling good, I'm not so bad, thank goodness.

Nora is a sweet, good creature. She suffers because she doesn't know much. I find it strange how we all attract each other, we who are so "self-critical." She likes Maciek. That would be great, wouldn't it?!

What's the day today? I smashed my head. Then everyone gathered and it was quite nice. Norka has given me the album, a complete one, beautifully bound, wonderful! Oh, there's something so sweet, so lovely, so good; something that lifts us, makes us better. Yet another fulfilled dream. Nora, I believe and you know that it's not the last one . . .

Zyguś has given me chocolates and two gingerbread hearts, Irka flowers and perfume, and Maciek sent me roses and a card, wishing for all my dreams to come true.

And I? What can I say, sometimes I dream about being famous, about reaching heights and flying across the world, and not just in my mind. And yet sometimes I just want to be an ordinary person—a townswoman, a mother. I want, I want so very badly to have children, happy and good, righteous, noble and honest children. Who knows which of those tasks is nobler, which one is harder?

Oh, I feel so good, Mama, and I know that you're sending many dear words through the air. Do you know that I am already 18? Yes, and I believe, and I love those whom I loved.

I have decided to work on myself from now on. There's still time, one can still become somebody. The one who has a spiritual life, who can have such a life, has to have something to build it upon. Not all lives rest on beautiful legs. And yes, yes, yes . . . Should I say it? Well, yes, I will, as it's like a grain of sand stuck in a shell, which becomes a pearl. Suffering is the pearl of love. I was angry at Irka and Zygu. I can't even imagine good moments not being poisoned by something. But he was so sweet, that's true, so lovely. He's coming tomorrow. If it's not a dream, then we'll soar high . . .

This goodbye has made me angry.

Tomorrow I go to Nora to get Kiciek.

Good night. Mama, I send you a kiss, I embrace you, as always. You love me the most in the world. Your wishes are my road to follow and my life's blessing. You will help me, Buluś and God.

JUNE 19, 1942, FRIDAY[25]

And God saved Zygu. Oh, I'm beside myself. They were taking people away all night long. They rounded up 1,260 boys. There are many victims, fathers, mothers, brothers. The sea of our blood is red, forgive us our trespasses, listen to us, Lord God! This was a terrible night, too terrible to describe. But Zyguś was here, my sweet one, sweet and loving. It was so good; we cuddled and kissed endlessly. I almost forgot about yesterday, though it was my birthday, so he could have spared me this. But that's the way he is. That's his disposition, his nature. He likes "women." Zośka, this "red-haired fog," was here as well. I was so stupid to show that poem. Even Z. said so. Well, tough, that's exactly what matters. There are times when one can speak and write, but not act. And it really was so delightfully pleasant that it was worth all the suffering. But sometimes I think it isn't worth it, that a loving woman has to pay too high a price.

> *June night*
> *pregnant*
> *with dense darkness*
> *night . . . stretches*
> *above my head.*
> *Night of solitude*
> *Came. The irresistible one stood*
> *at the end of the bed*
> *with a tormenting face*
> *dug its claws*
> *into the sticky brain*
> *and I dream . . .*

My naked thoughts
stripped of clothing
stretch under my skull
in silence
and for mercilessly long
the night goes on.

Heavy black shroud
dropped and clings
to the body
silent and stubborn
I shuddered.
The flower opens
in quiet
open lips
whisper words
fragrance of jasmine
of maturing buds.
Moan
exasperation slowly easing
senses sigh with relief
sweet fantasy
Dawn . . .

You will help me, Buluś and God.

JUNE 23, 1942, TUESDAY

Again words mean nothing; again words are ridiculous. Yesterday we experienced one of the wonderful symphonies of youth.

There was a kind of pogrom in our quarter. Buluś wrote and told me to leave the city for Tłuste* with Zyguś. She wrote "together." "Together"! It would be so delightful, so sweet! Though it's absurd for now. But nowadays even the biggest absurdity can become true.

---

* A prewar town in Poland (near Zaleszczyki), a district during the German occupation.

Oh, my dear Zyguś, we'll go away together, tra-la-la-la-la . . . aaah! Bimba says hello and I send you a kiss, Zyguś does too. Rena. You will help me, Buluś and God.

JUNE 25, 1942, THURSDAY

Where to start . . . Well. I'll just say it how it is. A wave of good and bad came. It's all right now, because it's all right to dream, to kiss. But today I don't "burn," I'm not like a dog trying to break free from its chain, even though I'm still full of longing. That's because Z has said a terrible thing today. He's said he wanted to read my diary, because that arouses him; it provides him with stimulation. Listen, my dear Diary, I love you, I love you, you're my soul, you're alive in a thousand of my bright memories, you cry the tears of my old worries, but I never ever wrote you for you to become stimulation in love! Am I to constantly tear the deepest parts of my soul apart, am I to make my heart bleed so that he can believe me and so that he can find pleasure in it? What about me, why do I love without any stimulation? (I find my stimulation in daydreaming.) I don't think life's so idyllic. Life is full of bitterness; one doesn't even need to look for it. And that's why Zygmunt was like that, exactly like that. It was because there was too much sweetness.

> *When your worry goes to sleep*
> *don't wake it up*
> *there's so much bitterness in life*
> *it's the source of the worst evil*
> *when your worry goes to sleep*
> *don't wake it up.*
> *Be happy, laugh and smile*
> *it only lasts a short while*
> *When your worry goes to sleep, don't wake it up*
> *there's so much bitterness in life!*

I think that even though Z is good and affectionate and sweet (today he was really sweet), there's something strangely calm about him. It's not the first time I thought this. I'm writing and thinking, and I'm angry, like today, but as soon as I curl up next to him, as soon as I hug him, I walk on air again. What am I going to do? Fantasies are the most wonderful too. They'll come true; they have to! Can one love somebody and dislike them at the same time? You will help me, Buluś and God!

THE FOLLOWING DAY

Most likely one can. No, I can't write about it today, because I'm angry. Z, the one who can be so dear, as warm as my own heart, can also be so distant. Yes, yesterday he was distant. It was hard for me, and strangely gloomy. I'm so glad I have my poetry! My poems. I love them so much.

It's not true, Z is not good for me at all! He says things, for example about my taste changing. He says that on purpose, he says that to hurt me and when one loves somebody, one doesn't want to hurt them. Life is overcast, but our tiny bit of sky was blue. Now there is nothing left. On days like today I think that we would be unhappy together. But this thought hurts so much. Oh, Lord God, why does it hurt so badly? It's terrible, it's so very hard; I wish it were Saturday already. You will help me, Buluś and God!

JUNE 27, 1942, SATURDAY EVENING

Good, peaceful, quiet, blessed Saturday evening. My soul has calmed down. Why? Because again I curled up against him, he caressed me and made me feel like his tiny little daughter. I forgot everything bad. It's a shame that Zyguś is gone now. I could lie curled up against him for a long, long time. You will help me, Buluś and God!

JUNE 28, 1942, SUNDAY

It's quiet and peaceful now; I'm well. I would like to curl up again, just curl up and sleep. It was something beyond words. He was. I don't know what I'm writing. Because it's dark. Oh, such a balmy night. This was a wonderful flight, devilish and heavenly at the same time. We took a big step forward. Toward this Z who is adored by people! Why, oh, why only in five years' time? After all today, already, already today. My legs couldn't cope. It was so very sweet what Z said—I am mature. And it was also very sweet with Marysia, because I really like this Daddy-Mommy sweetness. Perhaps I even prefer it. All of it is so wondrous. Divine and very human. Oh, how much I'd like to curl up against him again and say, "Oh, Daddy dear!" Off I go now to dream sweetly and in peace. You will help me, Buluś and God!!!

JUNE 29, 1942, MONDAY

So tell me, Zyguś, how am I to survive those two days, those two nights? Each hour lasts ten times longer. Oh, they go so slowly, they are so horrible, so excruciating, so oppressive. How did it come to that? How did it spill out, what was piling up, growing and growing? And will it always be like that from now on? Will we ever want more and if so, when, oh, when? Because today I don't want it, but my body does, it asks for it, it demands it. Won't it be like that every day from now on? Strange that I don't seem to be able to go back to what it was like before. I have ripened; I went overripe. It's good to think, to want and to complete—but how? It all scares me. Because it's a sober thought. Too sober. How can I think about it as a done thing or being done, but not about how to get there? No! No! I simply can't be bothered to think. And that's why this letter hit me like a sledgehammer. My lovely Buluś. My good, dear one, I know now that you have good intentions. I know, because I want it too, because it's my destiny. But do you know that it's highly absurd, it's the biggest illusion under the sun. Now, only now, when I read your letter, I thought that there are no real, serious reasons for it. You are a woman who's lived through a lot. You know a lot. And you tell me to be practical. You are such a child. Do you know that the way you presented it to me, I found it, well (to avoid committing a sin), simply in a bad taste. Think, two young people and . . .

Zyguś tells me bad things, he tells me sweet things too . . . He reckons we must part, he says that in five years' time I will be 10 centimeters taller and I will be prettier. But I won't be either of those things. I'm always prettier afterward—with shining eyes, with burning lips and flushed cheeks. Zyguś is also at his most beautiful then. I prefer to clear all obstacles and dream that it is already, that it is . . . You will help me, Buluś and God.

JULY 5, 1942, SUNDAY

We feared it, it threatened us and then it finally happened. What we were so afraid of finally did come after all. The ghetto. The notices went out today. We might stay here; we might not. Oh, Lord, You gave me so much hope, so much comfort—thank You for it.

It's so terrible. You don't know how terrible, you know nothing. You will come with me, because, of course, I will take my soul with me, my little looking glass. Just think, what remained in some old, yellowed books, in vellum scrolls covered with writing, what lived in legends, what one learned with surprise at school—has now come true. The truest truth of all. And it's so terrifying.

We fear deportation, supposedly they're planning to deport half the people. Oh, Dido, oh, Bimba. Great Lord God, have mercy. My thoughts are so dark, it's a sin to even think them.

I saw a happy-looking couple today. They'd been on an outing; they were on their way back, amused and happy. Zyguś, my darling, my love most sincere, when will we go on an outing like theirs? I love you as much as she loves him. I would look at you the same way. But she's so much happier, that's the only thing I know. Or perhaps—oh, Holy God, You are full of mercy—our children will say one day, "Our mother and father lived in the ghetto." Oh, I strongly believe in it. You will save us, oh, God Almighty. My Mama prays so hard for us. You will help us, Buluś and God.

6TH OF I DON'T KNOW WHAT, MONDAY

There is so much worry and concern, so much bitterness that I feel ashamed to write about our little nest. But ours is sweet, charming, wonderful. It's so good to talk about the nest. You will help me, Buluś and God.

JULY 10, 1942, FRIDAY

Goodbye, my little Diary! I will miss this abode. Let's hope Good God will let me see you here again. Give me your blessing from afar, Mama, and You, Lord God. Bring me back home soon (not in the ghetto). Our home . . . I've lived so many happy moments here, I'll always have fond memories of this flat where my love blossomed and matured. I'm in the middle of moving out, it's a terrible mess, I have to get going. You will help me, Buluś and God.

JULY 15, 1942, WEDNESDAY

Remember this day; remember it well. You will tell generations to come. Since 8 o'clock today we have been shut away in the ghetto. I live here now. The world is separated from me and I'm separated from the world. The days are terrible and the nights are not at all better. Every day brings more casualties and I keep praying to You, God Almighty, to let me kiss my dear Mama.

Oh, Great One, give us health and strength. Let us live. I feel horrible, Bimba is sick. Hope is shriveling so fast. There are fragrant flowers in front of the house, but who needs flowers? And Zygmunt, you know, I haven't seen him yet. I mean I saw him from a distance today, but he hasn't come over yet. Lord, please protect his dear head. But why can't I cuddle up next to him? Pity . . . Perhaps he . . . God, let me hug my dear Mama. You will help me, Buluś and God.

JULY 16, 1942, THURSDAY

You probably want to know what a closed-off ghetto looks like. Pretty ordinary. Barbed wire all around, with guards watching the gates (a German policeman and Jewish police*). Leaving the ghetto without a pass is punishable by death. Inside there are only our people, close ones, dear ones. Outside there are strangers. My soul is so very sad. My heart is seized with terror. Such is life.

I have missed Zyguś so much today, I thought about him all the time. I haven't seen him for a week, I've missed him so much and I still miss him, because his visit today wasn't a real visit. I longed so much for some caress,

---

* Within many ghettos there were Jewish police units, set up by order of the Germans. They guarded the ghetto, collected money and taxes, gathered labor forces, and more. While they were officially part of the Judenrat, they were often eyed suspiciously by them, as well as by the Jewish inhabitants of the ghetto.

nobody knows how much. After all we face such a terrible situation. Let me get some caresses. But it ended up being strange and cold, probably because there were other people in the flat and there was such a mess. Perhaps Saturday'll work out better . . . Yes, it must. We need a week's worth of caresses. I'll now dream like before. You will help me, Buluś and God.

JULY 18, 1942, SATURDAY

Days go by. They're all the same, like drops of rain. Evenings are the most pleasant. We sit in the yard in front of the house, we talk, joke and— breathing in the fragrance of the garden—I manage to forget. I forget what I want to forget. That I live in the ghetto, that I have so many worries, that I feel lonely and poor, that Z is a stranger to me, that despite all my longing I cannot get closer to him. It's not a relationship that other couples have, after all.

Here, in the yard, doves coo. The moon's crescent silently floats into the sky, flowers give a sweet fragrance and when I look at it all, I ask myself why. I was on the verge of tears three times today. I blamed the living conditions, but that's not true! Love can flourish anywhere, dear love, full of warmth . . . And yet, shadows always flit on my path. What is it? Where do those shadows come from? Are they shadows of clouds floating above? No, unfortunately not, these are shadows of a clouded face or, well, it's not worth mentioning. My heart aches so badly.

I don't want to ask God for anything else, only for our survival. But one can dream, why not? I dream about putting my head on Mama's bosom and crying so sweetly, it's good, just like now . . . Mama's not here, Norka is, so I'll go to her and cry my eyes out. She's a dear soul, she'll understand. I'll go. I don't want to see any other friends. Irka said she would stop by. What for? I can't stand her. I don't want to renew our relations. It's all stupid, calculated, contrived. Sometimes I just want to say that I don't care, but all I say is that I wish for the war to end! Bye-bye, dear Diary, my heart is heavy, like it's made of lead. You will help me, Buluś and God.

What scares me most are the shadows
When in the morning

a shadow flickers without a warning
on the road ahead of me
My heart trembles inside
and I look around
petrified
you can't look a shadow in the eye
you can't grasp it by its elbow
you can't touch it, ask it questions
you don't even know who casts it
This crawling, slithering grayness
That shimmers and strangely twists
What scares me most are the shadows.

You will help me, Buluś and God.

JULY 19, 1942

Tomorrow is Norka's birthday. Irka is coming, so it won't be the way it could be. But it'll still be sweet, because Zyguś, my beloved Zyguś, is again my beating heart; he's so delightfully sweet. The world's good to us, even in the ghetto. It's just that I'm always a bit silly, I get embarrassed about going there. But Z is truly the most beautiful and curling up against him, seeking his protection, is the best. So today I'm much calmer. In this apartment "it" is wonderful as well. Now I will have sweet thoughts about everything!

Tomorrow Norka is turning 18. I'd like to give her some of our dreams, something more than an album and flowers, something that nobody else will give her. I promised to buy her a wonderful camera when we leave here and to go hiking in the mountains, to make my friend happy. That would make me happy too.

in a little house
with green blinds
where flowers will bloom
where it will always be just the two of us

Zyguś, my beloved, the best. I send kisses to everybody and I thank Good Lord God for this and my dear Mama for praying for us. You will help me, Buluś and God.

JULY 20, 1942

Nora's birthday. Well? I knew it was going to be like that. But now I have talked to the neighbors and I feel a bit better. Holy God, protect us and save us. You will help me, Buluś and God.

JULY 22, 1942, WEDNESDAY

I have to write to silence the pain, to open the wounds and let worries seep out. Such a terrible, grim time. We don't know what tomorrow will bring. We expect families to be taken away. Bimba's sick and exhausted, Jarośka's terrible, not a word from Mama or Daddy. It's not good with Zygmunt, either. I didn't, I really didn't want to admit that I'm seething with venom. But I couldn't stop myself. Also because I'm right. I have tears in my eyes from grief and the tips of my fingers are tingling with anger.

I don't want to write about the details, as I might write surly, clamoring words, and what's the point? It will always be the same. It's his fault. He is right, I'm resentful and helplessly in love. One thing has to be changed though, just one expression—after all "the mug" might not tell anybody and . . . no! When I think about it, I get so furious that I don't want to see him ever again. I've had enough of it all. I cover my ears with my hands and close my eyes. I'd like to use my suffering to create suffering, to make myself ill. And he's right, he's the wisest of them all . . .

But in my dream it's completely different. My dreams are sweet . . . You will help me, Buluś and God.

JULY 23, 1942, THURSDAY

Well, Noruśka, my dear, dear child. I admire this world of yours, I love it too, but, you know me, one word shatters everything. Noruś, I'd like to study too and improve myself, but everything comes down to one word. I already know who is worth what, I know love and I told you the truth (although it's the first time I thought it)—he's not worth it. But it's not a question of him being worth it or not, one needs to love, one needs to go on loving, one can't say no!

I know, my dear, that you understand everything, but you don't understand how weak I am and how hopeless when faced with . . . this word. What I told you is true, even though he didn't say no, I know. I know he regrets it and is embarrassed. And (that's funny) I'm exasperated. If only hearts could be healed of love! But I don't even know myself if I'd like that. What I want, Noruś, is to go back to life and go hiking in the mountains with you. You will help me, Buluś and God.

JULY 24, 1942, FRIDAY

Dear God, help us. We need to pay our contribution by 12 o'clock tomorrow. The city is in danger. But I still have faith. My faith is deep and I beg You. You will help us, Buluś and God.

JULY 25, 1942, SATURDAY

The following day in the morning! Ordners* came last night. Dido hasn't paid everything yet. Not enough money. Oh! Why can't money rain from the sky? It's people's lives, after all. Terrible times have come. Mama, you have no idea how terrible. But Lord God looks after us and, though I'm horribly frightened, I have faith in Him.

I trust, because this morning a bright ray of sunshine came through all this darkness. It was sent by my Mama in a letter, in the form of a wonderful photograph of her. And when she smiled at me from the photo, I thought that Holy God has us in His care! Even in the darkest moments there is something that can make us smile. Mama, pray for us. I send you lots of kisses. You will help me, Buluś and God.

---

* Members of the Jewish Ghetto Police (Jüdischer Ordnungsdienst).

IN THE EVENING!

My dear Diary, my good, beloved friend! We went through such terrible times together and now the worst moment is upon us. I could be afraid now. But the One who didn't leave us then will help us today too. He'll save us. Hear, O, Israel,* save us, help us. You've kept me safe from bullets and bombs, from grenades. Help me survive, help us! And you, my dear Mama, pray for us today, pray hard. Think about us and may your thoughts be blessed. Mama! My dearest, one and only, such terrible times are coming. I love you with all my heart. I love you; we'll be together again. God, protect us all and Zygmunt and Grandparents and Jaróska. God, into Your hands I commit myself. You will help me, Buluś and God.

ZYGMUNT'S NOTES

JULY 27, 1942, MONDAY

It's done! First of all, dear Diary, please forgive me for wandering into your pages and trying to carry on the work of somebody I am not worthy of. Let me tell you that Renuśka didn't get the work permit stamp she needed to avoid being deported, so she has to stay in hiding. My dear parents have also been refused work permit stamps. I swear to God and history that I will save the three people who are dearest to me, even if it costs me my own life. You will help me, God!

JULY 28, 1942, TUESDAY

My parents were lucky to get into the city. They are hiding at the cemetery. Rena had to leave the factory. I had to find her a hiding place at any cost. I was in the city until 8 o'clock. I have finally succeeded.

---

* A reference to one of the most important prayers in Judaism, Shema Yisrael ("Hear, O, Israel: the Lord, our God, the Lord is one").

JULY 29, 1942

The Aktion *was prevented for the second time, because of a dispute between the army and the Gestapo.* I cannot describe everything that has gone on for the last three days. I have no energy for it after 12 hours of running around the city. These events have shaken me to the core, but they haven't broken me. I have a terribly difficult task. I have to save so many people without having any protection for myself, or any help from others. This burden rests on my shoulders alone. I won't last long and I will share the fate of my three doomed ones. I have taken Arianka to the other side.*

JULY 30, 1942

Today everything will be decided. I will gather all my mental and physical strength and I will achieve my goals. Or I will die trying.

5 O'CLOCK

Skrzypczyński will give me the final answer at 5 o'clock. At midday they took away our cards for stamping (along with the wives' cards). I decided to risk my document, because I thought it was my last chance to save Renuśka. No luck! They threatened to send me to the Gestapo. After a lot of begging, they finally withdrew that threat. But that forgery cost me my job at H.U.V.† for forgery. At 8 o'clock, I'll find out whether or not I'm going to stay. I set off.

IN THE NIGHT

Oh, gods! Such horror! It was all for nothing! The drama lasted one hour. I didn't get my card. Have I just slaughtered myself?! Zosia is gone! Now I am

---

* Most likely it refers to the attempt of stopping the destruction of the ghetto undertaken by the Wehrmacht lieutenant Dr. Albert Battel (1891–1952). For saving about one hundred Jews from the Przemyśl Ghetto, he was recognized as one of the Righteous Among the Nations by Yad Vashem in 1981.

† Heeres-Unterkunft-Verwaltung was responsible for managing military quarters.

on my own. What will happen to me? It's a great question. I wanted to save my parents and Rena, but instead I just got into more trouble myself. It looks like the end of the world is here. I still have hope.

JULY 31, 1942

Three shots! Three lives lost! It happened last night at 10:30 p.m. Fate decided to take my dearest ones away from me. My life is over. All I can hear are shots, shots . . . shots. My dearest Renusia, the last chapter of your diary is complete.

AFTERWORD

NOTES

ACKNOWLEDGMENTS

by
Elizabeth Bellak

AFTERWORD

I only spent about two weeks in the ghetto, which was in a poor, run-down quarter called Garbarze, northwest of our grandparents' apartment. The Nazis had given every Jew twenty-four hours to move there and allowed each family to carry only twenty-five kilograms. My grandparents, Renia, and I gathered together our most practical clothes for summer and winter, our sturdiest shoes, and a few coats in case we never got our furs back. My grandfather taped as many gold dollar coins as he could in a corner of his suitcase, hoping the guards wouldn't find them. The silver was safely buried in the basement; Granny and Grandpa would be back for it after the war.

On July 27, an *Aktion* began within the Przemyśl Ghetto. Unless you could prove you were employed in an essential labor or administrative position—and then get a stamp from the Gestapo on your work permit—you were going to be forced out of the ghetto to the camps or to your death. Only five thousand Jews were expected to receive this stamp, and Zygmunt and Maciek were luckily among them. Unfortunately, my sister, my grandparents, and I weren't.

Just one day later, the Gestapo surrounded the Przemyśl Ghetto and began rounding up the people who lived there; 6,500 Jews were loaded into cattle cars and shipped off to the death camp at Bełżec, about 100 kilometers northwest of the city. Another 2,500—who were determined to be too old or frail—were taken by truck to the Grochowce forest, which surrounded Przemyśl. There, they were shot in the napes of their necks and buried in a mass grave.

My sister and I were not in either group. Somehow—I don't know how, and he never told me—Zygmunt smuggled Renia and his parents into the attic of a three-story tenement house at 10 Moniuszko Street, where his uncle, a member of the Judenrat named Samuel Goliger, lived. I wasn't with them. Zygmunt had escorted me out just before them, and we'd snuck toward the checkpoint to try to get out to my best friend Dzidka's house.

I think I left in the early morning, but I say that only from a place in my mind where I've replayed every memory a thousand times. This is the same place I've searched for my last memories of my sister, though those have come up blank. How have I forgotten saying goodbye to her? What was the look on her face? What did she say to me? I'd give anything to remember our last words to each other. I'd give anything to know that I told her how much I loved her.

I do remember the last time I saw my grandparents. They were trying to be brave as Zygmunt motioned that it was time for me to leave, that I had to get out, that time was running out. My granny, whom I loved so much, turned away, raising her hands to her face. My grandpa kneeled down, placed his hands on my shoulders, and looked me in the eyes. Then he handed me a small, colorful box with a chain-link handle. It was the kind of compact suitcase perfect to carry lunch in, as if I were a little girl about to walk to school by herself for the very first time—not a child fleeing for her life.

"I've taped twenty gold coins inside," he said. "It's all I have. Wherever you're going, you can always sell these and get some cash."

My grandmother approached me, carrying a thin blue coat that I only wore on summer nights. She slipped my arms into it, being careful not to wrinkle the pink dress I was wearing, and then buttoned it up. Granny and Grandpa pulled me into a quick hug and then guided me gently out the door into the garden, where Zygmunt was waiting.

I don't know what happened to them, but I'm sure they ended up in that mass grave in the Grochowce forest. They were just too old for the Nazis to want to take them to a camp.

I'm not sure how Zygmunt got me out of the ghetto, but somehow, he took me directly to the Leszczyńskis' home. It was a walk-up apartment near the tinned coffee factory that Mr. Leszczyński owned, but in another part of town than my grandparents' shop, my school, and the ice-skating pond. Dzidka, my closest friend in the whole world, was there to greet me, along with her parents and her two sisters.

I didn't know how long I'd be there. I don't think I even understood why I was there. All I knew was that, even though I was with Dzidka and her family—whom I loved and trusted—I was terrified. A few times a day, someone pounded on the door, demanding to search the apartment. Mr. and Mrs. Leszczyński would motion for me to hide under a bed, whispering, "Do not say a word. Do not breathe. We'll be back for you." Then they'd close the door.

I crouched under the bed in a little ball, my chest heaving as I tried to choke back tears.

"Just a minute!" Mrs. Leszczyński would call to the person on the other side of the door.

Then, Mr. Leszczyński would open the door and say a few words, and silence would follow. The door would close. For the next two hours or half a day, I was safe.

I trusted Dzidka's family, and more than that, I trusted Zygmunt. I knew he'd do whatever he could to keep Renia safe—whether she was still in his uncle's attic, or whether he'd moved her like he'd moved me. He loved Renia, and he had promised our mom he'd protect her.

Of course, you know the rest of Renia's story. As hard as he tried, Zygmunt couldn't save her. My beautiful sister was murdered on July 30, 1942, alongside Zygmunt's parents.

It was several weeks before I found out what happened to her. Crouched in a ball in my best friend's apartment, I had no idea that someone had told the Germans that there were three Jews hiding in the attic of Mr. Goliger's tenement house, and that when the Gestapo forced their way in, Renia and Zygmunt's parents had been taken outside and shot.

The Leszczyńskis might have found out right away, but I don't know for sure. All I remember was that, as I hid in their apartment, desperately afraid that the Gestapo would come in, grab me, and take me far away from my family, my protectors, my best friend, and a life that had become increasingly bleak, I missed my mother desperately. It was a stabbing ache, like Renia had felt every single day since 1938.

After a week in the Leszczyńskis' apartment, Mr. Leszczyński told me it was time to leave.

"We're going to the railway station," he said.

I didn't ask why. I just slipped on the same pink dress I'd worn when I left my grandparents, wrapped my blue coat around myself, and grabbed the small lunch box that my grandpa had taped the coins into. I remembered his last words to me, his mustache, the kind twinkle in his eye, and I thought about how he must have felt giving it to me. He had to have known his life was over and that the lives of his two granddaughters might end soon as well.

I have no memory of the walk to the railroad station, nor do I recall where I sat on that train—or even if I did. It's been almost eighty years since I left Przemyśl, and I've cycled so many smells, visions, meetings, and conversations through my mind that it's sometimes hard to tell one from the other. I've also never returned to my grandparents' town. I can't. It's just too emotional for me.

We had to transfer in Kraków, and Mr. Leszczyński and I exited the train cautiously. He held my hand tightly, and we started to walk right toward a few Gestapo officers, dressed in their familiar gray uniforms with their ranks on their shoulders. They had German shepherds by their sides. Seeing the Gestapo wasn't unusual, especially in a public place like a train station, but this was different. I didn't have papers, so there was no way to prove that I wasn't Jewish. If Mr. Leszczyński was caught smuggling a Jew, he'd be sentenced to death.

We kept walking as my heart pounded in my chest. As we got closer, one of the Germans glanced at Mr. Leszczyński, seeming to miss me entirely, then turned back to the other officers and continued whatever conversation they were having. I let out a deep breath as we made our way past them, and then we waited for what felt like hours for the train to Warsaw.

Today, the train from Kraków to Warsaw takes about two and a half hours. In wartime Poland, it must have been twice that. I don't remember the ride—what passed me out the window, whether I slept, what Dzidka's dad said to me, or even if I knew where I was going. But we arrived in Warsaw at some point, and as the train came to a stop, I felt more anxious than I ever had in my life. Here I was in a familiar city, where I'd stood on the stage reading poetry when I was only eight, yet my mom—the person who made me feel safer and more loved than anyone else in the world—felt thousands of miles away.

When the train doors opened, I picked up my little lunch box and looked around. There were no Gestapo officers or dogs on the platform.

Instead, there was a crowd of people rushing from one train to another, and it seemed like no one was looking at the little girl in a thin coat carrying a tiny lunch box. But someone was. As Mr. Leszczyński and I walked down the platform, a young man in street clothes stepped forward and raised his hand to stop us.

"You came here with a Jewish child?" he yelled. "I'm turning you in!"

Mr. Leszczyński put his arm around me and pulled me close as he moved toward the man, towering over him. "Get the hell away from me, and if you don't, I'll kill you right here," he said.

What felt like five minutes of silence followed, but Mr. Leszczyński didn't move. He just stood there, looking down once to make sure I was okay. The man stared at him just a little longer, then turned and ran away. I don't know who he was. I don't know how or why he believed I was Jewish. All I remember is that Mr. Leszczyński and I walked off the platform, out of the station, and into the busy streets of Warsaw, my old home that was very much changed.

Mr. Leszczyński took me directly to my mom's friends, the Beredas. They lived in a nice building on Ossolinski Street, close to Saxon Garden State Park. I had never met Mr. or Mrs. Bereda before, so their smiling, tear-streaked faces were scary and unfamiliar. I trusted no one. But suddenly, I saw the face that had haunted my thoughts and my dreams, and I felt the longing I'd felt for months explode inside me. I dropped my tiny lunch box and fell into my mom's arms, sobbing. Then my heart broke, because I knew I was experiencing something my sister wasn't.

My mom probably found out from Mr. Leszczyński that day that Renia was dead, but she didn't tell me until she'd confirmed it herself weeks later. With the help and accompaniment of Mrs. Bereda's niece's husband, a Hungarian aristocrat named Von Anderle, she gathered together her papers and took the long trip to Przemyśl. That train ride must have been the hardest of my poor mom's life, hoping against hope that her oldest daughter might be alive, but knowing, deep down, the horrible truth.

She didn't go into the abandoned apartment where her parents had lived, so she didn't see that the piano was missing or that the cupboard in the living room didn't have any dishes and silverware in it. She didn't see the blank desk, where her father had signed all his contracts. But while she was in Przemyśl, someone gave her a small amulet that Renia used to wear. I think it was then my mom accepted that my sister was really gone.

Mom came back to Warsaw and retrieved me from the convent where I'd moved temporarily. Together, we took a trolley to the room she rented in an apartment in Zolybusz, a very nice neighborhood adjacent to Warsaw. Over the next few weeks, Mrs. Bereda's connections got me papers that gave me a new identity, and I was baptized by the same priest who'd baptized my mother. Just like that, I was Catholic, with a new birthday and a new name: Elzbieta Leszczyńska. Just like that, the Polish Shirley Temple disappeared.

Even though Mama and I lived outside the ghetto, disguised as Polish Catholics, we still saw and felt the war every day. Because my mom had to work, I lived and studied at a convent school during the week, and on weekends, she picked me up and took me home. On Sundays, we went to church, embracing the religion that had saved our lives. We took a trolley to the church and back, just like my mom did every working day. During the war, trolley cars were divided in the middle, and in the front sat the Germans. In the back, the Poles.

One day after church, we planned to have dinner at the home of my mom's boss, whose name was Kosiński. My mom worked at the Hotel Europejski as an assistant director. The trolley we'd boarded was moving along, with us seated comfortably in the back. It slowed down, then stopped, on its regular route, which took it next to the tall walls of the Warsaw Ghetto. There, a German army truck sat with its engine idling. Suddenly, the passenger-side door of the truck opened, and a Nazi soldier exited and walked up next to the trolley. He was holding a gun.

"Everyone out!" he yelled in German. "Germans on this side, Poles on this side. Exit!"

My mother grabbed my hand. At the time, there was something we called *Łapanka,* which meant "to round up people." This practice, which had been around since the Germans first occupied Poland in 1939, referred to the act of removing people from somewhere—like a trolley—separating them into groups, forcing one group onto a truck, and taking them off to a labor camp. There, these people would assist with the German war effort, digging, shoveling, paving roads, operating machinery in a factory, or, likely, being beaten, starved, and killed.

I'd witnessed this in Przemyśl, and my mother had seen it in Warsaw.

It was nothing new. My mom was having none of it, though. She was *not* going to lose another child.

Thanks to an education at universities in Berlin and Vienna and her work at the Hotel Europejski, my mom was fluent in German. Her head bowed, she grabbed my hand and started speaking to me in German, a language I couldn't understand. But I played along, nodding at everything she said. Holding his gun, a guard approached us, overheard my mom talking, and motioned for us to stand to the side with the Germans. As we turned around, I was sure I was about to be shot in the back.

But we weren't loaded onto a truck or killed. We were allowed to walk away, toward the Kosińskis' home, which was at the hotel. We walked what felt like all day, hiding in different doorways when we sensed danger. Passing trucks full of people—more than I'd seen at any other time during the war—we arrived at dinner late but before the 8:00 p.m. curfew. After we ate, I collapsed into one of the Kosińskis' beds. I lay there all night long, sweating from a fever, and the next day, my mom called the doctor. After he examined me, he told her that I'd developed yellow jaundice, and he believed it was brought on by fright.

After that night, Mr. Kosiński allowed my mom and me to live at the hotel. For weeks, I recovered there. When I was feeling better, we ate dinner with them. We went to church. We celebrated Christmas and Easter. My mother became friends with the girlfriend of the owner of a restaurant across the street, named Ziutka, and sometimes she fed us for free. She loved my mom. I went to *komplety,* which means I studied school privately, in secret. And day after day, my mother and I watched the Jews and Poles get trampled under the boots of the Germans. That's how we lived.

I didn't come to America immediately after the war. Sometime between the summers of 1942 and 1944, a German officer who lived at the hotel fell in love with my mom. He wanted to marry her. I don't think she loved him back; it was simply a very beneficial arrangement for a woman who'd used every bone in her body becoming resourceful enough to survive. But as the Soviet army advanced toward Warsaw in early 1944, an underground movement plotted a rebellion against the German occupiers. The Warsaw Uprising started in August 1944, and Germany fought back with everything they had. In sixty-three days, almost 250,000 Poles were killed, and half the city was destroyed by bombs.

The German officer begged my mom to leave Warsaw when the violence was at its worst. "It's too dangerous here," he said. "I love you, and I can help you get out."

My mom agreed, and the officer prepared papers for us. In the summer of 1944, my mom and I packed a few small suitcases. Before Warsaw surrendered, we escaped from Warsaw to Germany. Traveling through Germany was highly dangerous, and we passed Berlin and Dresden before finally crossing into Austria. Then we made our way toward a famous spa in Austria—where the officer told us wounded German officers and soldiers went to recover—via a Red Cross ambulance.

It was a dangerous trip. Fighting continued all around us as we traveled through the Austrian Alps. But when we arrived in the resort town of Bad Gastein, I realized the officer had been true to his word; there were thousands of wounded German soldiers there, and the hotels were all decorated with red crosses, signaling that they'd become convalescence hospitals. My mother soon got a job as a desk clerk at one of the hotels, called Straubinger, and we lived there from September 1944 to May 1945, when the American army arrived. Germany had been defeated by the Allies, and Europe was about to be liberated.

I'll never forget the first time I saw American soldiers. They were standing in a line, handsome men with smiles on their faces. I liked them right away, but there was something about them that seemed strange.

"What's going on with them?" I asked my mom. "Their mouths are moving, but they're not talking!"

My mom laughed. "They're chewing gum," she answered.

I was a teenaged refugee who'd barely survived the Holocaust, and I'd never seen gum, much less chewed it.

My mother got a job with the American Army and tried to secure papers that would let us move to the US. But she also knew someone in New York, and through the Red Cross, she located her. That woman helped my mom find a cousin of my grandfather, who wrote us an affidavit of support, allowing us to leave Austria for the United States. But we didn't go there directly; with the help of the Catholic Church, we ended up in a displaced persons' camp in Munich. Then we were sent north to Bremen. My mom had reestablished contact with her brother in France, and he wrote to her, begging us to come to France to live near him. When she wasn't responsive, he sent a car for us. It rolled up to the place we were staying, and when it stopped, a man named Major Zaremba, who was in the Polish army, stepped out. He was holding papers that gave us permission to settle in France.

Right then, my mother faced a decision.

"I've gone through too much in Europe," she said to him. "I've lost everyone. I want to start a new life, and that life is in America."

In December 1946, my mom and I gathered together our suitcases, plus $500 that my uncle Maurice had sent. We boarded a rickety boat called the *Marine Marlin,* and with the winds whipping and rain pouring as the boat tipped on its side, we sailed for five or six days across the Atlantic Ocean. We landed at a pier in Manhattan and were greeted by my grandfather's cousin's son, Dr. William Dubilier. He took us to New Rochelle, north of the city in Westchester County. We only stayed there for a few weeks, because my mom found a job in Greenwich, Connecticut. She worked there about a year, and then she moved us into a tiny room on West Ninetieth Street in Manhattan.

Other than a conservatory I'd attended in Austria sometime in 1944 or 1945, I hadn't gone to a real school in about three years. My mother valued education above all else, so she found me a Catholic boarding school called Nazareth Academy in Torresdale, Pennsylvania, and I moved there. I hardly spoke any English, and I had maybe two skirts to my name. I felt dirt poor next to all the other girls, but I couldn't tell them why. I didn't even want to tell my new best friend, who was a Polish girl named Ewa. The truth was too much for me—let alone another teenager—to digest. I told myself, *This is my new life. I'm in America, I'm Catholic, and I'm Elizabeth.*

I graduated and went to college, first in Manhattan, then in Missouri, and then back in Manhattan at Columbia University. But one day in the early 1950s, while I was home visiting my mom in her tiny apartment, Zygmunt Schwarzer came to visit. This handsome green-eyed man who had loved my sister more than anything in the world hadn't just survived the Holocaust; he'd become a doctor, just like he'd always wanted to be.

"I have something for you," he said, extending a thick, blue-lined notebook toward my mom.

It was Renia's diary, all seven hundred pages of it. My mom and I broke down in tears.

Zygmunt stayed for a little bit and told my mom and me how he'd survived after he'd smuggled me to Dzidka's house. In late July 1942, he had avoided going to the Bełżec death camp because he'd finally gotten his stamp from the Gestapo, confirming his employment. Between July and November 1942, he worked as a forced laborer at the German military base on the right bank of the San River. When the base got busier due to soldiers coming back from the front, Zygmunt became a carpenter, and he was assigned to building barracks where the newly arrived were disinfected before they left to go home to Germany.

In November 1942, there was another displacement *Aktion* of the inhabitants of the Przemyśl Ghetto. By then, Zygmunt had lost his work permit, and he was in hiding with a few other people in the attic of one of the ghetto's buildings. Somehow, they managed to survive until the end of the *Aktion*. I never confirmed it with Zygmunt, but I think this was when he left Renia's diary with a friend outside the ghetto walls.

After the final destruction of the ghetto in September 1943, Zygmunt was sent to the labor camp in Szebnie near Jasło, and from there—two months later—to Auschwitz. In October 1944, he was evacuated to the Sachsenhausen camp and worked at the Heinkel bomber aircraft works in Oranienburg. In December 1944, he was sent to the camp in Landsberg in Bavaria. In January 1945, he came down with typhus and managed to survive only thanks to the help of a doctor and a Lithuanian girl working in the kitchen. If you can believe it, that doctor was Josef Mengele, the death camp physician who's famous for conducting horrific experiments on Jewish prisoners.

On April 30, 1945, the camp was liberated, and Zygmunt was finally free. He met his wife, Genia—who was called Jean in America—at a displaced persons' camp, and that fall he started studying medicine at Heidelberg University. He graduated in 1949 and left for the United States, where sometime in the early 1950s he tracked down my mom and decided to pay her a visit.

Getting through college had been such a struggle for me. My mom and I had no money, and we lived in a fifth-floor walk-up on Third Avenue, where the rent was only fifty-five dollars a month and where elevated trains went by till 7:00 at night, every single day. I worked as a waitress when I wasn't in class, and I was always so tired. My mom was, too. It wasn't like her, but she even said to me once, "Why do you want to go to school? You're just going to get married."

"No," I answered. "I want my degree."

I finally got it in 1955—with a major in German and a minor in Russian—and I was so happy. I'd *finally* done it.

One day, just before I graduated, I got called into an office at Columbia by a man I'd never met. When I sat down across from him, he offered me a job.

"What kind of job?" I asked.

"Well," he said, "it's a job where you can't tell anybody what you're doing."

It was the CIA. They wanted me because I could speak and write Russian and German fluently. I didn't have to think for a second about what *I* wanted, though.

"Thank you," I said to him, "but I can't take it. I've lived all my life in secret. I don't want to do that anymore."

But it's hard to give up a secret life when it's protected you for so long, so my mom and I still didn't talk to people about who we were. She even married her second husband, Clyde, in the early 1960s and never told him about her past. I didn't talk about where I came from to my friends at Columbia, where I stayed to get my master's degree in child psychology. I made myself forgot the movies I'd been in, and I didn't even see them until 2014, when Tomasz Magierski, a Polish filmmaker who's been researching Renia's and my story, found them in some archives and showed them to me. At the elementary school where I started to work in 1963 as a German and Russian teacher, I didn't tell anyone I'd once been the Polish Shirley Temple. I just laughed when my students called me "Miss Niska" because they couldn't pronounce *Leszczyńska*.

One day in 1964—after I'd left a job teaching business at Newtown High School in Queens and settled into a sixth-grade teaching position on Staten Island—I got invited to a party for the United Federation of Teachers, a teacher's union. The party was at a friend's big house in Queens, and she had a piano in her living room. It might have been thirty years since I'd acted, but I was still a performer, so I decided to sit on the piano bench and start playing and singing my Polish and Russian repertoire songs. When I finished one, a tall, handsome man who was a few years younger than I approached me. He was George Bellak, a teacher from Newtown who I'd always thought was very nice. He'd been born in Vienna, so we'd sometimes spoken German to each other, but I'd never considered him more than a friend.

"You play very well," he said, then smiled. "How are you getting home from the party?"

We talked all night and got on the subway at 2:00 a.m. When we stepped off, George walked me back to my apartment. That's how our romance started.

Everything happened so fast after that. We got married at city hall in June 1965 on a weekday that we both had off. We laughed when the officiant stuttered my name, "L . . . L . . . L . . . shhh . . . ka," and we celebrated that night at the Russian Tea Room. Within a few months, I was pregnant with our son, Andrew.

It took a long time for me to tell my husband who I was. Even though George was so much like me—he was Jewish, though his family had fled Austria in 1939—I wasn't sure I could stand to face the pain of talking about my past. I also wasn't sure he'd accept me. The war was over, and I didn't want to think about it. I had spent years trying to forget that I was the little girl who'd made it out of Poland alive but whose sister had not.

That's why, when my mother passed away from cancer on November 23, 1969—just a few months before my daughter, Alexandra Renata, was born—I placed Renia's diary in a safe-deposit box at a Chase Bank in Manhattan. "The past is the past," my uncle Maurice had always said, and that's the way I treated it.

It wasn't until my kids started asking questions that I told Andrew and Alexandra the truth.

"I'm Jewish," I said to them, "and it's time I tell you my story. I think you're ready for it."

The past still makes my heart race and my stomach sick, and reading Renia's diary gives me panic attacks. George, Andrew, Alexandra, and I visited Poland in the early 2000s—the first time I'd been there since I'd fled—and I couldn't make it as far as Przemyśl or to my family's old estate on the Dniester. I saw Maciek after I got back in town and told him about the trip, and I mentioned that I was still anxious and struggling to breathe well. He looked me up and down, then shook his head.

"If I knew you were going," he said, "I would have stopped you."

I can't imagine the pain my sister went through in her last moments, seeing me leave for a new life while she was left to her fate. I can't explain why I was allowed to live, and that's why I've tried for so long to turn my mind away from it.

Before his death on April 1, 1992, Zygmunt had learned to process the past in a different way. He'd retired from his successful pediatrics practice on Long Island, and he'd created a space in his basement for Renia's diary. He'd photocopied all its seven hundred pages, and he'd laid them out carefully like they were treasures. Every few days or nights, he'd wander down to his basement, and he'd read and study the diary near a photo of Renia he'd hung on the wall. His son, Mitchell, said spending time down there was almost a spiritual experience for him—like Renia was his muse.

In one of the very few times I saw him, he opened the pages of Renia's diary and wrote,

> Another month of May is coming, the month of love . . . Today is 23 April 1989. I'm with Renusia's sister—Jarusia. This blood link is all I have left. It's been 47 years since I have lost Renusia. When I think about her, I feel so small and unimportant. I owe her so much. Thanks to Renia I fell in love for the first time in my life, deeply and sincerely. And I was loved back by her in an extraordinary, unearthly, incredibly passionate way. It was an amazing, delicate emotion. Our love grew and developed thanks to her.
> I can't express how much I loved her. And it will never change until the end . . . Zygmunt.

I think all of us—and I especially—can learn from Zygmunt's example. The past isn't long gone; it's present in our hearts, our actions, and the lessons we teach our children. For Renia and Zygmunt, the past stood for love, and I will thank Zygmunt till the day I die not just for saving my life, but also for opening that chapter of my life again. Facing what you thought you'd put behind you may be painful, but learning and growing from it is the only way I can live now.

I hope my sister's diary teaches you to do that as well.

NOTES

1. FEBRUARY 2, 1939

Renia was only fourteen when she started this diary, and she was pensive, thoughtful, sentimental, and everything else a "good girl" in middle school usually is. She was innocent. I think we all were. You could be at the beginning of 1939, before the Germans and Soviets invaded Poland.

Back in those days, I wasn't living in Przemyśl with my grandparents and Renia. I was traveling around Poland with my mom, acting in movies and on the stage. I was in a movie called *Gehenna* and one called *Granica*, and I had a steady job at Cyrulik Warszawski, a famous theater in Warsaw, singing, dancing, and reciting the poetry of famous Polish poets like Jan Brzechwa and Julian Tuwim.

Renia had lived with our grandparents since sometime in 1938. Our dad, Bernard, whom we called Ticio, still lived at our family's estate in Stawki. Our village was tiny, but it was near a bigger town called Zaleszczyki, which was in a bend in the Dniester about three hundred kilometers southwest of Przemyśl. Being separated from your dad wasn't strange in those days. Ticio had employees to look after, wheat and sugar beets to grow and harvest, and acres and acres to manage. He provided for us like any good father should, but he didn't have enough time to devote to us with my mom away. Besides, fathers were more removed then; mothers were the ones who raised the kids.

My sister and I loved to read poems in public, so when I was five, my mom took us to try out for a radio show based in Lwów (called *Lviv* today), a large city about two hundred kilometers northeast of Zaleszczyki. The producers thought we had a lot of talent, so we got a spot reciting poetry. Renia soon decided to devote herself entirely to writing, but my mom took me to Warsaw for more auditions. Within two years, I was a tiny star on the stage and screen. My mom became my manager, and I became her shadow.

Unlike Renia, I was always with her, and when we weren't on the road, we rented a room on a beautiful street in Warsaw. I thought the city was so big and grand, with ancient cathedrals, synagogues, symphony houses, and museums—almost all of which were destroyed during the war. Because I was on the stage so much, I didn't go to a regular, Monday-to-Friday school. Instead, I had a tutor named Mrs. Arciszewska, and she taught me how to read poetry. I also studied at a dance school, and every week I saw a lady who taught me how to play the piano. When I think about it now, I was so lucky, like a little celebrity. I was in magazines and on movie posters. People recognized me on the street. My mother had cute dresses made to order for me, and one of them had a row of six buttons down the front that read *A-R-I-A-N-A*.

Our mom was tall and elegant, with dark hair and bright blue eyes like mine. She also had these beautiful, straight teeth. People used to stare at her and ask, "Who made your teeth?" and she'd laugh and answer, "They are my teeth!" She had a tremendous presence, and she used to wear fancy shoes that made her long legs look even longer. Even though we'd lived in the country for most of my childhood, I never saw her wearing pants. She was always in dresses, suits, or coats, with a corset underneath that Renia and I loved pulling tight in the back.

She wasn't an aristocrat, but her friends called her "the Baroness." There was a very exclusive store in Warsaw called Telimena that employed a team of tailors, and my mother once had them make her a green wool suit with leather buttons. She wore it with a silk blouse. Even when she went out to run an errand, she'd look like a lady. "Dress for yourself!" she'd always order me. I still say that to my own kids.

Renia also had my mother's bright blue eyes, but she looked less like Buluś (the name we called our mom) than I did. Renia sometimes got a little plump, and our mom never did. Renia was smart and thoughtful, but she wasn't a big personality like my mom and I were. The differences didn't matter, though. Renia just adored our mom.

While I wouldn't call Renia beautiful in the classical sense, she was gorgeous and lovely, inside and out. She had a sweet smile that made everyone comfortable, and people always wanted to be around her. She wore her hair in braids that she clipped up at the back of her head and, in many of the photos I have of her, she has on button-up shoes that go up past her ankles. She sometimes complained that the other girls had nicer clothes than she had, but I did that, too. After all, by the time I got stuck in Przemyśl, our mom wasn't there to buy pretty dresses and coats for us.

I'm sure none of the other girls cared or even noticed what Renia was wearing, though. I think they were jealous of her because of her accomplishments. She excelled at everything she put her mind to at school: math, geography, Russian, Latin, French, Polish, and German. She also studied Polish at the house of a professor named Jerschina, and under him, she learned to write beautifully. At home and at school, she read all sorts of famous Polish writers and poets, and I think they inspired her own poems.

Her high school—called *gymnasium*—was on the corner across the street from my grandparents' apartment, and it was a huge place with a big yard surrounded by a high metal fence. In those days, a teenager's life outside the house revolved around school. Kids today either go out on the weekend—like to the movies or the mall—or stay inside and play on their phones. In 1939, it was more black or white. If you were in for the night, you were writing in your diary, drawing, playing an instrument, reading, or doing something else that was solitary. If you were out, you were at school, where there were always activities and parties. When Renia wanted to connect, she went to school—and it seemed like she was forever going there.

Renia had lots of friends, and everybody really loved and honored her. I know she writes about having problems, but I think that was just silly, typical teenager stuff. We've all had that, right? Her best friend was named Norka, and sometimes Renia would take me to her house. I liked it there, and I liked Norka. Our grandfathers worked in the same business, painting houses and doing construction, so we had a lot of history in common.

Around 1942, after my sister died, Norka wrote a two-page letter that she sent to my mom. She said that my sister was the most wonderful, deep, exquisite human being she ever knew and that they were devoted to each other. I know Renia sometimes fought with her, but Norka was her best friend, so she saw past that. That letter breaks my heart, and I cried when I read it.

Then there was Irka Oberhard. Renia complained about her, and I know why. She was a very snippy girl, with a lawyer father who I always thought was a very ugly little guy. Her mother had gone to gymnasium with our mom—I believe at the same school Renia attended—and they were so-so friends. Irka's mother had a very caustic way of talking, and I thought she was always trying to interfere in Irka's and her sister Fela's lives. They came from a nice home, but they didn't have the talent my sister had. Renia was president of the literary club. She won all the awards. She wrote beautiful poetry, which all her friends and teachers always wanted to read.

2. FEBRUARY 26, 1939

Before the German and Soviet occupation, my mother and I visited Renia in Przemyśl when we weren't in Warsaw or on the road. I don't remember how much we went there, but I know Renia loved it. I did, too. I'd missed my sister constantly, and being in my mother's hometown was magical. Przemyśl was a lovely, ancient city built at the place where the Carpathian Mountains and the lowlands met. The San River slowly wound its way through it, and the Przemyśl Cathedral towered above it, the focal point of the city. It wasn't a big place—before the war, there were about sixty thousand people living there—but it felt busy, with a big market in the center of the Old Town, which was on the eastern bank of the San.

I wish I'd known how much it broke Renia's heart that Buluś and I weren't always with her; if I had, maybe I would remember more. Maybe I would have shown her more how much I loved her. But I wasn't even ten, and who remembers day-to-day events before they're eleven or twelve? I recall the big things and the general impressions, like how the room in which we stayed in Warsaw was on a fancy street and how it was full of Biedermeier furniture. I remember how my mom and her big smile and fur coats seemed right at home there. I remember her dragging me around Warsaw from place to place, appointment to appointment. I had a performance a few times a week, and I had to be there on time! I remember studying poetry at night with Mrs. Arciszewska. She had smooth, porcelain skin and lived in what looked like a castle, with a gorgeous bed and jewel-covered walls inside. She had a butler, a cook, and a cleaning lady. She owned a big dog named Rex and a small dog called Toja, which means "This is I." These are some of my major memories before the war, and Renia missed all of them.

I'm not sure what was happening with my dad then. I'm sure he was busy doing what he'd always done—growing and harvesting wheat, tending to his sugar beets, and overseeing the peasants who worked for him, many of whom were Ukrainian and lived in the little town of Tluste (Tovste), which was a few miles from our house. We had horses and cows, and my father—who was tall and handsome, with green eyes and wavy, reddish hair—used to wake up early, put on his riding pants and leather boots, and walk out to check on the animals and workers.

I know my dad was a bit older than my mom, but I have no idea how they met. I only have one picture of them together, and it's framed and sitting on my kitchen counter next to my favorite photos of my kids, husband, and grandkids. The picture is from their wedding day, and on the back, someone wrote *1923*. This was one year before Renia was born.

But that's all the information I have. I don't know where my dad was born, and I don't know when. My daughter, Alexandra, has tried all kinds of ways to uncover something about him, but when you don't have birthplaces and birth dates and almost every piece of paper your family owned was destroyed in the war, finding your family's history is next to impossible.

3. MARCH 28, 1939

We were Jewish, but we weren't really observant. In Stawki, we'd celebrated the high holidays, and when I got stranded in Przemyśl in 1939, we did the same. I remember my grandparents' synagogue was down the street from their building, and in the congregation, the ladies sat upstairs and the men sat downstairs. But I wasn't there much—just the holidays.

My grandmother had a stationery store on the ground floor of the building that she and my grandpa owned. They lived above it. In that store, she sold books, pencils, notebooks, and cards. She'd collect food for the poor on Fridays, and our maid would cook chicken for Shabbat, when we'd light candles. My grandma also closed the store on Saturday. But as far as being religious, that was about it.

I didn't think all that much about being Jewish, in fact, until the Germans came. We never felt different. My father's workers were Polish and Ukrainian, and so were my grandfather's. Those men might have been anti-Semitic—at least a little bit—but I never witnessed it. In Przemyśl, my friends weren't only Jewish. My best friend, Dzidka Leszczyński, was Catholic. And when I was on the stage, no one talked about religion. My name was Ariana and nothing else. No one was interested in the fact that my last name was Spiegel.

All that changed during the war, of course.

4. APRIL 2, 1939

My mother had one sibling—a brother named Maurice, who was a few years younger than she was. Maurice was such a good-looking man—very dashing, with the same blue eyes as my mom, and a big, thick mustache. Sometime in the 1920s, he went away to school in Caen, a city in the northern part of France. He stayed in France, became an architect and an engineer, and married a French society lady. She was Catholic. I don't know if he even told her he was Jewish—I suppose he must have—but he got married in the church; I believe he converted.

Hitler annexed Austria in March 1938, and Sudetenland, the German-speaking part of Czechoslovakia, was taken over by Germany soon after. By March 1939, the rest of the country fell. Although some of this takeover was peaceful—Sudetenland's annexation was agreed to by the major European countries in the Munich Agreement—everyone knew that Hitler was a threat to all of Europe. The agreement had just been a way to try to get him to settle down for a little bit.

Uncle Maurice must have been worried about Hitler and the Nazis even before the Munich Agreement, because he came to Stawki around 1938 and tried to convince my mom to move to Paris. I remember he brought her a beautiful watch as a gift. But it was no use. My mom's life and family were in Poland, and she didn't want to leave.

Clearly, Renia did, even just to get away to see the world. She was so curious and interested, and she wanted to study in France, just like my uncle had. She never got to; the war got in the way of all her dreams.

5. AUGUST 15, 1939

Officials from Germany and the USSR met together secretly all during the summer of 1939, planning to form a political alliance that laid out each country's sphere of influence throughout Europe. By August 15, 1939, the beginnings of an agreement were in place, and by August 23, the Molotov-Ribbentrop Pact—also known as the Nazi-Soviet Pact—had been signed. It promised peace between the two countries and sealed their top-secret arrangement to split up Romania, Poland, Lithuania, Latvia, Estonia, and Finland between the two countries. Poland would be divided in half along the Pisa, Narev, Vistula, and San rivers. Germany got everything to the west, and the Soviets got everything to the east. On September 1, Germany invaded Poland, and sixteen days later, Russia marched in and began their occupation.

Our lives were never the same after that.

Mommy dropped me off with her parents one day that summer, when the talk of war was just that. She then went back to Warsaw, most likely to promote me. Our separation was never meant to be for more than a few weeks or months; I was her little girl, and I had movies to star in, lessons to take, and poems to recite. I was building a career in Warsaw. But August turned to September, and without warning, German troops marched toward Warsaw, bombs fell from the sky, and Warsaw fell to the Germans. Then the So-viets invaded Poland, and the half of Przemyśl that was on the east bank of the San went to them. The other bank became Nazi territory. The Germans destroyed the road bridge that went from one side to the other, but it didn't make much difference to us; you couldn't cross the river without official papers. We didn't have those, so we were cut off from our mother.

It took some time for me to understand that I wasn't going to see my mom anytime soon. I was just a little kid, and the idea of not having the person I loved more than anything in the world around was impossible. But Renia understood—she'd felt that pain of being without our mom for over a year—and she decided to tell me the full truth one day.

"Now, stop crying," she said, holding me tight. "I know you miss Mommy, and I do, too. But we have to get used to it. This is the way it is now. Life has changed."

I don't think my grandparents had had the heart to tell me. They were good, kind, hardworking people, and they always wanted to protect us, especially when we weren't with our mom and dad. My grandmother was named Anna, and my grandfather was Marek. My grandma had been born and raised in Jarosław, a town about thirty-five kilometers north of Przemyśl on the west bank of the San. I'm not sure where she met my grandpa, but at some point early in their marriage, they settled into a home on the second floor of a two-story building near the main street in Przemyśl. That's where they raised my mom and Uncle Maurice. That same apartment—located at 19 Slowackiego, just down from a major plaza—was where I lived from 1939 to 1942.

Their apartment wasn't very big. Renia and I slept in a corner in the liv-ing room, near the big wooden desk where my sister did her homework. That desk was also where Renia used to write the proposals for my grand-pa's work, drawing up estimates that he'd then give to potential customers. People didn't have closets like they do now, so in that same room stood a large cupboard that stored their dishes for Seder. I remember, one day, a cat crawled inside and had kittens. It was crazy! I still don't know where that cat came from.

Their building sat on the corner down the street from a synagogue and near Renia's school. My grandma's store occupied half of the ground floor, and in the other half was an apothecary. Her brother's wife had a cheese and milk store that took up the spot next to that. I never figured out that relationship; her brother and his family lived upstairs in the apartment next to ours, yet they never talked to us.

My grandma's other brother—who'd been president of a bank—had passed away before 1939, but his family ran away from Jarosław when the Germans came. His wife, his two lawyer sons, his daughter—who'd headed a school—and their families stayed with us for a little bit until they could find their own place. One of the sons had a small child of about six named Marylka, and she had flaming red, curly hair. We practically slept on top of each other till they left, but it didn't matter. We were just happy they were safe.

Granny was taller than my grandpa, and she was in her midsixties, which in those days seemed and looked much older than it does now. Like me, she'd been on the stage when she was young, and I wonder sometimes if she identified with me because of that. Or maybe she just knew I was a motherless kid who needed extra attention. Sometimes on the weekend, she'd get dressed up in one of her nice, fur coats and take me on a walk to Zamek, a castle on a hill just outside the city. She held my hand tightly the whole way, and I still remember how safe I felt with her leather gloves wrapped around my little fingers. I loved my granny very, very much.

Grandpa was quite short, with big, piercing blue eyes just like mine, Renia's, and our mom's. He was bald and had a small, neatly trimmed mustache, and he had a nice fur-lined coat like my grandma. Like most men back then, he wore hats when he left the house. The people who worked under my grandpa loved him, and I know why; he wasn't well educated, but he was kind. He treated his employees with the same respect he treated his family

He also did everything in his power to protect us.

On September 7, 1939, bombs started to fall on Przemyśl. The shopping center, Pasaz Gansa, caught fire, and as the Germans advanced, thousands fled—especially the Jews, whom the Germans began threatening, arresting, and killing. Many of them crossed over to the Soviet side looking for refuge.

The Polish army tried to fight back, but it only took a month and five days for the whole country to fall. The Germans and Soviets were well armed, coordinated, and much stronger than our foot soldiers, horses, bombers, and volunteers. We were targets—under attack and not safe in our own home—so my grandpa decided to take Renia and me out of Przemyśl when it went under siege. With no real plan, nothing except the clothes on our backs and a little money, we left the apartment and started to walk toward Lwów, which was about one hundred kilometers away. Lwów was where I'd gone with my mom and Renia to recite poetry on the radio, and I knew it wasn't close—at all. But I kept my mouth closed because I trusted Grandpa. He and Granny and Renia were all I had.

My grandma stayed home with the maid, whose name was Pelagia Palivoda. She didn't say why she refused to go, but I guess she was just too old and tired to walk that far. Pelagia would be good company, though. She and my granny were very different—Pelagia was a simple Polish woman who slept on a bed that folded down from the wall in the kitchen—but they were close. Pelagia had devoted her life to my grandparents.

As soon as we stepped onto one of the major streets leading out of Przemyśl, I remember seeing crowds of people fleeing with as little as we had, and those who could were running. There were more horses and carriages than cars where we lived, and we may have gotten a ride in a buggy at some point, but I can't recall. All I remember is that it was pitch black, I was hungry and terrified, and nobody knew where we were going. Even to a naïve little girl, it seemed like we had no direction. All we understood was that the Germans were here, they were bombing our homes, and staying put wasn't safe.

As we fled, we could hear German planes circling near us, the steady whir of engines roaring and the *bang-boom* of bombs falling on the ground. But we assumed that the enemy would bomb a town rather than outside of it. People lived in towns, in buildings, and if your goal is to kill as many of them as possible, the city is the place to bomb. We assumed we'd be safe in the fields or forest, so that's where we headed.

September was harvesttime for wheat, and wheat is rough when you cut it. As my sister walked through the fields, she sometimes fell or brushed against a stalk that had been missed, and she scratched up her arms and legs, which started to bleed. We couldn't stop for her, though; we had to keep moving away from the firing and bombing we could hear behind us.

We walked out from the wheat, passing the forest as we headed into another field. I looked around and noticed row after row of cabbages, round and ripening and almost ready to be picked.

"They look like heads," Renia said. "I mean, like human heads, not just cabbage heads."

Then Grandpa stopped, looked at us, and whispered, "Run to the forest, girls. Run! We can't be here, because the German planes will see the cabbages and think they're people. They'll want to bomb right here."

So we shifted directions and ran for our lives through the forest and toward Lwów.

6. NOVEMBER 6, 1939

I don't remember this postcard from my dad. In fact, I don't remember anything about him during the war. But it's clear he'd lost our estate. The part of Poland where I'd been born was occupied by the Soviets, and they were Communist, so our land was now the government's. Ticio had moved to Horodenka—a city just to the west of our old home—to find other work.

We weren't aristocrats, so we didn't have huge collections of art that the Soviets could steal like they did to so many other Polish landowners. We'd lived in a manor house, not a mansion. But we'd been comfortable. We'd had nannies and employees. We'd had a chicken coop and a place to store bushels and bushels of wheat. We'd grown sugar beets that we sold to the factories for sugar. But most important, we'd lived on acres of fertile land, and that's what the Soviets wanted.

7. FEBRUARY 17, 1940

I don't remember this visit from my father. I wish I did. I think it's shocking how someone so close to you—your own blood relative—can fall so far away from you in such a short period of time. Now, after all these years have gone by, much of my understanding of him is constructed from things other people later told me.

For example, Renia had a nanny named Klara when she and my parents lived on the estate where she'd been born. Apparently, Klara was a very skinny woman and wasn't beautiful like my mom, yet I heard later that my mother believed my father had an affair with her. I don't even remember who told me this; it was just family gossip, passed along from person to person, and now it feels as real as any other truth I know.

I was also told my mom lost a baby between Renia and me because she'd caught a venereal disease from my dad. Everyone suspected him of having an affair with a woman who worked on the farm and that she'd been the source of it. Was my dad a womanizer? I'll never really know, but I still believe he was just because of those two stories.

Regardless, my parents clearly had problems, and it must have been part of the reason Buluś moved to Warsaw with me. Or maybe my father just didn't take much interest in us girls. Maybe he wanted a boy to help him on the estate, which was what good sons did in those days.

8. OCTOBER 12, 1940

I never would have guessed that Zygmunt Schwarzer—or Zygo, as Renia sometimes called him—would play such a major role in my life. That he would change my life, really. But he did, and, more important than that, he made the last two years of my sister's life better in so many ways. With Zygmunt, she knew the strongest, most romantic love she'd ever experienced.

Zygmunt was born in 1923 in Jarosław, where my grandma was from. I didn't know his family well, but I understood that my mother had gone to gymnasium with his mother, and his father, Wilhelm Schwarzer, had been a respected doctor in Jarosław. When the Germans invaded Poland, the Schwarzers fled to Przemyśl, just like my grandma's family had. In Przemyśl, Dr. Schwarzer picked up his practice right away, even though he had a brand-new home and the country was in the middle of an occupation. That kind of toughness is what Zygmunt also possessed, though I wouldn't realize it for a while.

I always thought Zygmunt was so handsome, and that drove my sister crazy. "You're such a flirt!" she'd yell at me, and I'd say back, "He's your boyfriend, not mine!" I promise you I didn't have a crush on him. I was just a dramatic little girl who loved to follow my sister around and make friends with her friends. And Zygmunt was so easy to be friends with.

Zygmunt had black, curly hair, bright green eyes, and dimples on the sides of his cheeks that got deeper every time he smiled—which was a lot. Zygmunt was one year older than Renia, which made him seven years older than I was, but despite our difference in age, I always felt warm and comfortable around him. So did Renia. My sister liked him very, very much.

Zygmunt's best friend was named Maciek Tuchman. Maciek was about the same age as Zygmunt, and he was jolly and kind of plump. He always had a crush on my sister, and even though she loved being with him, Renia only had eyes for Zygmunt. Though I know there was some playful competition between Zygmunt and Maciek, they really were a team. "We were tied to each another and living each other's lives," Maciek—who was called Marcel when he got to America after the war—once said in an interview.

I don't know exactly how Zygmunt, Maciek, Irka, and Nora became such close friends. It must have been school, since my sister was now going to school with boys. But Zygmunt occupied all her thoughts. They fought sometimes, but it wasn't serious; their little arguments were just the ups and downs of kids in love.

9. DECEMBER 25, 1940

Between October and November 1940, the Nazi German government created the Warsaw Ghetto across 1.3 square miles of the northern part of the city, right at the center of the Jewish quarter. Immediately, the entire remaining Jewish population of the city—many of whom were refugees rather than Warsaw natives—were forced into it. About four hundred thousand Jews squeezed into a space that held about nine people per room, and a giant brick wall encircled them. A train line ran just outside the ghetto walls, with several stops to load passengers and take them away to the death camps.

The formation of the ghetto wasn't a surprise to anyone; the Jews had been persecuted ever since the Nazis invaded Poland in 1939. Starting that November, Jewish businesses had been forced to display the Star of David, Jewish bank accounts had been frozen, and Jews around the city had been ordered to wear armbands. All of this—plus a real fear of deportation or execution—was why so many Jews had fled the German-occupied portion of Poland.

Mommy was Jewish, so of course Renia assumed she was inside the ghetto walls. But she wasn't; she'd avoided the ghetto by securing false papers with a Polish, Roman Catholic name. Sometime after the Germans arrived, my mom had connected with an old friend named Halina Bereda, who was also Jewish but had married a wealthy Polish Roman Catholic and converted. One of Halina's husband's great-uncles was a cardinal in the Polish Roman Catholic Diocese, in fact. Halina and her husband knew people who could arrange for Polish papers, so they paid them to create some for my mom. In February 1940, my mom became Maria Leszczyńska, was baptized by a priest named Fajecki into the Roman Catholic faith, and—just like that—she blended in.

Renia and I knew none of this at first. If we were lucky, we received letters from Buluś maybe twice a year because it was almost impossible to send mail from the Nazi-occupied zone to the Soviet-occupied zone. All outgoing mail was read and censored by the Gestapo. That didn't stop my mom from trying, though. Around the time the ghetto went up, my mother paid a Polish man from Warsaw to cross the river San with a letter for us. When he showed up at our door, we were so excited! Then he went back to Warsaw, found my mother, and threatened to report her to the Gestapo if she didn't pay him more. She fled her apartment and moved to escape him.

My mother was charming, capable, intelligent—and fluent in German. She'd gone to university in Berlin, then Vienna, and she'd learned the language there during her years of study. Sometime after 1939, she became the assistant director of the Hotel Europjski, a gorgeous historical hotel with a grand staircase, a ballroom, and a large terrace that spilled out onto Pilsudski Square. During the German occupation, three hundred Wehrmacht officers lived there, and the German government had renamed it Europäisches Hotel. Mommy was dedicated to her job, and she was so good at it that she worked there several years during the war.

I know now she rented an apartment in Żoliborz, which was a neighborhood just north of the city center on the western bank of the Vistula River. She'd gotten the place thanks again to Mrs. Bereda. But other than Mrs. Bereda and her husband, I'm not sure who her friends were. Outside of working, I don't know how she spent her time. When I had lived with her in Warsaw, she'd had a male friend who I now assume was her boyfriend, but I don't know if they stayed together after 1939. Regardless of who she was with, I know she must have been lonely because the few letters that made it through to us said she missed us terribly. Imagine being a young mother separated from your children for two years because of war? I have two kids, and my heart aches just to think about it.

10. DECEMBER 31, 1940

As I said before, a teenager's life in Przemyśl revolved around school, and there were constantly parties, dances, and get-togethers. I know I went to at least one event with Renia—and I loved every single second of it—but most of the time, I was more interested in being with my own friends. The best of those was a little blond girl named Dzidka.

Dzidka Leszczyński—whose real first name was Zosia—was the youngest of three daughters in a Roman Catholic family that owned and ran a small tinned coffee factory at 41 Mickiewicz Street in Przemyśl. Her dad, Ludomir, was tall, slender, and aristocratic-looking, with a thick mustache and a confident way of walking and talking. I didn't know it till much later, but during the German occupation, he was in Żegota—a member of the Council to Aid Jews—and that gave him some influence. Mr. Leszczyński was devoutly religious, but he didn't see barriers among people. In his business and his life, Jews, Roman Catholics, Ukrainians, Poles, and more worked together for the good of society and their families, and for that reason, his youngest daughter's best friend might as well have been his own. Or at least that's how he always made me feel.

Dzidka was skinny, fair, and a little taller than I was. One of her older sisters—either Ludomira or Janina, I can't remember which—went to school with Renia, and they sometimes spent time together creating poems in their little leather-bound notebooks. Renia would write them and her friend would illustrate them. Dzidka and I were probably off together while they did. She and I used to sing songs, play with dolls, and walk hand in hand around town after school. We were inseparable.

Dzidka's dad saved my life, and I talk about that in the epilogue that follows Renia's diary. But, even though I never saw my best friend again after I escaped Przemyśl, being close to her is the single greatest bit of good fortune I've ever had. I don't know how Dzidka made it through the war, but I found out, thankfully, that she did. She moved to Kraków, married, adopted children, and died a few years ago from Alzheimer's. My dear Dzidka, I missed all those years.

11. MARCH 9, 1941

I had a diary? I don't even remember it! But I knew Maciek Tuchman for over eighty years, and if he had a crush on my sister, I am sure it was harmless. He and Zygmunt were the best of friends, and Maciek would never try to steal Renia from him. He was a joker then, and he was for the rest of his long life, too.

Maciek and I were friends in New York until he passed away in 2018 at the age of ninety-seven. He was also my internist until the end of his long career. When he came to America, people began calling him Marcel, and I usually did, too, because it became his identity in the same way Elizabeth became mine. But in my memory, he's Maciek, and in Renia's world, that's who he'll always be.

Like Zygmunt, Maciek secured a work permit before being sent to the Przemyśl Ghetto in 1942. He lived there with his parents until the ghetto was swept clean, the Nazis shooting the people who still lived there in the back of the head. His mother was one of them; she was taken out of the ghetto and murdered in the Przemyśl Jewish cemetery. Maciek and his father were hiding in an attic, listening all night to the sound of gunshots.

Sometime in 1942, he and his dad were shipped off to Auschwitz, and there, they were ordered to work in a Siemens factory that was just outside the camp. Along with a hundred other prisoners, they labored as slaves until the SS forced them out in a death march in 1945. They made it—alive— from Buchenwald to Berlin, where they were liberated at the end of the war. At a displaced persons' camp in Bergen-Belsen, he met his wife, a Czech woman named Shoshana.

Like Zygmunt, Maciek wanted to be a doctor, yet there were few opportunities for a survivor in Europe to get an education. Maciek and Zygmunt applied to and were accepted by a special program at Heidelberg University, and they, their wives, and eight hundred other survivors lived and studied surrounded by former Nazis. Maciek graduated with honors in 1949, then moved to New York City, where he because an internist at NYU. He was there for fifty years.

In 1963, I was working at NYU's medical school, and one afternoon, I walked into the cafeteria. Suddenly, I heard a voice yelling out. It had the same Polish accent I have.

"Arianka! Arianka!"

It was Maciek! Smiling, jolly, warm, familiar Maciek from Przemyśl, who had made it through the ghetto and the camps and had lost half his family just as I had. He was alive, and he was in a New York City cafeteria with his arms wide open, ready to embrace me.

Maciek was my internist for many decades, until he retired after he'd been diagnosed with Alzheimer's. I visited him at his home after he left his practice, and he didn't remember recent events, like the death of his son, Jeffrey, from cancer in 2017. But he could recall things from the time of the war. We held hands and sang a few old, traditional Polish songs, and he said each word perfectly. He could even recite Pushkin in Russian.

Maciek died on November 10, 2018, and I attended his funeral on my birthday, November 18. Afterward, my family and I went to my favorite Italian restaurant, where we toasted Maciek's ninety-seven years—and my birthday as well. What a miracle to have made it through so much and to have lived for so long.

12. JUNE 21, 1941

It's been almost eighty years since I last saw my sister. That's a lifetime since I heard her laugh ringing out from the kitchen, saw her looking up from one of her leather notebooks, her bright blue eyes shining, or felt the familiar touch of her hand holding mine. Yet her presence is one of the largest in my life. A photo of her hangs in the entry of my apartment, looking out over the center of my living room, and it's a constant reminder of the past. Seeing Renia's smile every day, I remember the good times, but I also remember how the world shifted suddenly and spared me, while it sacrificed so many others, including her.

I'm not sure I fully realized how traumatic my childhood was until I was well into adulthood. War is too big and too scary for most children to understand, and I was no exception. But in her deeply poetic way, I think Renia grasped what was happening around us. She just saw the world differently. Her fatefulness, her carefulness, her subtle, perceptive observations about the pace and meaning of every moment show me how she processed the passage of time. She realized she was witnessing the calm before the storm, and she captured it. She savored it, knowing it was fleeting.

The shaky sense of security we had in Soviet-occupied Poland slipped away on June 22, 1941, when war broke out between Germany and the Soviet Union. Nazi Germany decided it wanted to take over all of Europe and that the Soviet Union was the biggest thing standing in their way. That summer, German troops invaded Soviet-occupied territories on three separate fronts. The code name for this assault was Operation Barbarossa, and it was the largest German military offensive of World War II.

This German assault was what our secret, forbidden radios had warned us of, what the Communist propaganda we were taught in Russian class had put into verse, and what Renia had had nightmares about. At the end of June 1941, bombs fell fast on major cities in Soviet-occupied Poland, and Przemyśl, unfortunately, was one of the first hit.

13. JULY 1, 1941

Just like that, the German army came, bombs fell, lives were lost, and the Soviet army retreated. Then the Germans pushed east. To Lwów. To Kiev. And eventually, in the bitter, cold winter, to St. Petersburg.

Przemyśl was just a stop on the way for the Nazis, who'd been across the San River for two years, waiting for the order to attack. Almost immediately after they invaded, they began to suppress the Jews. First, they forced all employed Jews to register their names in the local labor office. Then they ordered all Jews over the age of twelve to wear armbands with a blue Star of David on them. If you were on the street and passed a German soldier, you had to show your armband. If you resisted, you could be imprisoned or killed on the spot.

I was not yet eleven, so I didn't have to put one on, but when I first saw one, something in me died. My family and friends and neighbors who wore them weren't people anymore. They were objects.

14. JULY 11, 1941

When the Germans came, getting work meant everything if you were Jewish. Maybe your work was dirty, unpleasant, or far below what you'd been trained for, but it didn't matter. Doing anything that proved you were strong and capable enough to support the war effort might save your life.

At first, Zygmunt worked at a clinic, as Renia described. I'm sure this was happy work for him because he wanted to be a doctor, but that was the last intelligent job he had. The next summer, when all Jews were ordered to move into the ghetto, he and Maciek found work in a German storage depot that was located just outside Przemyśl at an army labor camp. They both sorted and organized uniforms there.

In his book, *Remember: My Stories of Survival and Beyond*, Maciek writes that their time in the factory almost got Zygmunt killed. Knowing that there were hardly any supplies in the ghetto and that he could trade a good pair of pants for food, Zygmunt decided to take a chance. He looked around and realized that no guards were watching him, and he put on six or seven pairs of army fatigues under the pants he'd come to work in. As he started to walk toward the door, looking like he'd put on thirty pounds since that morning, he was stopped by a guard.

"What's going on there? What are you trying to do?" the guard asked.

Zygmunt knew he'd been caught and that he was going to be either beaten, jailed, or executed immediately, so he kept silent.

There was a young Jewish woman working in the administrative offices, and she liked Zygmunt. She also knew that the German soldier who'd just caught Zygmunt had a crush on her. Seeing that Zygmunt had gotten caught, she stood up from her desk and intervened.

"Please let him go. I can give you something."

It's unclear what she gave him—and I hope for her sake it wasn't much—but she saved Zygmunt. Just to be extra careful, Zygmunt also slipped the German soldier a gold coin.

That incident was the first of many things Zygmunt survived in the war. Between getting work, making connections, and being resourceful, he and Maciek had more lives than almost anyone I grew up with.

15. AUGUST 25, 1941

After the Germans took over all of Poland, my mom's letters came more frequently. As Renia wrote, it was one after the other after the other. I guess this was because mail didn't have to pass from one occupied zone to another anymore, but it could have been something else, like Mama becoming friendly with someone at the post office. I didn't ask at the time; I was just glad to hear from her.

With her new papers and name, my mom also had the freedom to travel to see us. It would be difficult and dangerous—she had to take time from work, she had to travel through a war zone, and, most likely, she had to lie about who she was seeing. The train trip was also over ten hours, with one transfer in Kraków.

But my mom hadn't spent a significant, uninterrupted amount of time with her children for two years, and she had to. She missed us terribly. And we missed her!

16. SEPTEMBER 29, 1941

In 1939, the Germans had bombed the bridge that connected Zasanie—a part of Przemyśl on the left bank of the San—so people crossed on the railway bridge instead. But by September 1941, Jews were forbidden to use that bridge. The secret Renia writes about died with her, so I have no idea how we got over the San. Nor do I know why I went to see our mom before she did. Did our grandpa or mom bribe a German soldier? Did we walk with Dzidka's father, who lied by saying, "These are my daughters"? I wish I remembered, but I don't. All I know is that, when I mention to people that I saw my mom a few times during the war in Przemyśl and that she returned to Warsaw without me and Renia—their only question is, "Why didn't you stay with her? You could have escaped!"

It wasn't that easy. Death lurked around every corner, and it was an expensive and dangerous endeavor to start a new life. We didn't have papers that would allow us to do it. Yet a new identity was the only way to get out, like Buluś had done.

17. OCTOBER 10, 1941

Soon after the summer of 1941, the Nazis began seizing the Jews' valuables and household items. If you didn't open up your door when they knocked, they forced their way in, and you were taken away and beaten or put in prison.

My granny and grandpa's upright piano stood next to the balcony Renia was on when Zygmunt blew her a kiss before the Nazis arrived. For two years, we'd played that piano almost every day, and practicing never felt like a chore. We liked playing, and Granny liked helping us. For my grandparents, my sister, and me, that upright piano was a symbol of something strong and permanent. It stood on solid ground, as it had since my mother and my uncle Maurice were babies.

But the Nazis took whatever they wanted. Your money, your dishes, your clothes, your silverware, your children, or your life. The first thing they stole from us was my grandparents' piano, a few soldiers entering the apartment one afternoon while I was out. They hauled it down the stairs and out the door, leaving a small pile of dust in the space where it had stood. When I came home, Granny was a different person, like her heart had been ripped out.

Not long after Germany invaded Przemyśl, they also forbid Jewish children from going to school. This policy wasn't new for the Nazis, just to those of us in Przemyśl. In April 1933, the German government ordered that only 1 percent of the population within German universities could be Jewish. The problem was that 5 percent of the German population *was* Jewish. Then, in 1938, Jewish children were barred from enrolling in any German public school. Although Jewish teachers—all of whom had been fired from the public schools—were allowed to form their own Jewish schools, many mothers, grandmothers, older siblings, or neighbors chose instead to tutor their kids at home.

Renia and I had always gone to public schools, and during the Soviet occupation, nothing had stood in our way. Our friends and classmates were Jewish, Polish, and Ukrainian, and we didn't distinguish among them. Our teachers didn't either. But when the Nazis came, I was forced to stay home. During those long days, I daydreamed or made up stories with my dolls. When I was so bored I couldn't stand it anymore, I'd put on my coat and go outside for a walk, counting the minutes until Dzidka was home from school and I could run over to her house.

Renia wrote in her diary, made up some poems, sent some letters, and looked out the window for hours, feeling nothing. Sometimes she'd sneak away to Norka's house to study French or ancient history, relying on books rather than teachers. Luckily, Jerschina still came by for Polish lessons, and Renia always looked forward to that.

In 1944, I still hadn't gone back to school, but I enrolled at a conservatory in Salzburg, which was as close to an education as I could get. I thought about my grandma the whole time. With my fingers stretched across the ivory keys, Granny would have been so proud of me. Today, I have an upright Steinway in my apartment, against the wall and near a large window just like my grandparents' was. When I'm feeling nostalgic, I play the Polish and Russian folk songs my teachers taught me in my youth, when patriotic music was hopeful and defiant. The Nazis might have tried to take everything—our identities, our passions, and our education—but they couldn't steal the music in our hearts.

18. NOVEMBER 7, 1941

The process leading to the creation of the Przemyśl Ghetto was slow, careful, and well thought out. In late autumn of 1941, the town quarter of Garbarze—which was bordered by the San on the west, north, and east, and on the south by the railway that connected Kraków and Lwów—was proclaimed to be a Jewish residential area. The quarter's establishment took until the summer of 1942, and up to that time, Jews were allowed to walk freely through the streets, but with their armbands on.

This area wasn't called a ghetto—yet. It was a residential area for Jews, and when a policeman came knocking at our door in early November 1941, he wanted us to move there. I don't know who bribed him, though I'm sure it was my grandpa. Maybe he appealed to the fact that he was Polish like us and that the Germans might be able to take our possessions and homes, but they couldn't take who we were. But I bet my grandpa didn't say much. He probably rummaged around in his desk, grabbed a few gold coins, and muttered, "Here, take these. Just please let my family stay. Please, just for now."

But I know my grandpa realized that the next time a soldier or policeman came knocking at the door, he might be giving final orders to go, now, with only twenty-five kilograms of our worldly possessions packed in a suitcase. Maybe my grandpa could attempt to bribe this next person, but you can only do that for so long. We were going to lose our possessions and our homes, and we had to prepare.

At some point during the fall of 1941, my grandparents boxed up all the silver they'd stored along with their Seder china in the large cupboard in their living room. Lining a big, wooden box with paper and cloth, they placed spoons, knives, forks, serving platters, candlesticks, and any piece of silver in the house and bundled it up tightly. Then they closed the lid and nailed it shut. Late one night, my grandfather crawled into their tiny basement and buried it with a shovel. For all I know, that box is still there.

19. NOVEMBER 24, 1941

I'm not sure what Renia meant by Buluś moving the house. Did my mom clear out the possessions she knew the Germans would take? The family photos, the silverware, and the articles of clothing that reminded her of home? That had to be it. Hiding your possessions was one small act of control and defiance, and if my mother did anything in her life, she took charge of a situation.

My mom died in late 1969 from cancer. It had started in her breast, but they didn't have mammograms in those days, so she didn't find out till it had metastasized into her hip bone. She had been sick since about 1960, and she'd married a man named Clyde because she knew he could help take care of her. He was kind to her, but he wasn't fond of foreigners, even though he had immigrant friends, one of whom had introduced him to my mom.

That wasn't the only secret she'd kept. When I cleaned out her apartment, I found two small suitcases she'd hidden away in her closet. Inside one of them were two tiny silver spoons, a stack of faded family photographs, a pair of pearl earrings, a few gold bracelets, and a beaded chain made of coral. These were the treasures from my childhood, the memories I'd stored in my brain, too afraid to dig up because they might make me cry. In the other small suitcase, I found the embroidered, beaded traditional Polish vests that Renia and I had worn at the harvest festival in Zaleszczyki. They were Krakowski Strój, meaning the traditional garb from the Kraków region. Right there in those suitcases sat my childhood. Right there was Poland. And I have no idea how my mother carried all of it from our estate to Przemyśl to Warsaw to Austria to all the dozen other places we'd lived after the war, without me knowing.

20. DECEMBER 8, 1941

The news about my father and Lila living in a ghetto is one of the few solid pieces of evidence I have about where my dad was at the end of 1941. Unfortunately, what Renia wrote doesn't give much away. I don't know which ghetto my dad and Lila were living in, though it was probably in Horodenka, where they'd fled when they were forced out of our estate. The Germans created the ghetto in Horodenka around April 1941, establishing it in a part of the city that was one-third the size of the area where most Jews had previously lived.

If my dad and Lila were there, I'm sure they didn't make it out. That's because, on December 5, the Nazis executed their "First Action" in Horodenka, assembling a murder squad to wipe out the ghetto. They lured out 2,500 Jews—which was half of the ghetto's population—telling them that they'd be receiving a typhus vaccine. Instead, everyone was murdered in the nearby forest. Those that were left in the ghetto were sealed off in a four-block stretch, living practically on top of each other until September 2, 1942, when almost all of them were shipped to the concentration camp at Majdanek, about four hundred kilometers northwest.

The Nazis kept meticulous records in the camps, but we don't have my dad's birth date, so we don't know if he was there. The same goes for Lila.

21. DECEMBER 28, 1941

On December 26, 1941, the Nazis announced that Jews had to hand over their furs because the German troops needed them on the battlefield. German and Polish police—like the one we'd paid off months before—entered homes and seized furs, and on the streets, German police stopped Jewish men and women, ripped out the fur linings of their hats or coats, and moved on. In some cases, women on the street were also ordered to remove their shoes. They took them off and walked home along the cobblestones in their stockings.

My grandma had hired a tailor to make our coats. My sister's coat was fully lined with a fur collar, my grandpa's went below his knees and was entirely fur lined, and my grandmother's was just the same. Mine was a smaller version of Renia's, and we always wore them out with tights and hats in the winter. We had other coats, but these were our best—what we wore on special occasions and when winter was at its worst.

When Grandpa heard the Germans had sent out an edict about our furs, he didn't panic. Some hopeful part of him decided that the war would be over soon. He'd survive. He might lose his family's furs now, but he could get them back when everything was all said and done and the Germans had retreated.

So he made a plan and asked a friend for a favor.

My grandpa sometimes worked with a Ukrainian man who had a business making keys. They liked and trusted each other, so Grandpa gathered together all our furs, placed them in a suitcase, and walked to the Ukrainian man's store, which was nearby.

"Take these coats," he said. "Please save them for me. I'll back for them after the war's over."

I guess I don't have to tell you that we never got those coats back. Everyone except for me and maybe the locksmith was dead before the next winter.

22. APRIL 9, 1942

When you were shut into your quarter, it wasn't with walls or barbed wire, like we'd soon be in the ghetto. Instead, you couldn't leave your neighborhood without special permission from the Germans. My grandparents' house was on the main street of town, and while I know Norka lived in a different quarter from the one we lived in, I don't remember which it was. I know she lived on a small street—not one of the main ones—but our town was small, so Renia could walk there easily. In any case, my sister's chances of seeing Norka every day, like she always had, were slim because she didn't have the right papers.

Around that time, though, even worse things were happening near where the main road made its way toward the suburbs. Przemyśl's Jewish cemetery is located just off Slowackiego and was built on a hill around 1860, when the old cemetery became full. I've heard it's still beautiful today: hilly, wooded, and overgrown in the middle where the oldest graves are, some of which have toppled a little bit to their sides over time. The newer graves are toward the outside, and you can usually find flowers or photos sitting at their bases.

This was one of the places where Gestapo officials decided to execute Jews starting in the spring of 1942, when Renia realized she'd never see Norka again. It was also where Maciek's mom was taken on September 3, 1943, after she'd been found hiding in a bunker in the ghetto with thirty other Jews. Before the Gestapo took her to the cemetery, where they'd force her to strip naked and dig her own grave, she looked at one of the guards and said, "Yes, you may have me, you bastards, but you will not catch my son and my husband."

23. MAY 12, 1942

I never understood my parents' relationship in the way that Renia did. In my earliest memories, my parents were separated because my mother was managing my career in Warsaw, and my father had his business on the estate. Was anything wrong? Not that I knew, but I was a busy little girl who'd never really had a relationship with my dad. What was there to understand? Renia was almost a teenager by the time my mom and I moved to Warsaw, so she had years and years before me to see things I didn't and feel things I never did. I think that's why my mom told her she was going to ask for a divorce. She knew Renia would understand it, even if it was hard for her to accept it.

Renia didn't tell me anything, but that was like her. Even though she complained about me being too flirtatious, annoying, or smart-mouthed, I was her baby sister, and she wanted to protect me. I also never asked my mom what made her want the divorce. Sure, she hadn't seen my father in years as far as I knew, but divorce was a major decision that would change her life. Women didn't do that in those days.

As for my dad . . . it breaks my heart to say it, but the letter Renia mentions was the last we heard from him. The war killed most of my wonderful family. God rest your soul, Bernard Spiegel, my Ticio. You were a man of few words, who tended to your fields, your leather boots shiny and green eyes sparkly under the summer sun. I wish I had known you longer and better.

24. JUNE 7, 1942

There's a quarter in Przemyśl called Zasanie, and before the war, it had one synagogue. During the war, the Germans turned the synagogue into a power station, and they forced the Jewish residents of the quarter to live together in one building. I've read there were about forty-five to sixty occupants, packed together like sardines.

On June 3, 1942, Germans murdered forty-five of these people. Just like so many others before them, they were loaded onto trucks, taken to a fort in the suburbs of Przemyśl, and shot one by one in the nape of the neck. Just before they died, many of them—just like Maciek's mom—had been forced to strip naked and dig their own graves.

I don't remember this, but other Jews—both in Zasanie and throughout Przemyśl—were beaten on the street for trying to steal a piece of bread. Others were chased by dogs while the guards—some of whom had their children with them—laughed. Then the Jews were hanged, a public spectacle that the children watched, too.

Writing this makes me sick. Renia had the full, open emotions to describe what she lived through, but most of the time now, I don't. When people ask me about the war, I just don't want to talk about it.

25. JUNE 19, 1942

In the early summer of 1942, news spread that there had been a series of anti-Jewish riots in the towns of Tarnów and Rzeszów, which lay along the road between Przemyśl and Kraków. Communication wasn't reliable between cities during the war, so the Przemyśl Judenrat decided they needed to investigate to figure out if the rumors about the riots were true. They were.

"This can't happen here to us," the Judenrat told the Gestapo. "We're going through enough without the whole community coming after us, too."

The Judenrat and the Germans worked together in two ways. The Judenrat was administered by the Nazi government, so they performed services for them like registering Jews and reporting those numbers. They also worked to protect the Jewish community, organizing food distribution, helping the elderly, and trying to simplify life in the ghetto. It wasn't unusual for them to come to the Gestapo with a concern; they knew the Jewish community needed protection, and they thought the Gestapo might offer it.

The Gestapo officials listened and nodded, seeming sympathetic. Then they told them they'd come up with a plan. A few days later, they announced it.

"If you behave well, we'll protect you," a Gestapo official said.

"But how is that?" the head of the Judenrat asked.

The Gestapo chief, whose name was Benthin, cleared his throat.

"If you provide me with one thousand young people for work at the Janowska camp in Lwów, they'll be safe. Nothing will happen to them."

On June 18, 1942—the horrible night Renia describes, which was also her birthday—1,260 Jews were loaded into cattle cars and transported to forced labor at Janowska. There, most of them slaved away doing carpentry or metalwork for the Nazis. To make things worse, the Gestapo shot many of their relatives right there on the tracks as they waved goodbye. The families that weren't killed were later charged the cost of their loved ones' transportation to the camps.

The Gestapo's words had all been lies, and they'd betrayed the trust of the Judenrat to help them with their dirty work.

ACKNOWLEDGMENTS

I would like to dedicate this book to the memory of my cherished sister, Renia. She was a mother figure to me during the war. Through this book, her memory will not be lost to history.

I am grateful to the renowned Holocaust scholar Deborah Lipstadt for writing the introduction to my sister's diary. I appreciate her insight into my sister's poetry, love, and humanity.

To *moja mamusia*, Bulczyk. You were the most beautiful, well-educated, elegant, and resourceful woman I have ever met. You knew how to maneuver through life. You knew how to survive. You gave me life. You gave me courage. You gave me hope. You gave me a life in America.

There are certain people to whom I owe my very existence. Their bravery is the reason I am alive today: Ludomir Leszczyński, a righteous Pole who, under the penalty of death, saved my life and brought me from Przemyśl to my mother in Warsaw; the Bereda family, who welcomed me in Warsaw, reunited me with my mother, whom I had not seen in two long years, helped me to obtain papers, and basically saved my life—again; Zygmunt Schwarzer, who risked his life and took me out of the ghetto in Przemyśl to safety. He saved my life. Again. He brought the last remnants of my sister in the form of the diary and miraculously found my mother in the United States. I am forever indebted to them for my life.

My deepest appreciation to Tomasz Magierski. Tomasz unearthed press clippings, movie reels, photographs, and countless other documents about Renia and me. He was captivated by Renia's story, and without his tireless efforts, her story would not have been brought to life. *Dziękuję bardzo.*

I would like to acknowledge with gratitude the support and love of my

ACKNOWLEDGMENTS

family: my son, Andrew Bellak, and daughter-in-law, Susan. My beautiful grandchildren, Theo, Nicholas, and Julian.

A special note of gratitude to Marta Dziurosz and Anna Blasiak, who had the painful and arduous task of translating over seven hundred written pages of my sister's work, including sixty poems.

Thank you to Jennifer Weis of St. Martin's Press for taking an interest in this story and believing wholeheartedly that it needed to be told!

To my recently departed husband of fifty-three years, George Bellak, I miss you dearly. You understood me implicitly. George was my Viennese-born wunderkind, who showed unwavering support and love and devotion to me and our children.

I would like to thank all those whose assistance proved to be a milestone in the accomplishment of my end goal: to tell the world what happened.

I would like to pay tribute to my extended family, who were not as lucky and perished in the Holocaust.

But there is one person more than any other whose never-failing dedication and perseverance have ensured that my sister's words would not be lost to history.

That person is my beloved daughter, Alexandra Renata.

Renia's spirit lives on through her and it is to her that generations of future readers will be indebted.

—*Elizabeth Bellak*